PERGAMON INTERNATIONAL LIBRARY
of Science, Technology, Engineering and Social Studies

The 1000-volume original paperback library in aid of education, industrial training and the enjoyment of leisure

Publisher: Robert Maxwell, M.C.

In-Service Education
and
Teachers' Centres

Other Books of Interest

CHAPMAN, L.R. The Process of Learning Mathematics

COPPEN, H.E. Aids to Teaching and Learning

CROSS, G.R. The Psychology of Learning

DAVIES, T.I. School Organization

DIXON, K. Philosophy of Education and the Curriculum

FELDMAN, K.A. College and Student: Selected Readings in the Social Psychology of Higher Education

GRAINGER, A.J. The Bullring: a Classroom Experiment in Moral Education

HALSALL, E. The Comprehensive School: Guidelines for the Reorganization of Secondary Education

HOPSON, B. & HAYES, J. The Theory and Practice of Vocational Guidance

HUGHES, M.G. Secondary School Administration: a Management Approach, 2nd Edition

HUGHES, P.M. Guidance and Counselling in Schools

HUNTER, S.L. The Scottish Educational System, 2nd Edition

JOHNSTON, D.J. Teachers' In-service Education

KING, E.J. Education and Social Change

KING, E.J. The Teacher and the Needs of Society in Evolution

MARSHALL, S. Adventure in Creative Education

O'LEARY, K.D. & O'LEARY, S.F. Classroom Management: The Successful Use of Behaviour Modification

RAVENETTE, A.T. Dimensions of Reading Difficulties

RENFREW, C.E. Speech Disorders in Children

SEGAL, S.S. No Child is Ineducable, 2nd Edition

The terms of our inspection copy service apply to all the above books. A complete catalogue of all books in the Pergamon International Library is available on request.

The Publisher will be pleased to receive suggestions for revised editions and new titles.

In-Service Education and Teachers' Centres

Edited by
ELIZABETH ADAMS

PERGAMON PRESS

OXFORD · NEW YORK · TORONTO · PARIS
SYDNEY · BRAUNSCHWEIG

U. K.	Pergamon Press Ltd., Headington Hill Hall, Oxford, England
U. S. A.	Pergamon Press Inc., Maxwell House, Fairview Park, Elmsford, New York 10523, U.S.A.
C A N A D A	Pergamon of Canada Ltd., 207 Queen's Quay West, Toronto 1, Canada
A U S T R A L I A	Pergamon Press (Aust) Pty. Ltd., 19a Boundary Street, Rushcutters Bay, N.S.W. 2011, Australia
F R A N C E	Pergamon Press SARL, 24 rue des Ecoles, 75240 Paris, Cedex 05, France
W E S T G E R M A N Y	Pergamon Press GmbH, 3300 Braunschweig, Postfach 2923, Burgplatz 1, West Germany

Copyright © 1975 Pergamon Press Ltd.

First edition 1975

Library of Congress Cataloging in Publication Data

Main entry under title:

In-service education and teachers' centers.

Includes index.

1. Teachers—In-service training. 2. Teacher
centers. I. Adams, A. Elizabeth.

LB1731.154	1975	371.1'46	75-6719

ISBN 0-08-018291-7
ISBN 0-08-018290-9 flexicover

Printed by A. Wheaton & Co., Exeter, England

Contents

Contributors

ELIZABETH ADAMS, Educational Consultant, former General Inspector, Surrey County Council

JOHN BRAND, Warden, Hipper Teachers' Centre, Chesterfield, Derbyshire

JOAN DEAN, Chief Inspector, Surrey County Council

ARTHUR DUCKERS, Senior Lecturer in Education, La Trobe University, Melbourne, Australia

MATTHEW MILES, Senior Research Associate, Center for Policy Research Inc., New York

JAMES PORTER, Principal, Berkshire College of Education

MALCOLM SKILBECK, Professor of Education and Director of Education Centre, New University of Ulster, Coleraine

JO STEPHENS, Staff Inspector for in-service training, Surrey County Council

NANETTE WHITBREAD, Principal Lecturer, City of Leicester College of Education

Acknowledgements

AFTER a professional lifetime of teaching, inspecting and taking responsibility for the in-service education of teachers, it was a pleasure to be invited by Edmund King to look around at the field of play and bring together the considered opinions of a good team of friends and colleagues.

Each of the authors who has contributed to this book is concerned for the educational welfare of pupils and students, for the betterment of the classroom situation in schools, for the means by which this might be effected and for the recognition of the crucial place of teachers themselves in that task.

For myself, and I suspect for many teachers, work and in-service education are inextricably mingled. What has so often helped me has been the support of a network of contacts: people at home and overseas to use as a sounding board, people with whom to work on ideas, people who, however eminent in the educational hierarchy, will treat me as their equal for the purposes of the discussion.

In acknowledging my indebtedness to the authors my hope is that more and more teachers, each in his own way, will find support in the multifarious ramifications of the in-service structure which they are helping to shape.

My secretary, Leila Hammond, also belongs to the network but deserves separate and special thanks.

Wimbledon, 1974   ELIZABETH ADAMS

CHAPTER 1

Editor's Introduction

THE book opens with an historical perspective by John Brand and Nanette Whitbread giving some indications of how the present state of the teaching service has been reached, and in particular of the ways in which, during the past century or two, first initial training and then in-service needs came to be identified and in some measure met. In the early days "training" had a poor connotation. The only trained teachers were ill-educated and badly paid and their pupils were the children of the poor. The authors of this initial chapter provide a number of insights as to how this picture changed over the years. Although the old elementary tradition based on the inculcation of skills and moral precepts persisted until the 1944 Education Act, side-by-side with, but largely separated from, a tradition of liberal or at least cultural studies for a restricted group of children, many influences were at work preparing for the break-through to a national policy of primary and secondary education for all. Among these influences the authors instance the writings and example of some enlightened heads of schools and of some of Her Majesty's inspectors; the support to their members of professional associations of all kinds; the progressive movement and its philosophers; and the clarification of ideas deriving from the dialogue which every official enquiry or educational report stimulated.

Their story, brought up to the present time, is continued in the next two chapters by authors with positions in the advisory service of a local authority. Jo Stephens opens up the whole spectrum of opportunities which contribute to in-service education in a chapter full of check lists and challenges. She accepts the need for universal in-service education and rejects easy options with regard to its provision. She brings out some of the pros and cons of school-based staff development; of the professional implications (in terms of teacher's salary, job specification and holidays) of systematic in-service education; of what teacher trainers or teacher tutors, operating from perhaps

1

a variety of bases, will have to do; and of what a consultancy-based approach to in-service education will call for in terms of time, organization and intellectual probity.

In the following chapter Joan Dean examines a number of main questions linking local authority advisory services with the in-service education of teachers. The issues she clarifies are the ways in which teachers need to grow professionally, how such growth comes about and the part that local authority advisors play in this growth; all leading to a concluding section on the kind of advisory service an authority needs. Much of the wisdom here is relevant to any group of tutors, lecturers or consultants. The only difference between such groups and bodies of advisers is the double role which the latter are normally appointed to fulfil. Advisors or inspectors are seen by teachers not only as educational consultants but also, and perhaps primarily, as persons with a degree of influence at the educational office in matters affecting either preferential treatment for the school or personal promotion or both.

Neither of these two authors would give priority of place in the provision of teachers' in-service education to institutions of higher education. The author of the fourth chapter, however, would do this, and he makes a case for professional centres in colleges of education. As a member of the James Committee, James Porter relates his chapter closely to the report, *Teacher Education and Training*, and to the government White Paper issued in the same year, 1972. He argues pungently for the mutual benefits to college and school of some college staff with responsibility for initial training being also seriously involved in in-service education. The help needed by teachers during their first year of employment (now referred to as their induction year) should be provided by an "assigned" tutor who would be mainly field based but would be on the staff of a college of education or other comparable institution. For the in-service needs of practising teachers, colleges would provide regional resource centres and would offer courses (on the units/modules plan) leading, where appropriate, to degrees. Additionally, colleges would support innovations; and in this connection James Porter is critical of the extent of the impact of Schools Council projects, recognizing the difficulties of diffusion of curriculum innovations which have been developed by a central group.

Two other authors write from positions in higher education regarding the in-service education of teachers. Neither, however, is suggesting that institutions of higher education have a particular responsibility for the in-service education of teachers as teachers. Both are concerned rather with what has to be done mainly by the teachers themselves to put their own house in order.

Malcolm Skilbeck concurs with James Porter's reserves about the appropriateness — even the cost effectiveness — of the sponsored projects approach pursued throughout its 10 years of existence by the national Schools Council. Concentrating on curriculum development as distinct from in-service education in general, he traces the origins of two major thrusts in curriculum development: one, the Nuffield Schools Council approach; the other, school-based or teacher-centred activity. He makes the case for curriculum development within the school and at the local level: not because it is easy but because nothing else works.

As he sees it, the teacher is the key to curriculum development as to any other educational reform. He has no use for groups of outside experts making decisions about what should go on in school classrooms and his observations on public examinations in secondary schools are a logical extension of this point. It is clear to him that the operation of the examination system inhibits progress towards school-based curricula and teacher-centred schools: progress which cannot be easy in any case. He is convinced that when the secondary school is as it should be, it will no longer find it possible to assimilate the public examination system.

Malcolm Skilbeck recognizes the need for local, regional and national structures of support, and in doing so calls for appropriate in-service education not only for teachers but for heads of schools and for all those who work with teachers from whatever college, advisory or consultative base. Towards the end of his chapter comes a summary of three separate modes of in-service education. His last word is on the teachers' need to learn about themselves and their relationship with others in intensive group work situations.

The author of the next chapter, Arthur Duckers, sees the pivot of the entire educational enterprise as the interaction in the classroom between teacher and pupil. What concerns him particularly is that practitioners find that they have to relinquish their foothold in the classroom if they are to reap rewards in salary and status commensurate with the enhanced competence achieved by dedication, experience and the application of theory to daily practice. Those remaining faithful to their calling have to be satisfied with intrinsic rewards while career-orientated teachers may reach positions of some power. He quotes an Australian authority on this point to the effect that right impressions on significant people pay off better than significant impressions on the right people (that is, on the children).

Arthur Duckers' remedy for this situation is professionalization. He analyses what the term means and shows that no benefit accrues to the teaching force from pretending that it is already a bona fide profession. He deals with five major impediments to professionalism and scans the literature for the attributes of a profession. The remedy that he proposes is that a proportion of practising teachers having reached doctoral level in their formal qualifications could become control groups in their district. Retaining part-time contact with pupils at school, the time-table of each member of such a local control group should enable him to form part of a connecting link between classroom teachers and members of the academic and administrative superstructure of education. What he proposes is a strategy for the prac-titioner to meet all comers in the educational field on terms of equality, and for the teachers to give substance to their claim for recognition as profes-sional persons.

The next three chapters are devoted to the teachers' centre, the new in-service education institution. Some teachers' centres, attached to institutes or schools of education in universities, have existed almost throughout the post-war period as part of area training organizations. In recent years, however, there has been a sudden flowering of teachers' centres set up by local authorities in schools, colleges or free-standing. In general these are the outcome of Working Paper number 10 published in 1967 by the Schools Council: *Curriculum development: teachers' groups and centres.* This document provided local education authorities with a certain amount of guidance for action — a teachers' centre was a firm proposition needing accommodation and staffing, that is, a place in the estimates.

In the operative working paper the idea of teachers' centres was put for-ward in the context first of the need for secondary teachers to meet to discuss the Certificate of Secondary Education, and secondly of the ex-perience of some teachers with Nuffield mathematics and science projects. The suggestion was made that teachers needed to meet locally in groups in a workshop situation. The local education authorities were asked to cooperate with existing in-service agencies such as a college of education or a university, even to cross authority boundaries in the attempt to make suitable new in-service education opportunities. In its conclusion the working paper en-joined that local groups of teachers should provide the motive power, without "hierarchy of initiative or control". As the paper then gave a couple of pages to practical considerations including financial implications the local education authorities recognized that a new institution was being mooted for which they might choose to make provision.

Appointed as warden of one of these new local authority centres, John Brand experienced the satisfactions and the frustrations of establishing a new institution. Sustained by enthusiasm, common sense and good relations with all comers, he learnt the new job on his feet. In his chapter he conveys something of these experiences in the light of wide contact with other wardens and of academic research on teachers' centres. To him, teachers' centres are the appropriate agency for the development of new school curricula. It is a disappointment, therefore, that they are less used by secondary than by primary teachers. He is critical of the job specification for some wardens and especially of joint appointments: wary also of the formulas used for setting up management committees in some areas. Without describing the warden's position as a career trap, he scorns alike those who use it as a means of escape from classroom realities into the busy trivia of office life and those who see it as a shop window for their own specialisms and as a step on the career ladder. On the whole, however, John Brand's focus is firmly on service to teachers, not on prospects for wardens. He makes a summary of three levels of involvement by local teachers in centres, and does not despair of harnessing staff from secondary as well as from primary schools.

What he describes approximates to the classic British model of a teachers' centre to which Matthew Miles, the American author of the next two chapters, frequently refers. Both these chapters are adapted from a report of a conference on teacher centres held at Syracuse University in 1972. The question to which conference members addressed themselves was whether, in America, a new institution, the teacher centre could be looked at as a means — not quite of salvation, but of "effecting educational change through teacher development". Miles' two chapters correspond with the two sections of his report. Chapter 8 is a somewhat abridged account of the conference proceedings with the main omissions from the text indicated by Editor's notes. Apart from the deletion of some footnotes and references, Chapter 9 is the final section of the report in its entirety: it constitutes the author's reflections and commentary.

Soon after the conference opened the high-level educators (no school teachers were present) gave voice to deep concern verging on despair about the state of public education in the United States. They admitted that schools could not succeed without effective teachers and said that existing institutions appeared to be unable (or unwilling) to provide teachers with serious learning opportunities. After such setting of the scene, the conference gave attention to an account by Audrey Griggs, a Schools Council field officer, of the "British model" of teacher centre. This account has been omitted as much of the information is readily available through Schools Council publications. Included, however, is Matt Miles' list of what teachers' centres were for: a check list of ten functions that "seem crucial in the process of professional renewal".

Having thus established the "quintessential Teacher Centre concept" the chapter continues with a section on recent developments in American teacher education with reference to teacher centres. Practically none of the assumptions on which Americans established their large, complex training centres had been found relevant in Britain. Matt Miles suggests that "a major block to successful diffusion of something like the Teacher Centre concept is the tendency to giantize . . . rather than developing pragmatically and organically from small-scale success experiences, as in the British model".

Following all this discussion about recent developments there is an account of "alternative" models of teacher centre. Those included in the chapter are the Teachers' Active Learning Centre in the San Francisco bay area and the Philadelphia Teacher Centre (both rather "British-type"); the Oakland Schools Centre in Pontiac, a large consulting and service-supplying agency a few miles from Detroit; and one centre at Syracuse itself supported by the United States Office of Education. Matt Miles concludes the chapter with a gloss on some devastating quotes from the final address, and with a summary of what had happened since the conference, especially regarding finance, to most of the bright hopes and national plans for the diffusion of teacher centres.

In Chapter 9 full advantage is taken of the invitation of David Krathwohl, the Chairman, to relate the discussions about teacher centres to theories of change in such a way as to have maximum impact beyond the conference group. These theories of change are used by the author to give a series of different perspectives. First he discusses the teachers' centre as an innovation and considers what redesigning of the British model might suit America. Next he considers the teachers' centre not just as an innovation in itself but as a strategy for encouraging a wide variety of changes in such areas as curricula or teaching methods. From these considerations of change strategy he develops some generalizations as to how the teacher centre ministers to motivational needs — of which the most striking is the one identified in the Coleman report([1]) as "fate control": the sense that the individual is not a pawn but has ability to act on the environment and not simply be run by it.

A second perspective is that of person change and system change, in the course of which Matt Miles points to the weakness of centre work unless teachers are also supported in their schools. What follows as the third perspective is a discussion of three metaphors for setting up centres: the oasis, the designed building, and linkage of existing buildings. The consideration of the teacher centre as a social movement comes next; and finally, their possibilities as an alternative situation. This last perspective seems to the author to be a fruitful line of thought which he develops somewhat before venturing into his view of the future. For this he offers fourteen predictions, none of them startling. As he says: "there is little that is apocalyptic or visionary in the air at the moment". He concludes, however, that the teacher centre movement is worth pushing if only in the hope that it may "help schools and schooling shift in a more human, productive direction".

The final chapter in this book begins with some indications of current public opinion concerning in-service needs in relation to the kinds of provision which were fairly normal until recently in Britain. There follows an account of modern in-service developments deriving from the Beloe and the Lockwood reports. This leads to some comments on the effects of an external examination system on the British teacher's traditional claim to freedom in matters of curriculum and school organization, and on the principles by which teachers exercise such of these freedoms as they actually have.

These questions of principle and of what teachers think their schools are for are illustrated by reference to a study of a secondary school in process of change and development: the Nailsea project. Suggesting that a report of such a research provides good in-service study material, other examples of relevant reports are instanced. An account of a conference on educational administration leads into questions about management and what teachers can learn from theory built up mainly in the context of business. The chapter ends with some reminders about the nature of in-service education.

Reference

1.   COLEMAN, J. S., *Equality of educational opportunity*,Washington, D.C.: United States Government Printing Office, 1966.

CHAPTER 2

An Historical Perspective

THE aim here can be to identify only some key factors and influences which have contributed to the emergence of present-day in-service education provision as it is presented elsewhere in this book. The limitations of space preclude a thorough analysis, and therefore necessitate a high degree of selectivity.

Periods of accelerated social change have usually been characterized by intensified interest in educational reform, revealed in attempts both to introduce legislation and to influence teachers through the publication of a spate of books and pamphlets on educational theory and practice.

The seventeenth century was a period when Samuel Hartlib and his circle were involved in both activities, as Charles Webster has described in some detail.[1] The early stages of the Industrial Revolution in Britain, coinciding with ideological repercussions from the American and French revolutions, was another such period extending from the late eighteenth to the early nineteenth centuries: the educational ideas of Rousseau and Pestalozzi were constantly under discussion; the philosophical radicals, utilitarians and Benthamites concerned themselves with many aspects of education and acted as pressure groups; the Sunday School movement flourished for a while; Joseph Lancaster and Andrew Bell promulgated their respective versions of the monitorial system; Robert Owen opened his unique school and adult education centre at New Lanark, and the first infant school movement was started; there were parliamentary committees of inquiry, debates and Bills concerning the education of the masses.

The last three decades of the nineteenth century, when England became a predominantly urban society, again saw a spate of educational inquiries, legislation and reform accompanied by much public discussion of the curriculum at all levels and the emergence of a variety of pressure groups. And the social dislocation of the First World War was followed by the relative success of the

Progressive Movement in education which profoundly affected some teachers in both the private and public sectors. We are once again witnessing another such era of intensified efforts to influence the schools through the teachers at a time of greatly accelerated social change.

Though particular periods can be highlighted in this way, it should not be forgotten that outstanding teachers have always striven to influence other teachers with whom they come in contact and have written their advice to achieve a wider impact. Roger Ascham, Richard Mulcaster, Charles Hoole and John Dury are examples as important in earlier times as Friedrich Froebel, John Dewey, Maria Montessori or A.S. Neill in more recent times. Innovative schools from Abbotsholme to Summerhill to Countesthorpe have made an impact well beyond their own walls. In this sense the in-service education of some teachers has been on-going.

Moreover, conscientious and enthusiastic teachers have always made it their business to widen or up-date their knowledge of the subject matter of their teaching, availing themselves of specialist literature, societies, conferences and courses of lectures. Adult education from the later nineteenth century has been well patronized by teachers who have participated in the Literary and Philosophical Societies, University Extension, the Workers' Education Association and now the Open University. Elementary and college-trained teachers have thereby raised their own academic level, often with a view to improving their salary and status within the profession.

The growth of a central authority during the last century, and the emergence of a state system after 1870, made possible attempts at deliberate intervention in the in-service education of teachers. The Education Department through Circulars, the Inspectorate and the Codes, the Science and Art Department through its approved syllabi and examinations, and both departments through their control of grants paid on the basis of results, as well as the Endowed School Commissioners as they devised and amended schemes for the reform of grammar schools, were all three engaged upon some form of in-service education of teachers and schoolmasters. Adventurous school boards and their more powerful successors, the local education authorities, were able to seize the opportunity of providing limited in-service training, controlling the curriculum and fostering restricted innovation.

Teachers and central government agencies have been the targets of educational pressure groups which have sought to promote change in curriculum content and teaching methods. Two prime examples from the later decades of the last century were the science lobby of H. E. Armstrong and T. H. Huxley, recently described by W. H. Brock,([2]) and the Froebelians.([3]) This century has witnessed a plethora of such single-minded pressure groups among which the various subject associations and the Nursery School Association may be considered particularly influential in their in-service work. The non-streaming and comprehensive school lobby of the last twenty years has had considerable in-service implications and repercussions, largely school-based but with support from such journals as *Forum* and *Comprehensive Education* and their annual conferences. The urgency with which the Community Relations Commission is pressing local education authorities to instigate in-service education for a multi-racial society is testimony to the new recognition of in-service education as a force for effective change. Indeed, teachers may now be exposed to pressure from a variety of sources.

The term "in-service education", as it is now generally used, refers to the entire process of curriculum review and any consequent modification of practice. Yet less than 5 years ago there was heated debate concerning what constituted involvement in curriculum development in contrast to participation in the lower order activity of in-service training.

The written word

Initially, in the absence of in-service activity on an organized basis, the communication of new ideas and approaches by means of the written word was a significant feature of teachers' in-service education. Thus Barnard,([4]) referring to the impact on the education scene of Thomas Arnold (1795-1842), the eminent head of Rugby School, pointed out that he was fortunate in his press, for he had been referred to in three works which spread his fame far and wide — Stanley's *Life of Arnold*, the novel *Tom Brown's Schooldays* and his son Matthew Arnold's poem *Rugby Chapel.*

Similarly John Ruskin (1810-1900), who for 12 years was Professor of Fine Art at Oxford while being actively associated with the Working Men's College in London, was a prolific writer. His books were not specifically concerned with educational topics, but most of them contained many passages on the subject of education. He has been described as a destructive critic of the existing education system, which appeared to him to be based on the principle of competition and to give a wrong outlook on life. As Barnard noted:

> We have by now become converted to so much of what Ruskin advocated, that it is easy to underestimate his importance as an education reformer; but it is largely to his influence that we owe the development of art teaching in schools, interest in nature study, the extension of playgrounds and playing fields, more imaginative methods of teaching history and literature, the realisation of the educational value of handicrafts, the medical and physical care of school children.

The whole infant school movement of the 1820s and the subsequent characteristics of the urban infant school, with its tiered gallery for simultaneous instruction of vast numbers of little children, owed much to the writing of Samuel Wilderspin (1792-1866) whose handbook *On the importance of Educating the Infant Children of the Poor* was reprinted eight times after 1823. This ensured that Wilderspin's rather than Robert Owen's became the model for the nineteenth-century infant school, for it provided untrained infant teachers with techniques for handling the situation with which they were then faced.

These examples serve to illustrate the impact of the written word as a stimulus to thought and action in the field of education: Thomas Arnold's reputation and influence were both aided by the written work of others, while John Ruskin created his own literary platform, and several practising exponents of the early nineteenth-century infant school furthered that movement.[5]

From the monitorial system to the pupil-teachers

The initial impetus for curriculum change and the consequent stratification of the teacher's professional standing resulted in the main from the work of outstanding individuals or various forms of state legislation.

One such individual who has assumed major significance as an early influence on the developing aspirations of the state education service is Sir James Kay-Shuttleworth (1804-77) who, apart from being responsible for the setting up of one of the very first training colleges for teachers, was also the first secretary of the first government department to be given a specific responsibility for education in 1839.

Barnard's appraisal[4] undoubtedly emphasized the positive aspects of Kay-Shuttleworth's contribution. As Barnard indicated, it was because Kay-Shuttleworth recognized the shortcomings of the earliest forms of training that he introduced the pupil-teacher system to take their place. Under this system pupil-teachers were selected at the age of 13 and underwent a 5-year apprenticeship with the headmaster concerned. Those who were successful could sit for a competitive examination and, if they passed high enough, were awarded Queen's Scholarships which entitled them to a 3-year course at a training college, at the end of which they could qualify as certificated teachers. Thus initial training was itself an in-service process for most elementary teachers in the nineteenth century. This became a sharply controversial issue by the time of the Cross Commission in 1888, which published Majority and Minority Reports respectively favouring and castigating the pupil-teacher system.

Kay-Shuttleworth laid the foundations of English elementary education; for he had stimulated public interest and his pupil-teachers gradually brought the mechanical monitorial system to an end. To him education meant an inculcation of habits, a training of skills and a development of intelligence; the school was to be a centre of social life and culture. At the same time it can be seen that there had been a significant step forward in the professional development of the teacher.

It was during the 1830s that the State began to support the voluntary efforts of the Churches in educating the working class on a large scale. As Barnard([4]) has it, "The educational ideal of the time was the training of the poor to an honest and industrious poverty which knows its place and was duly appreciative of any favours received". At the time there were no formal arrangements for training teachers and the problem was how enough teachers could be found within a largely uneducated population. The immediate solution both abroad and in this country appeared in the shape of the method known as the "monitorial system", promoted here by Joseph Lancaster (1778-1838) who described it as "a new mechanical system for use of schools" and Andrew Bell (1753-1832) who had been forced by staff shortages to put classes in the care of some senior pupils, while serving as a missionary in Madras. The system was quite straightforward; the older children in a school taught the younger. As Andrew Bell put it, "give me twenty-four pupils to-day and I will give you twenty-four teachers tomorrow". The system was inexpensive and it meant that the absence of teachers need not mean an absence of instruction. This state of affairs lasted for a generation simply because no better alternative emerged. Attempts to establish a training college for teachers were thwarted, because of the interdenominational religious controversy.

The squalid state of education as revealed by the inspectors of schools led to a public outcry and the establishment in 1846 of Kay-Shuttleworth's scheme of apprenticeship for pupil-teachers, which itself eventually came under attack in the Minority Report of the Cross Commission.

The public and grammar schools

The endowed grammar school was where the classical languages were taught, for this was the technical meaning of the term "grammar". The masters at such schools were normally required by the statutes to be graduates and were supposed to hold a teaching licence, which was granted by the bishop of the diocese. The first great public schools were simply those grammar schools which had outgrown their local origins and achieved national renown.

It is perhaps significant that although masters in grammar schools needed a bishop's licence to teach, no such requirement was enforced for those employed in elementary schools. However, as the nineteenth century progressed, the Church influence became less apparent and the licence to teach was not always required, but it was not finally abolished until the Endowed Schools Act was passed in 1869.

Although the classical languages were no longer the key to all human knowledge and the ability to speak and write Latin was no longer a vital vocational asset, they remained the hallmark of a gentleman and a prerequisite for university education. Barnard[4] maintains that the curriculum of the endowed grammar and public school remained much the same as it had been at the time of the Renaissance. Thus Latin and Greek language and literature virtually constituted the secondary curriculum, and the methods of teaching remained largely traditional. The public and many of the endowed grammar schools were at a low ebb in the early nineteenth century, and yet there was a growing need for extensive educational provision to meet the needs of the various sections of the rising and ambitious middle classes. This was met partly by the establishment of a significant number of new schools through the 1840s to 1860s and by the dramatic reform of the old public schools. David Newsome[6] has vividly portrayed the transformation of the latter into more civilized and well-organized communities with a new professional ethos under the leadership of several outstanding headmasters. The closed network, within which masters who served under their influence subsequently became headmasters of other schools in the same category, itself provided an informal process of in-service education.

Thomas Arnold wrought many changes in the school curriculum, including methods of instruction which would encourage self-activity while training the power of self-expression, at the same time adjusted to the needs of the individual pupils, with consequent implications for the manner in which the teachers would approach their work both in his school and elsewhere. Arnold carried out his ideas by applying the full weight of his own vigorous moral personality. The mere fact of his high reputation increased the prestige of other headmasters and that of the profession generally. This in turn improved the standing and facilitated the independence of the public schools to resist state intervention by clubbing together in the Headmasters' Conference. Otherwise it is possible that higher secondary education might have succumbed to state control and a source of potential curriculum innovation have been lost.

There has been a tendency wholly to attribute the emergence of a rash of new and more progressive schools during the forties and fifties of last century, including Cheltenham (1841), Marlborough (1843), Rossall (1844) and Wellington (1853), to the influence of Arnold alone; but this would do less than justice to the work of such men as Samuel Butler (1774-1839) who was elected to the headmastership of Shrewsbury in 1798 and his successor Benjamin Hall Kennedy (1804-89).

Elements of a rudimentary in-service pattern were clearly present, by virtue of the fact that Arnold's influence was transmitted via members of his staff and old pupils, who became headmasters of many of the public and endowed schools. As Barnard notes, "He was very careful to appoint as his assistants, men whom he could trust to carry out his ideals".

Elementary schools under the revised code

Robert Lowe had been Vice-President of the Education Department for three years, when he introduced the Revised Code in 1862. He was a liberal free-trader and was determined to solve the then current educational problems by applying his own economic theories. The Royal Commission under the Duke of Newcastle estimated that most of the 2,535,462 working-class children in schools of any kind left by the age of 11 and over a third attended for under a year. Lowe tried to change this situation by basing the Education Department's grants, not simply on the amount raised by local effort, but on the attendance of pupils under a certificated teacher, and subject to the results of an examination of each child in the "three R's" by an inspector. "Hitherto", Lowe said, "we have been living under a system of bounties and protection. Now we propose to have a little free trade." The teachers' pension scheme, grants for apparatus and pupil-teachers' stipends were withdrawn, and grants to training colleges were cut down. These measures constituted the revised code of 1862 — a legally binding document issued by the Education Department. It was a system designed to try to ensure value for expenditure of public funds on schools over which the state could exercise only indirect control.

This development possessed a special significance for the professional aspirations of the teacher. Certainly the teachers' pay scale was altered in the sense that it now became common practice to pay the teacher on a commission basis, with a basic salary and a proportion of the government allowance earned by the children. Obviously the intention was to give teachers an incentive to obtain good results at the annual examination and in the process improve the grant, hence the description of "payment by results". This mode of payment predominated for more than 30 years and was phased out to a great extent with the emergence of the larger school boards in the 1890s, which according to David Wardle([7]) took this step mainly as a result of continual pressure from the teachers' organizations.

The "results" achieved under this scheme were far too often mechanical in nature. Whereas the older order was charged with neglecting the less able, the Revised Code encouraged neglect of the intelligent and the reduction of all pupils to the level of the lowest capacity in a given school or class. The retrograde character of the Revised Code, from the standpoint of curriculum development, is immediately apparent, when it is realized that under this system "cramming" became a desirable educational procedure and the stereotyped false idea that the three R's were the all-important rudiments of education gained general acceptance.

As Adamson([8]) observed, on the credit side, the establishment of a qualified body of practitioners would lead inevitably to a certain levelling up in standards. Nevertheless the long-term implications for the teaching profession were inescapable, for the Revised Code resulted in teachers who were industrious and competent, but uninspired and not favourably disposed towards originality and experiment. In short, the emphasis from the curriculum point of view was on the achievement of measurable results in a limited field.

The repercussions of the Revised Code on curriculum development were entirely negative. Thoughtful inspectors such as Matthew Arnold noticed a marked tendency for teachers to resort to the drill and minute subdivision of material, which had been characteristic of the monitorial system. Experiments in curriculum exploration and extension were brought to a grinding halt. Hitherto the inspectorate had been a support to teachers, encouraging reform and experiment. Now relationships between teachers and inspectors became so strained that the scars remain to this day, for under the 1862 Code teachers had no alternative but to attempt to deceive the inspectors in order to secure a living wage.

The school-board period (1870-1902)

By 1870 there was increasing evidence and a growing awareness of the inadequacy of voluntary provision in meeting the educational needs of the working class. For every child to be found in school there was at least one other at home, or more likely at work. It was in such a climate that the Government passed the Elementary Education Act of 1870, introducing the school boards; for as W. E. Forster, the Vice-President of the Committee of Council, observed while introducing the Bill, "Notwithstanding the large sums of money we have voted, we find a vast number of children badly taught or utterly untaught, because there are too few schools and too many bad schools, and because there are large numbers of parents in this country who cannot, or will not, send their children to school".

During the school-board period, there were some interesting developments in the status and function of teachers. Employment by a school board tended to invest a teacher with a certain semi-official standing, especially if the board was in a large city. Salaries increased rapidly for the more successful teachers and for the first time, a career structure and a stratification in status became factors in the situation. With the construction of large schools in urban areas, it became necessary to appoint headteachers possessing administrative ability as well as teaching skill, and such men acquired a rise in status almost unknown to the head of a small rural school.

David Wardle writes that the school-board period witnessed a growing maturity in the function of teacher associations and a corresponding increase in professional awareness among teachers. Unfortunately the developments were noted for their piecemeal and uneven nature and rate of progress, so that any review of, or experiment with, the curriculum tended to be restricted There was also a great discrepancy between the different boards over the matter of a pay structure for their teachers. The contrast was most noticeable between urban and rural schools.

In effect this profoundly influenced the quality of intake into the teaching profession. Thus in urban areas better pay often, but not always, attracted superior candidates for the job to those applying in rural areas. The mere existence of these differentials was enough to ensure that the possibility of cooperative deliberations on the practical problems in teaching remained a dim, distant prospect. Likewise the distinction between the pay of heads and that of assistant teachers had an adverse effect on recruitment of assistants, particularly since as schools tended to become larger and fewer, there was less chance of promotion to a headship. In fact the head of any school earned twice as much as his senior assistant and three times as much as the ordinary qualified teacher. Consequently a majority of the school boards soon began to experience difficulty in the recruitment of male pupil-teachers.

The school-board period was one when the relationship between teachers and administrators often reached breaking point. This could be partly attributed to the growing professional maturity of teachers, but also to the fact that administrators possessed little or no understanding of the classroom situation.

Hardly any members of school boards had the benefit of practical teaching experience, and even fewer possessed first-hand knowledge of elementary schools.

According to Adamson,[8] ex-elementary school teachers were very rarely called to higher service during the school-board period as inspectors or organizers. The administrators were generally prejudiced against such appointments on the grounds that such men possessed a doubtful academic background and their understanding of the education process as a whole lacked breadth of vision. However, teachers' professional organizations showed signs of increasing solidarity as could be seen by the way they defended their position.

An important influence on the curriculum for the younger child during the school-board era was the thinking of Friedrich Froebel (1782-1852). As early as 1851 a private kindergarten was started in Bloomsbury by one of Froebel's disciples, and in 1854 his method was demonstrated at the Society of Arts' exhibition in London. This attracted much attention from teachers and inspectors, and during the next 20 years more schools of this type were opened both in London and the provinces, although in the main they were confined to children of rich parents. By 1784 a Froebel Society had been founded by Maria Grey, who had previously done so much to bring the Girls' Public Day Schools into being. This society has prospered ever since, providing a challenging range of course activities and publications for its members. Whether initially Froebel-trained or not, most infant and many junior school teachers must have encountered its influence.

Froebel's ideas were not so easy to adapt to the vast numbers in the infants' departments of public elementary schools, even after they had been released from the restrictive practices associated with "payment by results". Kindergarten exercises were introduced in many infant classes by the 1890s, but the manner of their operation was of necessity mechanical, because the teachers concerned were dealing with extremely overcrowded classes, as contemporary photographs show. As early as 1874 the London School Board appointed a Froebelian to give in-service lectures to infant teachers.

Teachers' associations

The founding of teachers' associations was a feature of the second half of the nineteenth century. The activities of the Schools Inquiry Commission caused widespread concern among the heads of the endowed schools and, as a result, the Headmasters' Conference was established in 1869. It has met regularly ever since. The headmistresses formed their own association in 1874, but did not adopt such an exclusive policy as the headmasters over membership.

Meanwhile the National Union of Elementary Teachers was formed in 1870 and the word "Elementary" was dropped from its title in 1889. Among other sectional societies which came into existence were the Independent Schools Association (1883), the Headmasters' Association (1890), which included those secondary school heads who were not eligible for the Conference, the Association for Secondary School Assistant Mistresses (1884) and Assistant Masters (1891). Apart from these there were numerous professional or semi-professional societies concerned with purely educational matters, or with particular subjects of the curriculum and methods of teaching them.

From 1902 to World War I

It soon became apparent that teaching was beginning to make steady progress as a profession. This could be seen by the way in which differentials between the payment and conditions of teachers in rural areas and those in urban situations largely disappeared. During the period when he was effective head of the Board of Education (1902-11) Robert Morant reintroduced a sharp distinction between elementary and secondary education, which had begun to be blurred by some urban school boards' development of higher-grade schools. Higher elementary schools were excluded from secondary education which was to be the prerogative of grammar schools alone. This policy was bitterly attacked by the National Union of Teachers but supported by the secondary teachers' association. Wardle[7] describes the emergence of secondary school masters as an élite in terms of payment, conditions of service and social status, thus one split in the ranks of teachers' unity was substituted for another.

Curiously enough, having dealt a body-blow to the notion of education as a continual process, Morant proceeded to soften the hitherto harsh attitude of the Board of Education and of local authorities towards elementary schools and their teachers. The *Code for Public Elementary Schools* of 1904 and the *Handbook of Suggestions for the Consideration of Teachers* (1905) demonstrated a heartening attitude towards the teacher, which was virtually the opposite to the one in evidence under the old régime. The latter publication urged that "each teacher shall think for himself, and work out for himself such methods of teaching as may use his powers to their best advantage and be best suited to the particular needs and conditions of the schools". In addition the appearance of the large school with many qualified teachers demonstrated quite clearly that the administrator's view of the teacher had changed, for now the close and careful scrutiny with which the old-style headteacher had supervised the work of his pupil-teachers was no longer possible. A new concept was emerging, which visualized the assistant teacher as a competent professional, capable of a considerable degree of autonomy in his work in the classroom.

According to Selleck[9] the First World War proved to be a setback to the accelerating growth of a dynamic curriculum and the search for status on the part of the teacher. J. A. Pease, who at the time was President of the Board, addressed an open letter to "my colleagues in the national service of education" which attracted a great deal of attention. Mirroring his attitude and outlook, the *Journal of Education* stated that "The first duty of teachers . . . is to keep the system of education going; to fill up the gaps in our ranks; to continue makeshifts and be ready to work double spells when called upon".[10]

It was not possible to function normally, for no money was available for school buildings; schools and training colleges were taken over for military purposes despite the Board's successful protest against the over-enthusiastic requisitioning that marked the early days of the war. Over 20,000 teachers had served in the forces by the end of the war, many never to return, which only served to increase the acute nature of the staff shortage. The Board admitted that "the system as a whole, undoubtedly has suffered . . . the war has imposed on educational resources a continual and increasing strain as regards both personal and material conditions, and has entailed many sacrifices".[11] Such statements sum up the disorder brought about by the First World War.

Between the wars

Selleck[9] relates how in 1918 Caldwell Cook illustrated most effectively the state of the progressive cause and the degree to which the notion of a wide and free exchange of ideas on practice between teachers had progressed. The war was finished, the Perse School was prepared to welcome his return and his book had been well reviewed by the press. His conception of the educational process had been enthusiastically received and, therefore, he had every reason to be optimistic. Yet by 1933 he suffered a nervous breakdown, partly because of belated shellshock. He never taught again and he lived alone. A man who had wished to inspire others could not face anyone but his closest friends and eventually he died in 1937, broken and disillusioned.

While there are clearly much earlier examples of systems and legislation, which have influenced the way in which teachers have responded to the challenges implicit in providing educational opportunities geared to the needs of an increasingly dynamic society, few demonstrate this process of adaptation so aptly as the arrival of the Dalton Plan from the United States of America in the early 1920s.

Selleck relates how from many points of view the Dalton Plan was the most encouraging and stimulating development to emerge between the wars. Basically it was a simple and economic reorganization of the schools to enable both children and teachers to function to better effect. It did not add to or change the curriculum, it did not necessitate the purchase of expensive resources. It disposed of the notion that there was any one method of teaching children, while attempting to view the curriculum from the child's standpoint. Thoroughness could be accomplished without damaging the learning opportunities of either the slow learners or the brilliant children. It gave the uncertain teacher, who had come to realize that his present practice was not satisfactory, an opportunity to join the progressive ranks without forsaking all his more traditional leanings. He could experiment, while retaining the security of some of his valued habits and procedures.

Unfortunately this comparative victory for the progressive cause, with its attendant growth in some teachers' professional development, needs to be seen in relation to the shabby treatment handed out to the teachers in the same period by the government and the local education authorities. In addition, although the Dalton Plan was a positive development, it tended to reveal how thoroughly the teachers were insulated against reform by their reliance on the procedures which matched their limited educational background and which provided them with professional security.

Too often innovators were united in their opposition to the old order, but were divided on what should take its place. However, on the whole the progressives succeeded in gaining the initiative in educational discussions. They might not have radically altered practice in the classroom situation, but they had made an impact. Their problems were now the focus of educational debate. Their ideas found ready acceptance by the bodies committed to the provision of courses and study groups for practising teachers, such as the College of Preceptors, which was originally awarded a Royal Charter for what amounted to teacher training and in-service activity in 1848. The Educational Development Association tapped teachers' increasing need to understand the practical implications of progressive ideas, while the growing number of subject associations were gaining support and increasing their influence on the secondary curriculum. The views of the progressives were taken up in the training colleges and passed on to the new generation of teachers. Revised editions of *The Handbook of Suggestions for the Consideration of Teachers* and the 1931 and 1933 Hadow Reports were clearly permeated by their thinking, as were the pamphlets published by The Board of Education.

Yet this diffusion of progressive ideas was effected with little systematic in-service work among teachers, though HMIs were encouraging and had begun to run residential courses. Books and journals were the chief medium, supported by conferences run by various pressure groups. The American progressive movement was an important source. John Dewey's writings were published in Britain, W. H. Kilpatrick's "project method" was introduced in infant and junior classes and *The Child-Centred School* (1928) by Harold Rugg and Ann Shumaker was enthusiastically received. English progressive headteachers, such as E. R. Boyce in Stepney, wrote of their experiments with the new child-centred methods. The *New Era*, journal of the New Education Fellowship, began publication in 1920 and Susan Isaacs contributed regularly as "Ursula Wise" to *The Nursery World* from 1929 to 1936. One of the few ventures in specific retraining was undertaken by Maria Montessori who ran 6-month courses for teachers every other year in London from 1919 to 1938, and published detailed prescriptive handbooks on her methods. Individual local inspectors, such as Miss E. W. Miller in Leicester's nursery and infant schools, exerted their influence on teachers in their area. Not surprisingly, though the views of the progressives became widely known, classroom practice was slow to change and innovation tended to be confined to certain localities. Moreover, competition for free places in grammar schools through the scholarship examination inhibited experiment and reinforced mere instruction.

Educationalists, who had been encouraged by the Fisher Act of 1918 in the belief that long overdue reforms were now to be carried out, found that by April 1919 the Board had decided to confine the activity of the local education authorities to "the provision of minimal statutory services".

Within 2 years the Geddes Committee on National Expenditure had recommended raising the school admission age to 6, reducing free places, increasing class sizes, cutting teachers' salaries, school meals and medical inspection. Local expenditure became the subject of a close scrutiny, programmes of development were blocked and drastic building economies were introduced. Geddes were also responsible for a cut of 5 per cent in teachers' salaries in 1922. Further attempts were made to economize, some successful, others not; but the damage had been done. The atmosphere of continual pressure upon educational budgeting and the way in which governments and local authorities in equal measure were prepared to sacrifice the life-blood of the education service inevitably brought about a fall in teacher morale. During this period the teachers' main concern was to protect their falling standard of living and in-service activities became a secondary consideration.

The Second World War and the 1944 Act

With the outbreak of World War Two, the country once again stripped education of its resources, both teachers and facilities. An added hazard was the need to evacuate teachers and children, an operation which made new, round-the-clock demands on many teachers. However, this was one development which revealed an unexpected bonus, namely the increased extent to which teachers were involved with children's all-round welfare which led many to see their own commitment in a new light. As a consequence, the movement of the teacher from the authoritarian "front of the class" situation to the more democratic "within the class and among the children" stance had begun. Moreover, evacuation of teachers itself facilitated diffusion of ideas and practice.

The 1944 Education Act disposed of the "elementary" education format and provided a framework in which the recommendations of the Hadow Report, with its emphasis on "parity of status" for all post-primary education, might be achieved. The Act did not refer to the "types" of secondary school, with which the Hadow, Spens and Norwood Committees had been so much concerned, but most local education authorities planned for selective and non-selective schools. Consequently the crucial problem of *how* to select children for post-primary education was not raised as the existing "types" of school were retained. Nevertheless the Education Act, 1944 offered opportunities for progress in national education which had never been offered before.

The efforts of the new secondary schools to provide their children with opportunities equal to those available in grammar schools imposed a daunting task on their largely non-graduate teachers. Many attended evening classes in colleges of further education and extra-mural departments or wherever they could find useful courses. They joined subject associations and attended week-end and vacation courses. Little official help was forthcoming: they had to fend for themselves.

Motivated partly by the desire to raise their own academic level to meet new teaching demands, but also by the need to upgrade their salaries and professional status, many studied for London External Degrees. Here Birkbeck College served teachers well in London and the Home Counties.

The sixties were noted for the way in which in-service course provision accelerated, as well as the means by which it could be measured. The 1964 National Survey for the Plowden Report showed that as a national average two-thirds of primary teachers had attended at least one course during the previous 3 years, whereas Brian Cane's Three Counties Survey[12] showed that during 1964-7, teachers' participation in course activity in the counties of Durham, Norfolk and Glamorgan were not as great as this, and varied considerably from one county to another, and from primary to secondary groups of teachers. In one county, only 50 per cent had ever participated in in-service activity of any kind. Particularly notable here was the overwhelmingly positive attitude of the responding sample towards their need and desire for in-service activity.

Perhaps even more significant was the Department of Education's large-scale survey of the in-service situation in 1967,[13] which revealed that over one-third of all teachers had not attended any courses between 1964 and 1967. Apart from this the figures demonstrated an annual growth which tended to double itself in terms of course attendances.

Subject associations

The various subject associations have made a continuing contribution to curriculum development in the schools. They have been more concerned with the secondary curriculum, but they have not neglected the primary schools where some have made a significant impact in the post-war period. Their membership has come from both the public and private sectors, and they have acted as effective pressure groups for the reform of content and teaching methods. Their weakness has been their relative isolation from one another, so that they have not acted in concert to develop a consensus on the curriculum as a whole.

Their activities have included publication of pamphlets, bibliographies, handbooks and journals as well as running courses, conferences, study tours in Britain and abroad and in fieldwork centres. Thus they have acted as agencies for the diffusion of new ideas and research, bringing together teachers from a variety of types of school and other educational institutions. But for their work, some now well-established subjects might never have found a place in the school curriculum. New associations are continually being formed to promote new subjects, particularly for sixth-formers.

Local branches have been very active in some areas, collaborating with the university or local education authority specialist advisers. Innovatory schemes for Certificate of Secondary Education, Modes 2 or 3 have sometimes resulted.

To single out the work of any particular subject association would be unfair and improper. Let it suffice to note that the continuing contribution of these bodies is a positive factor of in-service education.

The McNair Report

This document[14] in describing in-service course provision immediately before and after World War Two, indicated that available opportunities for practising teachers to attend refresher courses to prepare them to teach particular branches of the curriculum, lacked system. A teacher, whether trained or untrained, was not then required to attend a refresher or any other type of course. Despite this and various other discouraging factors — expanding classes, contracting pay scales and resources — the demand for courses actually exceeded the supply. These courses run by Her Majesty's inspectors could be full-time lasting 2 or 3 weeks or even a full term; or part-time, held in the evenings, at weekends or in the holidays.

The McNair Committee realized that many teachers employed full-time in grant-earning and recognized schools before World War Two had remained untrained. In addition the system had been largely disorganized by the recruitment of more than 20,000 teachers into the Forces. In order to meet the needs of the immediate post-war situation, it proved necessary to arrange improvised, abbreviated and intensive courses for the training of teachers.

The Report also contained some recommendations that showed a desire to lay foundations for future growth. One such proposal produced the University Institutes of Education, one of whose numerous inherited responsibilities was the provision of a range of services for practising teachers in their areas. These services have tended to vary in nature, quality and scope in relation to the available resources and sense of priorities in the area. University involvement in teacher training dates from a recommendation of the Cross Commission which resulted in several day training colleges for elementary teachers in the 1890s. These were remodelled as 1-year post-graduate courses for secondary teachers by the end of the century.

The development of award-bearing in-service courses has tended to vary in relation to the outlook of each particular institute of education and its perception of local needs. In many cases award-bearing activity has been notable for its scope and variety although it is in the field of the short course and the study group that a number of institutes have made major contributions towards interpreting changing teachers' attitudes towards the curriculum and in-service education. Certainly poorer local education authorities, particularly in rural areas, have often had good cause to welcome the growing and imaginative contribution of the institutes of education.

More recently collaboration between the Department of Education and the institutes of education has resulted in intensive workshop-style long residential courses, which are generally thought to be effective. Inevitably, with the growth of teachers' centres, attendance at some institutes of education have tended to fall and the need to reconsider their function has been recognized.

The Nuffield Foundation and the origin of teachers' centres

The pressures on the curriculum in the past 15 years have been such that a measure taken to meet one immediate need has tended to create the necessity for further measures. The Nuffield Foundation developed a procedure for mathematics projects whereby teams of teachers, college lecturers and university consultants, backed by advisory committees, devised new trial courses and as a result of feedback from the schools, the materials were revised and then put on extended trial prior to publication.

In this way a wide selection of learning aids was produced, including books, apparatus and audio-visual material. In the process the teams found it necessary to have somewhere for the teachers from a trial area to meet together to discuss their reactions to the materials. A central meeting point within a trial area meant that displays of the developing materials and apparatus could be provided. Consequently the climate was created for the emergence of the first single subject teachers' centres, which at that time were known as Nuffield science or mathematics centres.

Having also taken on curriculum development in French and other foreign languages, the Nuffield Foundation was clearly in danger of being overloaded with specific subject development work, which would overstretch its resources and undermine its autonomy to determine its areas of research. It had helped to set in motion an irresistible demand for extensive curriculum reform and had formulated a procedure for action research. The time had come for a more publicly responsible body to undertake this work.

The Schools Council, teachers' centres and the Certificate of Secondary Education

The Schools Council arose from a report by a working party which met in 1963 under the chairmanship of Sir John Lockwood.([15]) It absorbed the Curriculum Study Group originally established by the Ministry of Education in 1962 which had aroused suspicions of a return to central control. In creating the Schools Council the express intention was to "uphold and interpret the principle that each school shall have the fullest possible measure of responsibility for its own work, with its own curriculum and teaching methods based on the needs of its own pupils and evolved by its own staff; and to seek through a co-operative study of common problems to assist all who have individual or joint responsibilities for, or in connection with, the schools curricula and examinations to co-ordinate their actions in harmony with this principle".

In its early days the Council's influence was more noticeable on the examining than on the curriculum aspect. Credit for the effective launching of the Certificate of Secondary Education examinations must be shared with the Secondary School Examinations Council for its preparatory work before it was taken over by the new body, and with the fourteen regional boards which administer the examination under the national guidance of the Council.

The CSE was recommended by the Beloe Committee in 1960 and introduced in 1965. It is a school-leaving certificate, assessed so that the top grade is equivalent to the Ordinary level of the General Certificate of Education. The organization is mounted on a regional basis, with teachers represented on the regional committees and constituting the local subject panels. New panels can be established in response to local demand.

The three modes of CSE all involve teachers in syllabus and assessment design, but modes 2 and 3 invite teachers in groups of local schools or in individual schools to design their own syllabus and, in the case of mode 3, design their own examinations and other forms of assessment. The administrative means has thus been created for realizing the abortive hopes of the Norwood Committee for teacher-controlled, school-based examinations.

Sadly, only a tiny minority of teachers have ventured to make use of mode 3. To do so is not only very demanding and time-consuming, it also requires supportive facilities and resources that are often lacking. Where mode 3 is undertaken, the subject teachers necessarily become engaged upon mutual in-service education. This is also true to a lesser extent with mode 2.

Nevertheless, even mode 1 has proved an interesting development from an in-service education standpoint, because the teachers on a particular subject panel have to meet periodically to review the subject content and examination procedures. In this situation they have an opportunity to make a direct impact on the curriculum and the manner in which it is used. The fact that such meetings are often held in teachers' centres means that there is always a likelihood that the teachers concerned will encounter colleagues from primary schools and improve the pattern of communication in the process.

It is still too early to evaluate the Schools Council's achievement as an influence on the developing curriculum. Its numerous subject committees and curriculum development projects have worked independently to encourage new thinking both within and across discipline boundaries, as well as on either side and across the primary-secondary division. The high priority it gave to preparing for the raising of the school-leaving age, and the series of working papers that resulted, may have contributed to the notion that pupils who leave school at the minimum age constitute an identifiable group with particular characteristics. Its working parties on examinations and its Examinations Bulletins may well have reinforced this by generally assuming those below the 40th percentile are unexaminable. As Parry[16] has observed: "While it repeatedly protests that it merely offers a service to be accepted or rejected as teachers wish, it continues with money provided by the Department of Education and under local education authorities to build up an organisation that could be used dogmatically." Conscious of the need to allay suspicion, the inspectorate is ambivalent about purveying information from the Schools Council to the teachers, and hence the lines of communication between the two have not been satisfactorily worked out.

Schools Council Working Papers Nos. 2[17] and 3[18] recommended the establishment of local development centres for the promotion and encouragement of school-based curriculum development. Nuffield project work had seen the creation of teachers' centres in a supporting role, but by 1965 the

Schools Council proposed the establishment of separate centres for different areas of the curriculum.

Within 2 years the Schools Council thinking had changed as demonstrated by Working Paper No.10([19]) which suggested that a local centre would be more effective if it could cover the entire curriculum at all levels. This would reduce the tendency for subject specialists to work in isolation and ensure that the centres brought primary and secondary teachers into closer contact.

By favouring teachers' centres controlled by the local education authorities as the growth point for in-service work on curriculum development, the Schools Council — and, by implication, the Department of Education — seemed to wish to undermine the university institutes of education. The James Committee's([20]) proposal for dismantling the area training organizations and thereby curtailing university institutes' in-service functions, can be seen as a further threat to autonomous influences on curriculum development and in-service education. That some local education authorities are evidently planning to exclude colleges of education from in-service provision, placing it all in the hands of their advisers and basing it on their teachers' centres, lends further substance to this danger.

Colleges of education and the James Report

Some college of education lecturers have been actively involved in all aspects of in-service education for some time. However, even the most optimistic survey([13]) recorded the in-service involvement of hardly more than one-fifth of education department staff from colleges of education, disregarding a negligible contribution from all other departments combined. In recent years, colleges of education have encountered mounting criticism regarding their handling of initial teacher training, let alone their in-service education commitments.

This was recognized by the decision to set up the James Committee in 1971 whose Report urged an extensive restructuring of the colleges of education. The main stress in the Report's proposals for restructuring initial education and training was on in-service involvement referred to in the report as the third cycle. "To none of our recommendations do we attach more importance than to these, for they determine a great deal of the thinking which underlies the report as a whole."([20])

More recently a government White Paper([21]) was published which, while accepting some of the James Committee's proposals, ignored or rejected others. Where both were in firm agreement, however; was in their common concern that there should be greater opportunities for the continued education and training of all teachers at intervals throughout their careers. The proposal was for all teachers to be entitled to release for in-service education for periods equivalent to one term in every 7 years of service. The estimate was that the actual take-up of such an entitlement would result in 3 per cent of the teaching force being seconded at any one time, amounting to a four-fold increase in present opportunity. The Government made this suggestion on the grounds that the expenditure to achieve such an expansion of in-service education was "a necessary investment in the future quality of the teaching force".

The teaching profession and the training institutions long complained of the unsatisfactory nature of the new teacher's probationary year with its lack of any systematic induction process. Consequently there was wide acclaim for the White Paper's[21] commitment to an induction year comprising in-service continuation of initial training for new entrants under professional tutors at professional centres. Pilot schemes were to be run from 1973 so that the new scheme could be fully operational in 1975, but cuts in public expenditure already curtailed these early in 1974.

The Inspectorate

Old attitudes die hard, transmitted from one generation of teachers to the next as a professional mythology. Disguised as defensive hostility, teachers' fear and distrust of the inspectorate has stubbornly persisted despite the latter's efforts to create a more democratic atmosphere of partnership. Her Majesty's inspectors were originally highly supportive, but under the Revised Code they were forced to play the role of critic and judge in a forbidding and authoritarian manner. The invention of "the full-dress formal inspection"[22] after 1902 for grammar schools, and its extension after 1944 first to all secondary and later to primary schools too, served to perpetuate old attitudes. Recruited by patronage until 1926, their social background distinguished and divorced them from the majority of teachers. Nevertheless, many were closely identified with the interwar progressive movement which they undoubtedly helped to diffuse. Democratization of recruitment and internal organization has facilitated a change in the role of Her Majesty's Inspectorate which is now more generally seen as helpful and constructive, though some ambiguity remains as was shown in the 1968 report by a Select Committee of the House of Commons.([22]) From small beginnings in the 1930s, the post-war growth of the Department's long and short courses, bringing many more teachers into closer and more informal contact with inspectors, has done much to break down old attitudes.

Many local education authorities changed the titles of their inspectorate from organizers to advisers in an attempt to make explicit the implicit change in their function. During the past 10 years they have been increasingly involved in local curriculum development within the growing network of teachers' centres as well as in individual schools. A predictable bonus has been an all-round improvement in relations between them and the teachers in schools and colleges of education.

Selected influences on the in-service education process in Wales

(a) Some significant aspects of the evolution of secondary education in Wales

Basically the evolution of the elementary school in Wales tended to run parallel with the English state system, although the rural nature of so many of the schools produced the same drawbacks which have plagued the English rural areas. However, the Aberdare Report on Secondary Education which appeared in 1881 revealed the unsatisfactory nature of intermediate and higher education in Wales. A more recent report([23]) describes how "the conscience of the country was stirred and a body of reformers set out to improve the situation".

In the last decade of the nineteenth century sixty-four intermediate schools were opened in Wales and the number of children receiving secondary education nearly doubled. These new schools were inspected and examined by the Central Welsh Board, created for the purpose in 1896.

The 1902 Education Act enabled Welsh local education authorities to set up secondary schools as distinct from intermediate schools. Some authorities which had experimented with higher-grade schools made some of them secondary schools with the encouragement of the Board of Education.

As new secondary schools were built, the general trend towards a grammar-school-styled curriculum became most marked. By 1939 Wales had sufficient grammar schools to cater for the needs of its population. As the Central Advisory Committee Report points out([23]) the fact that in one year in one Welsh county, almost 60 per cent of the children in the 10 to 12 age group entered that type of school, tends to create misgivings regarding the suitability of a grammar school education for such a wide range of children. As it happened the policy of the local education authorities favoured the grammar school rather than central and technical schools and the Welsh people supported this policy.

However, the impetus of the 1926 Hadow Report stimulated interest in the development of central or senior schools and clarified their aims. In the years that followed local education authorities were encouraged to make separate provision for children of 11-plus who did not proceed to secondary schools. As the report[23] observes: "in spite of the difficulties, some of these schools overcame the strong prejudice against them and established a tradition as valuable in its way as that of the grammar school".

(b) In-service education during the last decade in Wales

The Gittins Committee[24] observed that provision of in-service activity in Wales varied considerably in relation to the locality, the resources of the local education authority, the college education department and the demands of the teachers. The course activity seemed to depend on the availability of help from university department of education staff and local education authority advisers. Very few Welsh authorities ran their own local residential courses, and only one possessed a residential centre which permitted continuous, planned use for courses related to the needs of teachers in the area.

The Gittins Report suggested that during 1964-67 most Welsh authorities achieved only limited development of their own in-service pattern, and that this might be related to the slow development of the advisory services advocated in the report. Many authorities were too small to carry their own provision and as Morgan[25] observed: "It seems likely, too, that the emphasis in present provision (up to 1967) fell on short courses of lectures, most often without arrangements to follow up in schools or teachers' centres. Nevertheless this development still appears to vary considerably between areas."

Conclusion

Overall, in-service education is now more freely available than at any other time in the history of the state education service. Similarly at no time have teachers as a body been placed in such a favourable position to take advantage of the increased provision, although it is necessary to point out that activity and provision are still very uneven. There is a tendency for richer, but not necessarily larger, authorities with high density populations in industrial areas to make better and more thorough provision than those covering mainly agricultural areas. The 1974 reorganization of local government may be expected over the long term to result in more equitable provision.

From the days when religious fervour and vocational dedication were assumed, teachers have been expected to make sacrifices in the interest of the children. The expectation was reinforced as teaching conferred professional rather than artisan status. Teaching became subject to the ambiguity inherent in the concept of a professional vocation. Growing professional confidence and autonomy, officially encouraged in this century, has enabled teachers to respond to increasingly complex demands involving professional judgement. Universal secondary education, particularly under comprehensive reorganization, has blurred social class distinctions among both pupils and teachers while highlighting outmoded vestiges of the old order. Frustration with these, especially in the matter of salaries, has inevitably led many teachers to reject vocationalism when this is taken to imply subservience and inadequate remuneration. It is partly on this account that the staffing situation in London schools is fast reaching crisis point. Refusal to cover up deficiencies is a sign of professional maturity.

Teachers are also demanding greater participation in the formal structures of decision-making and control. This is a logical concomitant of grass-roots involvement in curriculum development.

Expected to cure many of society's ills, the education service has responded with community schools, educational priority areas, raising of the school-leaving age, compensatory education programmes and so on. All such responses impose heavy demands on the teaching force which has to re-educate itself on the job. The need for supportive in-service education — courses, study groups, action research — is pressing.

At a time of acute economic crisis it is difficult to view opportunities for in-service education with sanguine enthusiasm. Even so, an optimistic outlook is justified by the range and extent of provision that has never before been matched. There is the Schools Council without which the current reappraisal of the secondary curriculum could not have reached its present stage of development. Teachers' centres are now firmly established as part of the education scene. Local authority advisers and Her Majesty's inspectors no longer merely inspect but run courses and are working out the changing nature of their roles. Uncertainty, however, shrouds the future of the colleges of education and the area training organizations concerning the contribution they will be allowed to make. Independent bodies such as the Nuffield Foundation take a practical interest in developing more appropriate curricula for children in a constantly changing society. Television and the rest of the mass media have turned their attention to the learning process, with the Open University making a distinct and significant contribution to the in-service education of teachers and others.

As after the First World War, horizons seem high and wide; but governments from now on must recognize that education can no longer be the victim of perennial economy cuts. Innovations such as the Bachelor of Education degree, the Council for National Academic Awards and the Open University clearly represent new potential. In the case of the first, however, the tendency to base qualifications on the academic content of a teacher's specialism at the expense of emphasis on the theory and practice of teaching is perhaps reminiscent of a bygone age; but the Council for National Academic Awards has proved willing to accept more directly professional courses for in-service B.Ed., and the Open University post-experience courses have been found relevant to the needs of practising teachers.

In earlier days some teachers' concern for their professional commitment found expression in the formation of local associations, and in the process created the first organized in-service education. The teachers' centre movement now seems to have inherited that responsibility and has rightly been described as the main hope for the future. To fulfil that hope it will need to safeguard itself from undue control by local or central government agencies, and ensure the continued injection from independent sources that has so far been secured by the involvement of universities and colleges. Teacher control of in-service education requires a professional maturity that can transcend intra-professional vested interests and mutual suspicion.

References

1. WEBSTER, C., *Samuel Hartlib and the advancement of learning,* Cambridge University Press, 1970.
2. BROCK, W. H., *H. E. Armstrong and the teaching of science 1880-1930,* Cambridge University Press, 1973.
3. LAWRENCE, E., *Frederich Froebel and English education,* Routledge & Kegan Paul 1952.

4.   BARNARD, H. C., *A history of English education from 1760*, revised edition, University of London Press, 1970.
5.   TURNER, D., 1870: The state and the infant school system, in *British Journal of Educational Studies*, vol. xviii, no.2, 1970.
6.   NEWSOME, D., *Godliness and good learning*, Murray, 1961.
7.   WARDLE, D., *English popular education 1780-1970*, Cambridge University Press, 1970.
8.   ADAMSON, J. W., *A short history of education*, Cambridge University Press, 1922.
9.   SELLECK, R. J. W., *English primary education and the progressives*, Routledge & Kegan Paul, 1972.
10. PEASE, J. A., A letter to teachers in time of war (1914), in *Journal of Education*, vol. 46, no.543.
11. Report of the Board of Education for the year 1914-1915.
12. CANE, B., *In-service training*, National Foundation for Educational Research, 1969.
13. *Statistics of Education*, Special Series No.2, Survey of in-service training for teachers, 1967, Department of Education and Science and Townsend, H. E. R., Her Majesty's Stationery Office, 1970.
14. Report of a Committee appointed by the President of the Board of Education to consider the supply, recruitment and training of teachers and youth leaders (the *McNair Report*), Her Majesty's Stationery Office, 1944.
15. *Schools Council, the first three years: 1964/7*, Appendix C, Her Majesty's Stationery Office, 1968.
16. PARRY, J. P., *The provision of education in England and Wales*, Allen & Unwin, 1971.
17. SCHOOLS COUNCIL, *Raising the school-leaving age*, Working Paper number 2, Her Majesty's Stationery Office, 1965(a).
18. SCHOOLS COUNCIL, *English*, Working Paper number 3, Her Majesty's Stationery Office, 1965(b).
19. SCHOOLS COUNCIL, *Curriculum development: teachers' groups and centres*, Her Majesty's Stationery Office, 1967.
20. DEPARTMENT OF EDUCATION AND SCIENCE, *Teacher education and training* (the James Report), Her Majesty's Stationery Office, 1972.
21. *Education: a framework for expansion*, Cmnd. 5174, Her Majesty's Stationery Office, 1972.
22. BLACKIE, J., *Inspecting and the inspectorate*, Routledge & Kegan Paul, 1970.
23. *The future of secondary education in Wales*, a report of the Central Advisory Council for Education (Wales), Her Majesty's Stationery Office, 1949.
24. *Primary education in Wales*, a report of the Central Advisory Council for Education (Wales) (the Gittins report), Her Majesty's Stationery Office, 1967.
25. MORGAN, G. A. V., *Aspects of primary education: the challenge of Gittins*, Evans/Methuen, 1970.

CHAPTER 3

Some Current Issues for Teacher In-service Education

IN the context of this chapter I use the term in-service education to mean the development of the individual which arises from the whole range of events and activities by which serving teachers can extend their personal academic or practical education, their professional competence and their understanding of educational principles and methods. This is a slightly expanded version of the definition of third-cycle education used by the James Committee in its report *Teacher Education and Training.*([1])

It is necessary to make this point at the outset so that provision of teachers' courses shall be recognized as only one part of the complex. In practice many people still regard courses or other externally provided activities as virtually the only medium for in-service education. I say "in practice" because usually when questioned about this teachers in fact subscribe to other means but only occasionally are these developed in any structured way. We face, I think, *the issue of securing recognition, by both teachers and providers, of a whole spectrum of opportunities which contribute to in-service education. Recognition must then be followed by the maximization of the professional development to which the opportunities can give rise.*

It will be useful to pin-point parts of the spectrum by quoting the results of a recent survey amongst teachers. Thirty primary headteachers and 179 primary teachers undertook an exercise in which they were given the list of items in Table I and asked to tick those which were likely to improve a teacher's personal skill in the teaching of reading. Some of the items included seemed unlikely, in themselves, to improve personal skill although they might be helpful in making more effective the skill possessed. The percentage of heads and teachers marking each item is shown in the right-hand columns.

The high rating given to smaller classes (in this context) is disturbing if it is an expression of teacher preoccupation with the idea that better staffing ratios will automatically improve teacher skills. Such a view can cause some teachers to rationalize their failure to take responsibility for improving their skills through personal study in one form or another. One sometimes suspects

TABLE 1. Items ticked by (1) heads and (2) other teachers as likely to improve a teacher's skill in the teaching of reading

	Heads	Other teachers
Provision of relevant teachers' books in individual schools	67%	78%
Provision of relevant teachers' books in teachers' centres	33%	23%
Experience	27%	28%
Courses of lectures by class teachers	33%	41%
Courses of lectures by advisory or college staff	27%	35%
Courses of lectures with follow-up of study groups	63%	55%
Watching experienced teachers in own school	40%	53%
Watching experienced teachers in other schools	53%	37%
Provision of more equipment and books for children	50%	73%
Study groups led by teachers	47%	38%
Smaller classes	73%	92%
Personal reading of relevant literature	63%	61%
Television or radio programmes on the subject	33%	49%
Opportunity for regular structured discussion with own head and colleagues	83%	75%

The three items marked most often by heads were
    83 per cent regular structured discussion with head and colleagues,
    73 per cent smaller classes,
    67 per cent provision of relevant teachers' books in individual schools.
For teachers the same three items came out best but in a different order
    97 per cent smaller classes,
    78 per cent provision of relevant teachers' books in individual schools,
    75 per cent regular structured discussion with head and colleagues.

that "if only we had . . . then we could" is an excuse for inaction. The two other high-ranking items point clearly to the need to review school-based provision for in-service education. There are, of course, other tentative conclusions which could be drawn from the results of this survey.

An exercise like this can be a useful starting-point for a discussion with teachers about the extent of the range of teacher learning situations. In particular it usually leads to recognition of staff development opportunities within the school. At this point I want only to to expose *the potential of the professional community in a school as a learning resource for individual teachers* as an issue worth exploring by the teaching profession.

As a practical contribution I would suggest the following check-list as a starting-point for any head who wanted to evaluate or promote staff development systems within his own school.

> To what extent do the staff share in the overall curriculum and organizational planning of the school?
>
> Do staff work alongside each other with pupils or do they always work in isolation?
>
> Are there regular structured discussions of educational and pedagogical matters?
>
> Is there a staff room climate in which teachers are encouraged to discuss their work and can share problems constructively without fear of exposing ignorance or uncertainty?
>
> Have staff developed a theoretical basis for their methods which they can communicate effectively to the local community?
>
> Have the staff developed the skill of learning from each other and from teachers in other schools?

There is ample evidence of the effectiveness of some schools as staff development communities. We see staff in them develop into heads and senior teachers who act in their turn as in-service educators for new colleagues in other schools. We may be disappointed from time to time at setbacks in such schools when key staff move away but this is counteracted by the spread and growth of good practice elsewhere. When all schools give proper attention to staff development then the effects of teacher movement may be diminished. In fact movement itself may be curtailed by the increase in job-satisfaction which might emerge from such a general policy.

My discussions with heads based on this check list often produce a common response. "But we've always done that", is a predictable starter. Closer analysis of particular items may, however, reveal an unjustified faith in the weekly staff meeting or in informal conversation over coffee! When working in an area to which most people pay lip-service it takes a courageous head to expose and examine exactly what happens. In setting up a staff development system there are in any case some professional taboos to overcome; in particular those which imply a judgement of one teacher by another or which threaten the privacy of the classroom.

It is important not to underestimate the possible effect of such taboos on the ability of some adults to learn from one another in a professional setting. Are these impediments to personal development shared by any other isolated professionals such as the general practitioner or the parish priest? If so it could be significant that in both these fields, as well as in teaching, the idea of training completed before employment is still widely held in practice if not in theory. It may also be significant that a real or imagined status gap exists between the professional and his client in each case. This may force the professional to develop self-reliance to a level where it may interfere with his ability to assume a non-dominant role or to tolerate the feelings of inadequacy which are the price we pay for learning to do the job better.

Furthermore, the isolation in which such professionals actually perform may create unfounded feelings of indadaquacy or guilt which could be dispelled if there were more opportunities for colleagues to provide models for each other. In underplaying public evaluation we are deprived of opportunities for private evaluation which could lead to personal professional development. Teaching is not, of course, the only situation in which the more isolated the individual becomes the less likely he is to be able, or to have any desire, to accept opportunities to share experiences with others. It is a common feature of everyday life in many so-called civilized parts of the world.

I have said that the old idea of training before employment is still widely held in practice and many would no doubt challenge this. My evidence is drawn from repeated comments from established educators concerning what "ought" to be covered by initial training. Often they seem to me to indicate a totally unrealistic conception of the enormity of the training task and the capacity and maturity of 18 - 21-year-olds. Occasionally the comments belie basic beliefs about learning to which, in other circumstances, the speakers would subscribe; such as the need to develop understanding through real experiences.

Sadly even the James Report([1]) falls into the trap when in paragraph 2.1, after pointing out that the new initial training proposals would take time to be fully effective, it says "meanwhile established members of the profession need opportunities to improve their professional status and standards". Fortunately the rest of the report makes it clear that the committee favoured on-going in-service education as a principle and not just as a stop-gap or remedy.

The need for in-service education has become widely accepted when changes in curriculum or a teacher's role are involved. *The belief that initial training only fits the teacher to make a start and that means for development from then on must be part of the job specification must be reflected in practice and not remain ideology. Furthermore, responsibility for securing a teacher's professional growth must be shared by the teacher himself, by his seniors and his employers.* These two issues are even more fundamental than those previously discussed.

I have come to the conclusion, somewhat ruefully, that such fundamental changes in attitude and practice are unlikely to come about in the normal course of professional innovation with anything like sufficient strength. That is not to say that groundwork has not been done of course. We already have the Plowden([2]) idea of the teacher-consultant in the school; the "training-the-trainers" approach of some in-service courses; the setting up of teacher-run and teacher-controlled local centres with emphasis on teacher-led activities — all these can help to change attitudes and to change practice. The fact that many such innovations have not been as successful as was hoped is, I suggest, due to the failure to recognize the time and support necessary for their introduction. This failure is widespread throughout the profession including consumers, organizers and financers. Potentially worthwhile provision can be jettisoned by the providers' anxieties about coverage, enrolment and subsequent external signs of change. The most supportive, generous and far-sighted provision, however, will continue to be partially wasted until all teachers recognize, in practical terms, that their professional education is all part of the job and until they are seen to organize their work and their institutions with this in mind.

The thoroughly professional teacher has already done this as far as an individual can. He will not, however, get all the facilities and conditions he needs nor will he find his proper status, including financial status, in society until all teachers and all schools have done the same. I believe that such a change in recognition by society of the teacher's job will only come about as the result of legislation concerning conditions of service. A salary agreement which gave teachers a professional salary and professional working hours and holidays would achieve this at a stroke and would do away publicly with the idea that school pupil hours and school teaching hours are the same. Such an agreement would bring recognition to lesson preparation, marking time and staff consultations within the teacher's working day and would in addition provide the equivalent of at least 30 days a year for specific staff development and curriculum development activities mainly in the school itself.

It is interesting to speculate on the reasons for the present low financial status of teachers and most of us have our pet theories. Non-teachers point immediately to long holidays and short hours — the pupil time and teacher time confusion again. Teachers counteract this by pointing out the preparation time, the time for professional development and all the other "out-of-school" activities. They spoil their case, however, when they label these as "extras" or "overtime" and when they demand that in-service training should be provided during pupil hours. We can't have it both ways!

The view that school-based in-service education of teachers is unlikely to develop very far within the normal pace of educational advance, in competition with other, less threatening, innovations does not mean that there is no hope of reaching my objective. There are externally created situations which, whether we agree with them in principle or not, could precipitate widespread behavioural changes amongst all concerned. I illustrate by two of a number of current examples. Firstly, I will take the case of reorganization of institutions (for example, the combination of a grammar school and a secondary modern to make a comprehensive school). Secondly, I use the forthcoming development of the induction year programmes for probationer teachers. These two examples have at least two common elements. They both demand an individual diagnostic approach and they both demand the acquisition of knowledge as it is needed as opposed to the transmission of knowledge as it is discovered or as a course organizer thinks fit.

When an educational institution is reorganized there is need for both group and individual preparation. It should be obvious, for example, that in the individual school or groups of schools affected various staff groups need to examine possible changes in objectives and consequent organizational or pedagogical matters. I say deliberately that it *should* be obvious for there are undoubtedly cases when this has not happened. In some instances where a head has himself undertaken considerable personal preparation it may not have occurred to him, or he may not have considered it part of his role, to engage his staff in such a programme. In the current state of practice in staff development I think it is probably quite unreasonable to expect that the majority of heads will recognize this need and even if they do that they will have the resources to meet it effectively. We must as a profession discover how key people, like heads, can be helped to recognize and fulfil these needs.

In addition to changes in the ethos and objectives of the community there will undoubtedly be changes for individuals in their teaching and their responsibilities other than teaching. It may well be that a teacher who has worked with a restricted age or intelligence range will need to work with pupils outside this range. Suitable preparation, such as a few weeks working with teachers in another school, may prevent him from either overestimating or underestimating the problem which could arise. Who will foresee the possible changes in the individual work pattern? Who will diagnose the need of the individual teacher? Who will be responsible for seeing that those needs are actually met?

Another type of change may occur in that the teacher may find himself responsible for the work of many more adults than before. Such a change may well occur at any other time in his career but seldom at the same time as major changes in a school, as occurs on reorganization. The supervision of other professionals will bring him head on with the taboos of judgement of colleagues and professional privacy already discussed. For the first time then he becomes a manager of adults as well as of children. He may simultaneously become part of a management team and be required to look beyond his own curriculum or pastoral area in order to work with broader issues. He may well need help in recognizing aspects and responsibilities of the new role as well as in learning to supervize colleagues and assist their development. Who will offer this help and see that his needs are fulfilled?

My second example concerns the induction year and the work of professional tutors as proposed in the government White Paper (1972) *Education: A Framework for Expansion.*[3] It is suggested that teachers in their first year: " . . . should receive the kind of help and support needed to make the induction process both more effective and less daunting than it has often been in the past", and also that: " . . . they must be released for not less than one-fifth of their time for in-service training". I shall discuss some aspects of an induction programme in detail partly because the idea supports the major issues which I have so far delineated and partly because it usefully reinforces the idea of consultancy based in-service education. I have yet another reason for taking this section in such detail and that is my belief that *the setting up of good models for the new induction programme is another vital issue for the profession.* I fear very much that lack of motivation, lack of money, lack of careful thought will result in hotch-potch schemes which do little more than pay a small bonus to designated teachers and which produce the minimum of professional growth. The potential of the induction year as a vehicle for some of the objectives I have stated convinces me that a poor start would do more damage to in-service education than a postponed start or even no start at all on a national basis.

Since the publication of the White Paper there has been much discussion about the idea of professional tutors and professional centres to undertake the necessary work with the new teachers and to provide some of the expansion of in-service opportunities for all. This discussion has gone on despite the failure of the Department of Education and Science to set up immediately the regional committees which were to co-ordinate the work and should therefore have been involved in the reorganization of the colleges and the forward planning of the local education authorities. The major participants in the early public discussions have been the colleges, who quite naturally tend to regard the work of the professional tutor as their province and are anxious about the future of their staffs, and the teacher associations who tend to favour school-based professional tutors at least for induction purposes. Indeed the National Association of Schoolmasters in its policy document on this matter specifically rejects the suggestion that the necessary expertise is to be found in colleges and asserts that the probationer needs the help of the experienced practising teacher.

A contribution to the overall discussion which begins to look at possibilities with some objectivity and gives some thought to the detail of the professional tutor role is a pamphlet called *The In-service Education and Training of Teachers* produced by the University Council for the Education of Teachers (UCET).[4] Parts of the pamphlet are based on the work done at the Cambridge Institute of Education which organized a conference for the purpose of thinking out the role and training of professional tutors well before the White Paper was published. Such an event would seem to be characteristic of what is good in the offerings of the institute at this point. Less helpful in this context is the paper of the Association of Institute and School of Education In-service Tutors entitled *The universities and the in-service education of teachers.*[5] The university paper which most catches my imagination is an unpublished one from the University of Surrey Educational Studies Division: *University involvement in the in-service education of teachers: some future possibilities.*[6] Perhaps a new university with no statutory responsibility for in-service education of teachers and no long tradition in it can more easily take a fresh look at this field. The local education authorities themselves have remained relatively silent, in public, oppressed perhaps by local government reorganization and justifiable cynicism about finance. With notable exceptions, however, much of the discussion since the publication of the White Paper has been concerned with territory, salary and with traditional well-recognized in-service activities.

The findings of the Bristol project([7]) on the needs of the probationers prompted me to initiate a local survey which would also serve to help heads and teachers consider the whole matter of induction. Probationers, heads and college lecturers responded to a questionnaire in which they were asked to rate eighteen items for possible inclusion in an induction programme as follows:

  (a) Definitely yes.
  (b) Could be useful.
  (c) Not very important.
  (d) Definitely not necessary.
  (e) No definite opinion on this.

Some of the results are shown in Table 2 which gives, for each of five categories of respondent, the percentage rating them either "a" or "b". The bracketed figure in each column gives the rank order for that group of teachers/lecturers. Only those themes which scored over 50 per cent from every respondent category are included.

The figures hold much of interest for any study group. The response of primary heads and teachers to further work on the teaching of reading is a pointer to a well-known anxiety. The same urgency at this stage would not be expected from college staff who would no doubt recognize this field as one in which expertise builds up slowly by a combination of experience and further study based on foundations laid, if not always fully appreciated, during initial training. It is in such a field that we see most clearly any conflict related to the issue of initial training and continuous professional development. Nevertheless, a need which primary teachers and heads express so strongly must be seen to receive attention if they are to be confident that the induction programme is valuable and this item has, therefore, enormous implications for the choice and training of professional tutors concerned with primary teachers.

The high rank given by heads and lecturers to the development of class control is in contrast to that given by the teachers themselves. The same discrepancy was found by the Bristol Survey.([7]) Is this a failure by the probationers to diagnose a problem or could it be an outcome of different standards of what constitutes acceptable classroom behaviour, between one generation of educators and another? Here is a useful tonic for staff room discussion!

There are other issues arising from the figures one could discuss at length in another context. At this point, however, I want to pick out particularly the three items ranked most highly by the lecturers. This choice was reflected in the head teacher ratings too. In rank order they were:

Help with and time for preparation of lesson material;
Support in learning to organize pupils and materials;
Assistance in developing good class control.

TABLE 2. Items proposed by teachers in Surrey for inclusion in induction programmes for newly appointed teachers. Percentages show the degree of emphasis. Bracketed figures give the rank order for the group of teachers/lecturers.

	Primary probationary teachers		Secondary probationary teachers		Primary heads		Secondary heads		College of education lecturers	
Opportunity to learn about county resources, services and procedures	90%	(1st)	86%	(1st)	88%	(9th)	85%	(7th)	93%	(4th)
Study of the teaching of reading	90%	(1st)	41%	(16th)	97%	(1st)	55%	(13th)	83%	(8th)
Help in learning to diagnose pupil and group problems and find solutions	81%	(3rd)	80%	(3rd)	93%	(4th)	95%	(2nd)	93%	(4th)
Sustained advice in relation to your own particular job in your school	80%	(4th)	82%	(2nd)	92%	(6th)	95%	(2nd)	93%	(4th)
Purposeful visits to other schools of same type	79%	(5th)	74%	(4th)	88%	(9th)	70%	(11th)	85%	(7th)
Help with overall curriculum planning	79%	(5th)	72%	(6th)	86%	(11th)	50%	(15th)	85%	(7th)
Study of display and improvement of school environment	76%	(7th)	52%	(14th)	89%	(8th)	60%	(12th)	72%	(9th)
Help with and time for preparation of lesson material	75%	(8th)	74%	(4th)	93%	(4th)	95%	(2nd)	100%	(1st)
Support in learning to organize pupils and materials	73%	(9th)	68%	(7th)	97%	(1st)	95%	(2nd)	98%	(2nd)
Help in learning to consult and advise parents	73%	(9th)	65%	(10th)	92%	(6th)	75%	(10th)	85%	(7th)
Assistance in developing good class control	61%	(11th)	66%	(9th)	96%	(3rd)	100%	(1st)	96%	(3rd)
Regular meetings with a senior member of the school staff	60%	(12th)	60%	(12th)	85%	(12th)	95%	(2nd)	83%	(8th)
Further training in observation and assessment of individuals	58%	(13th)	61%	(11th)	76%	(13th)	85%	(7th)	87%	(6th)
Opportunity for further study in an academic or practical subject at your level	52%	(14th)	68%	(7th)	51%	(16th)	45%	(16th)	54%	(11th)

I highlight this because these are all areas in which teachers with a few years experience frequently criticize new teachers and which they often imply should be mastered during initial training. The views expressed by the college staff support my own feeling that such an expectation is totally unrealistic. I think that we have here another clear example of the need for the whole profession to recognize initial training as a starting point only and therefore to accept the necessity for every teacher to undertake an on-going professional development programme related to his own career stage and existing skills.

The results of the survey as quoted in Table 2 provide useful data for planning the induction year curriculum. They help to pinpoint the various roles of the professional tutor and hence to indicate some of the skills which he must have or must develop. This in itself will help to guide the first preparation programmes for the professional tutors themselves. We are still left, however, with the dichotomy between a college/centre-based programme and a programme conducted by a school-based tutor.

I have already quoted the view of the National Association of School-masters. It is worth looking at the views of the Joint Council of Heads who propose that every school should have a professional tutor appropriately prepared for the job and paid on Scale 5 or Senior Teacher Scale in secondary schools and in primary schools at the level of the highest paid scale post in the school. These views show how greatly the headteachers value these posts. Nevertheless I wonder whether it was realistic to express them in 1973 with the intention (first announced by the Department of Education and Science) of having the posts provided and suitably filled by September 1975. These proposals are discussed in a paper called *The role and status of the professional tutor*[8] which firmly puts responsibility for staff development in the hands of the head.

There were over 900 probationer teachers in my own local education authority in the 1972/3 academic year. Tables 3 and 4 below show their distribution amongst primary and secondary schools respectively.

TABLE 3. Primary schools in Surrey in 1972/3

Number of probationers in a school	0	1	2	3	4	5	6	7
Number of schools	159	113	59	26	9	9	2	1

TABLE 4. Secondary schools in Surrey in 1972/3

Number of probationers in a school	0	1	2	3	4	5	6	7	8	9	10	11	12 to 17
Number of schools	0	8	9	7	11	9	8	13	8	3	3	2	6

The number of probationers in any one school fluctuates, sometimes wildly, from year to year and in this particular year the tutors in approximately 42 per cent of the primary schools would have had no probationers with whom to work and only 3 per cent would have had more than four. Even in the secondary schools about 50 per cent of tutors would have had five probationers or less.

These figures make nonsense of the proposals to train and appoint (or vice versa) over *470* high-level tutors in this one local authority to start their work by September 1975 even if they were to have responsibility for advising on in-service education for all staff. In any case the latter point is a contentious one amongst teacher associations. The quick action alternative of asking all schools to designate an existing teacher as professional tutor in addition to any other work he may have would almost inevitably lead to low-level appointments and a poor model for the induction year from which we might never recover. I repeat my contention that it would be better to phase in good practice slowly but consistently rather than to rush into a low-key operation before the profession and the resources can cope with it.

In an attempt to shed light on the school/centre problem the results of the induction programme survey were discussed by a group of centre leaders and centre advisory staff and by a group of secondary headteachers and senior staff. They were asked to give their views on whether each particular item would be predominantly covered in school under a school-based tutor or whether it would be likely to be covered at some form of professional centre by a centre-based tutor. The overall consensus was as follows.

School based

Help in learning to diagnose pupil and group problems and find solutions.

Sustained advice in relation to your own particular job in your own school.

Help with and time for preparation of lesson material.

Support in learning to organize pupils and materials.
Help in learning to consult and advise parents.
Assistance in developing good class control.
Regular meetings with a senior member of the school staff.

Centre based

Opportunity to learn about county resources, services and procedures.
Purposeful visits to other schools of the same type.
Study of display and improvement of school environment.
Opportunity for further study in an academic or practical subject.

Either base

Study of the teaching of reading.
Help with overall curriculum planning.
Further training in observation and assessment of individuals.

Regardless of whether one agrees with the placement of individual items it is clear that we should make both types of provision with the consequent need for closely defined links and responsibilities.

This conclusion leads me to another major issue: that of the *structure and control of in-service education.* It will be useful to continue to use the induction-year proposals as an example; but the issue arises equally strongly when we consider existing patterns of in-service education and the White Paper proposals concerning its development for all teachers to the point where everyone is entitled to the equivalent of one term "release" in 7 years.

On the basis of the previous discussion it appears that personnel will be needed in connection with the induction year for the following purposes:

Personal and group counselling.
Work alongside the probationer in the classroom and during preparation.
Leading discussions/seminars.
Assessing teacher skills and diagnosing classroom and teacher problems.
Helping in problem solution and skill acquisition.
Presentation and guidance in curriculum development and theory.
Organization of meetings and visits.
Gathering of curriculum information and materials.
Training of teacher colleagues in supportive action.
Final assessment.

Administration and servicing of induction centres.

These roles contain administrative and co-ordinating functions as well as functions of consultation and assessment. They do not all need to be done by people who are at that time school teachers and some of them would be done best by professional administrators.

I would hope that the educational aspects of the induction programme would be in the hands of professional-centre tutors, with this responsibility as a full-time one for a specified period, and that they would be assisted by school-based teacher tutors with specific responsibilities for this, in addition to their role as teachers. I think it is important that the centre-based tutors should be employed by or seconded to the local education authority for this purpose in order that they can be fully effective as recognized members of the authority's structure and as party to the policies and financial restraints pertaining at any time. I believe that it will be undesirable if, during their time as full-time professional-centre tutors, they are responsible to other institutions or non-authority departments and that mere liaison with the local education authority will be insufficient. I am not suggesting that the probationers should not have the opportunity to work with and to learn from non-authority staff and I would expect the professional tutors to arrange this. I simply feel convinced that a system of this complexity cannot work unless it is part of the same hierarchy as the teachers and the local authority advisory and administrative staffs.

I imagine that one full-time centre-based tutor would have a case load not exceeding thirty. In my own authority the average case load of probationers per inspector is about forty and the time available for dealing with them is very small. Nothing can be done much beyond offering assistance in difficult cases. Even if local authority advisory staffs were very much increased they could still not provide the support which I am envisaging. The professional tutor could undertake the educational aspects of the functions listed previously and would also be responsible for training a school-based tutor and delegating all or part of some aspects to him. The school-based tutors would then form a pool of suitably experienced teachers for secondment for a period as a full-time centre tutor thus making an adequate career structure within the training field if one regards posts as teachers, centre leaders, inspectors/advisers and college lecturers as all part of it.

It is important that the centre-based tutor should have time for his own professional development (otherwise how can he continue to offer the necessary guidance?) and that he should have time for liaison and consultation with heads and senior staff and with other agencies. I would anticipate that on one day a week the tutor would have a programme of work at the centre for all his group of probationers and that three of the remaining 4 days would be spent with them in school. The case load of thirty may have looked generous but in fact this works out at only the equivalent of half a day in 5 weeks in the classroom with each one.

Thought needs also to be given to the needs of the professional tutors to extend their skills by being members of an interacting group of colleagues. This need is often unrecognized amongst inspectors and advisers, for example, and heads too can suffer from isolation unless they take steps to avoid it. College lecturers, like teachers, have their colleagues about them every day. I would hope to see four or five professional tutors working from one centre under the direction of a senior tutor. This would also be economic from the resources point of view. In my own authority with 900 probationers one such centre would therefore cater for about one-fifth of them.

Obviously the number, sizes and location of the professional centres must also depend on the geography of the area. It is also obvious that the role of the local authority adviser, traditionally responsible for probationers, must be recast and his role in relation to the professional centre well thought out. Thought must also be given to college of education staff who will be working in the schools with student teachers and may be linking up with the school-based tutors in particular. I see the colleges of education as providing, perhaps on secondment to the local authority, a very suitable pool of potential centre-based tutors, along with the school-based tutor already mentioned.

One overwhelming contribution to the education service which all these structures could make is *to extend and to provide for the consultancy based approach to the in-service education of teachers.* Inevitably I go much further than probationers in my support for a consultancy-based system for professional development. With adequate staff, in both quantity and quality, the professional centres could offer a service to all teachers. In practice most of the take-up would be from primary schools, which traditionally draw on local support more easily than secondary schools partly because the same problems are recognized as common to many primary teachers in an area. Even so the centre, if it were able to draw on sufficiently committed consultants from other, more powerful or academic institutions, could also make a significant contribution to local support at other levels.

It must not be thought that I am ignoring the value of the existing advisory services and those teachers' centres which already undertake some consultancy work. It is common knowledge that local authority advisory departments are, in most subject areas, hopelessly understaffed for such a purpose. This is partly because advisory staff are often at the beck and call of so many schools and officials for purely routine matters. This means that local authority advisory staff seldom have enough time for deep inquiry, observation, diagnosis and follow-up work.

Her Majesty's inspectors also have, on paper, a consultancy function but in practice do not even offer as much long-term commitment as local authority staff. Their best consultancy role might emerge if they could direct it to local advisory and administrative staff to whom they could offer a knowledge of practice and problems country-wide in the same way that local authority staff should be able to draw on local area practice in consulting with schools. Similarly Schools Council field officers could look again at their work and perhaps do more long-term work with groups and individual centre leaders over a period of time. At the present time they have developed a style rather like Her Majesty's inspectors and local authority advisory staff of spreading their time too thinly in an effort to meet something of all demands. A public servant may be justified in believing that he must be available to all on demand but must recognize that he is unlikely to be very effective if this is the case.

Teachers' centre leaders could also have potential as consultants but in some cases are slow to move away from the traditional centre-based course or workshop pattern and into working with teachers in schools. This is a status as well as a time problem no doubt. Within my experience the best example of a consultancy-based teachers' centre is the Mathematics Centre at Abbey Wood in South-east London. It has, however, taken a good deal of vision and determination on the part of the director to develop the work in ways which are different from the traditional expectations of most consumers and local education authority officers. Even now this is still only a one-man operation. A useful account of the development of this centre is available in *Feedback*, the bulletin of the centre.[9]

The method of operation of this centre owes something to the fact that it developed as a result of the thinking expressed in a report of the Joint Mathematical Council in 1965.[10] Most other mathematics centres which began in the 1960s were the result of local authority undertakings given to the Nuffield Mathematics Project and hence in general became trial and feed-back points for the writings of a central national team. The Nuffield Project model, like most early national curriculum development attempts, did little to help the teachers to diagnose their own curriculum problems and neither did it enlist their creative help in solving them to any extent. The Joint Mathematical Council report, although it now appears relatively cautious, was based on the idea of linked local through to regional and national consultancy support systems. It is scarcely surprising that a centre devoted to problem-solving in a relatively small geographical area should flourish and that many centres initially set up to transmit ideas from a national project should radically change their role or disappear altogether soon after the project's publications were complete.

Whatever good intentions there are, however, consultancy work cannot succeed without *time*. The consultant must be able to commit himself to the client over a specified period. Examples are the Mathematics Advisory Unit([11]) of the University of Nottingham School of Education and the Shell Centre for Mathematical Education at Nottingham where tutors have worked with small groups of teachers over some years.

Not only must time be allocated to the tutor for consultancy work but he must be capable of defending himself against temptations to widen his clientele beyond his useful limits no matter how strongly pressed. It is all too easy for a tutor to get into the same impossible situation as Her Majesty's inspectors and local authority advisers. Such a position is easily assumed by an independent tutor on the apparently reasonable grounds of wanting to help as many teachers as possible. Is it too cynical to suggest that this could be a way of rationalizing an escape from the depth of involvement which the successful consultant must reach?

It is part of my hope for the professional centres of the future that they will be places to which leading teachers, college lecturers, and inspectors can be seconded full time for a reasonable period, at least a year, and that from there they can undertake consultancy-based work with a limited number of clients. The developmental benefits for the consultant for his normal "back-home" work would, hopefully, match those for his clients.

The idea of consultancy support for schools and individuals is dealt with in depth in the pamphlet *In-service education for innovation* published by the National Council for Educational Technology.([12]) So far this publication has received little attention in the educational world; perhaps because it is a little ahead of much current thinking. The two major messages it discusses, namely *the problem-solving approach to innovation and the consultancy and support systems of in-service education,* constitute major issues in the field of educational development.

The allocation of time for in-service education is not just a problem for consultants but for teachers too of course. I have touched on this already and suggested that a new concept of conditions of service, which would involve both public and professional recognition of teacher hours as opposed to pupil hours, would improve the status of teachers as well as provide some of the necessary time.

For the last 20 years educationists and society itself have been changing the job of the teacher. The consequences of this have not been fully faced by the community, through its elected representatives, nor by the schools themselves in their allocation of those human and material resources which are available. Our failure to meet the changing situation adequately is most marked in secondary schools. Almost unresolved problems have been created by the emergence of larger schools. As the size of an institution increases the management and administrative functions increase proportionately faster — this is common experience in any walk of life. In the absence of a reasonable complement of non-teaching staff necessary routine work is not only supervised but actually executed by the head and senior teaching staff. At a lower level special teacher responsibilities may be created for examinations, careers, stock, and most secondary teachers know that these usually mean examinations clerk, careers librarian and meeting organizer, and stock control and order clerk. In all these areas there are educational jobs and there are administrative jobs. In the absence of time, and sometimes of vision, only the administrative side develops. Project yourself into the future, however, and imagine the value in terms of staff and pupil development of an examinations officer who would act as a consultant on development of objectives and methods of assessing them; of a careers officer who would have time for personal and group discussions and activities, who would keep colleagues in touch with career developments and keep the needs of consumers in view as his contribution to the head's curriculum planning group; of a resources and materials consultant who would help colleagues to diagnose and solve problems of presentation. All of these key people would need operational non-teaching support and all would take personal responsibility for the development of their own skills, knowledge and resources so that they could interpret the possibilities to their colleagues.

This vision, which is coming alive in places, pinpoints one important change in the teaching job. More and more teachers can now expect to have some responsibility for and to their colleagues. Where will the time for this come from? Now add to it the time for teachers to take part in public examinations, perhaps through assessment of course work in their own schools or in local groups or perhaps through teacher-control mechanisms such as subject panels, executive committees and so on. Add also the time which is needed to select or even prepare materials for individual pupils which is such a time-consuming move from the one-textbook-for-all days and then add the time for participation in the corporate management of the school. Most of the non-classroom work contributes to the in-service education of teachers. Much of it needs to be done during school terms and some of it during the pupil hours of the school day.

It is my experience that most heads see improved staffing ratios as the answer to these problems. I doubt if this alone would, in practice, have a significant effect as I think that there would be a tendency at present for any increase in staffing to be absorbed into the normal school timetable to provide more options at 14-plus and/or smaller classes and that the situation concerning non-classroom work would be as bad as ever. My own attempt to solve the problems would also involve an investigation into possible changes in methods of grouping pupils and teachers in schools and changes in the nature of pupil/teacher contacts and teaching methods.

Radical changes in the use of teacher time, groupings and resources are not unknown of course. Departmental heads may at first be given responsibility for allocating one block of time for the work of several traditional size "classes" of pupils and may discover that there are other ways of grouping them than to split them equally amongst the teachers. Such a department may soon find itself able to develop flexible modes of working which permit small group development, private study time, workshop sessions with several teachers (and students) available and some time for non-classroom work too.

In a book containing a collection of independent chapters under the general title *The secondary school timetable*[13] there is a chapter on changing management ideas and the timetable which develops this theme. The author is a secondary headteacher and he points out that a school of 1400 pupils which has seventy teachers all teaching for 90 per cent of their time will have an average class size of about twenty-two pupils. He calculates that if the class contact time of the teachers is reduced to 80 per cent then the average class size becomes twenty-five. He recommends a re-examination of staff activity and deployment. It is certainly possible that pupils might be better served if more of the non-classroom role of the teacher were recognized in school timetables.

Such fundamental changes in practice develop slowly in individual schools and take time to percolate through the system. It is my view *that the need to re-examine patterns of timetabling and grouping of teachers and pupils is yet another issue related to in-service education which is demanding attention in the next few years.*

I have as yet paid no attention to courses in in-service education yet they still play the largest part in recognized staff development programmes and many organizations and individuals see the major expansion of in-service opportunities in course terms. By speaking of "release for in-service training" for the equivalent of one term in 7 years the White Paper([3]) reinforces this idea in some measure. The word "course" can have a number of connotations but I shall use it to describe those activities in which teachers meet in groups with a tutor for some specific study related to their work or personal development. The reader will readily see that this can cover a number of arrangements such as some day conferences, evening study groups at centres, one-year diploma courses, Open University studies and so on.

The style of work on courses has changed over the years, usually following teaching methods in schools. It is rare for a course to consist only of lectures now, for example, and there is a lot of emphasis on learning through discussion, practical work, individual projects, etc. — just like school!

The evaluation and improvement of the teachers' course aspect of in-service education is an important issue at present. It is my observation that courses are frequently over-rated as a means of teacher development. That is not to say that they have no value in terms of bringing teachers into contact with each other and with a variety of thinking and/or materials or even as a psychological break but they do not, in the main, seem to create improvements in educational practice concomitant with their cost in time and money.

I do not dare at this point in my chapter to delve into this issue in depth. It is my hope that as school-based staff development and consultancy services gain in importance so "courses" will be seen in perspective and yet at this point in time I am pessimistic. My pessimism comes partly from the observation that the pre-packed course, put together before the course members are known, can conveniently shift responsibility away from the consumer and offer an easy scapegoat for the course member if for any reason he is dissatisfied with the outcome in terms of personal learning. It also comes partly from the realization that there are so many people with a vested interest in attracting teachers to enrol on courses that alternative forms of teacher education, with their threats both on the financial front and in terms of personal commitments, conflicts and problems, will have difficulty in gaining ground.

It can fairly be said, in my view, that the government White Paper proposal that all teachers should become entitled to the equivalent of one-term "release" in 7 years for in-service training and its acceptance that the proper venue for teachers so released would be the reformed colleges of education, acting as professional centres, will make courses once again too important a part of the picture, Moreover, the weight given to this method of teacher education could tend to narrow still further our already blinkered outlook.

Not only, therefore, must we face the issue of evaluating and improving teachers' courses at all levels but we must ask: "When is a course likely to be the most effective method of learning?" — using the word "when" in the senses of "at what stage" and "in what circumstances". These are questions to which there are no convenient general answers and which must therefore be asked at *every* level and by *every* party when courses are planned or participation considered.

A further issue to which I must draw attention is *the role of the local education authority in the in-service education of its own teachers*. I will not trespass on Chapter 4 in which the role of the local inspectorate is very fully discussed in terms entirely compatible with many of my earlier comments. I want to identify three aspects of this role: first, the local education authority as the employer of people who can undertake consultancy and other work directly related to in-service education; second, as the provider of funds and opportunity for its teachers to develop their own teacher-controlled in-service education activities and to take advantage of those offered by bodies other than the local authority; third, as a body which is in a position to survey the whole field to try to ensure that all needs are recognized, and that appropriate provision is made somewhere and is subsequently used.

The first of these is the one which creates the most divisions between the traditional providers of in-service education. The view is sometimes expressed by universities and colleges in particular, that those who are concerned with the promotion of teachers ought not to be involved in their professional development. This is like the view still held by a significant proportion of the teaching profession that the teacher should not take part in the assessment of his own pupils for public examination purposes. This view is entirely at odds with the beliefs and practice of the certificate of secondary education and, in fact, with the assessment methods of some universities and colleges themselves. Personally I think that it would be a pity if the *only* organized in-service opportunities were in the hands of the employers or if *all* the consultants were answerable to the same authority, for I readily acknowledge the need to be able to discuss problems freely with people who are known to be unconnected with the hierarchy at work. (I wonder, as I write, what implications this has for the work of teacher-counsellors in schools, both counsellors for pupils and counsellors in the guise of school-based professional tutors, for staff!) Nevertheless teachers expect, rightly I think, that their local authority will provide advisers and leaders and that through them the teachers can if they so choose develop education within the overall philosophy of the local community; and conversely can influence through them both that philosophy and the provision which the local community (through its elected members) is willing to make.

The second role, as provider of funds for teacher control of their own development and for participation in non-authority opportunities, is undertaken by all local education authorities, as far as I know, at least in the provision for financial support for attendance at courses other than local authority courses. A system by which teachers in an area have financial support to provide their own in-service education is rare but increasing. In the main this is done through teacher-controlled local centres. I do not mean those which are just convenient venues for the local authority's own courses or courses imported from the area training organization, but centres in which the leaders and/or a local committee ahve decision-making power on action and spending within the usual budgetary control.

My own authority has set up a teacher body called the Surrey Schools Council to develop this aspect of provision and this council has the appropriate finance and powers of decision to enable it to operate effectively. Looking to the future I envisage a day when part of the allocation of money to schools comes under a heading for staff development – perhaps the innovation of professional tutors will bring this about. Perhaps too we shall see the day when school staffs are together taking decisions about the attendance of their colleagues at courses and that in these cases all local authorities will respond to this responsible planning by paying all the expenses and not just a proportion of them.

My third suggested role for the local education authority concerns its potential in a scanning capacity. We are faced with diversity of need from the teachers and we have developed a system with many providers. As far as I can tell the local authority is in the best position to see where there are gaps because it is the body expected to put the teachers in touch with suitable opportunities. It is forced therefore to be concerned with both the needs of the teachers and schools and with the provisions in a most practical way and it is motivated to do so by its accountability to the public in a way that neither the teachers themselves nor the other course providers are accountable. I am not recommending local education authority control of all in-service work but I am recommending positive recognition of the employer's role in recognizing need, in helping teachers to diagnose need and in helping to provide, often through other bodies, for those needs to be met. Further, I do not believe that this is likely to be done with any thoroughness unless it is a specific responsibility of one or more of the authority's officers — but I recognize that my own post makes me a very biased commentator!

A practical example of the sort of coordinated provision which can be developed has arisen in my own authority in connection with the skills of teaching reading. As it is recognized that there is a constant need for teachers to develop skills in teaching so-called basic subjects, even disjointed provision for learning more about teaching reading normally succeeds from the point of view of a course organizer who has to fill his courses in order to maintain his resources. There is circumstantial evidence to suggest, however, that occasional courses on teaching reading have little effect and may serve to convince some teachers that nobody knows the answer. Once we recognize that learning to teach reading is a skill which teachers usually learn slowly, through experience, structured discussion and help at the right moment, then the need for a multi-level and continuous learning programme for teachers becomes obvious.

The development of a county-wide screening programme for 7-year-olds, aimed at finding those whose reading ability did not match up to their general ability for one reason or another, has served also to focus the attention of most primary teachers on diagnosis and action in the teaching of reading. As a result a carefully structured course covering diagnosis, action, organization, etc., was mounted in many areas of the county. These have led to the setting up of study groups in the teachers' centres. The groups are led by teachers who have special skill in the teaching of reading and experience of working with other teachers which is enhanced by their attendance at a university course designed for those involved in the in-service training of other teachers. Some of the study groups are intended especially for teachers who are taking some responsibility in their schools for helping other teachers in the teaching of reading. This pyramidal structure of leadership and learning is discussed with local headteachers prior to each course and this in itself serves to reinforce, or even start, the idea of consultancy and structured support systems in schools as a means of in-service education.

This example serves then to illustrate the potential of a broad look at needs which a local education authority should be able to supply. It also serves to pinpoint the differences in roles of various providers. Firstly, the school as a provider of consultancy skills within its own staff; secondly, the teachers' centre as a provider of continuous study groups for its local teachers; thirdly, the local advisory staff as providers of a practical structured course with a specific objective; fourthly, the university as the provider of a special course dealing not only with the subject of reading and its teaching but with the specifics of teaching teachers. I am not suggesting that these reflect the only roles that each body can play but I do suggest that *more recognition of the special contributions of different sorts of institutions could lead to a much more satisfactory structure for in-service education.* There is a tendency, but I *think* we are overcoming it, for every provider to want to be all things to all men. Regrettably the need to prove success (through enrolment) in order to maintain supply of resources encourages this. We must work towards a situation in which each provider is developing its own particular offerings within a coherent whole and in which it is common practice for one to recommend the work of another. Hopefully this could be one of the major advantages of regional planning for in-service education. We must rid ourselves of the situation where the offerings of the teachers' centres, the in-service course programmes of the local education authorities and the area training organizations based at the universities are undifferentiated, and hence in competition; in favour of a system which develops special roles for each and which encourages teachers to recognize the issue with which I began — namely, the need to develop the whole spectrum of opportunities for in-service education.

The second chapter of this book traced the development of in-service education to the present time. The purpose of the third has been to delineate some current issues, the resolution of which must be the concern of the entire profession in the next decade. Some of these issues are discussed in depth in subsequent chapters and others are still on the periphery of our thinking. It is appropriate, I think, to end by drawing them together on this page in order that they shall serve as a foundation for what is to come.

We need to
    secure recognition of the whole spectrum of situations and activities which contribute to teacher in-service education;
    maximize their value, in terms of professional development;

recognize and use the professional community in a school as a learning resource for individual teachers;

establish the practice of initial training as a starting-point followed by on-going in-service education throughout a teacher's career;

set up good models for the induction of new teachers;

investigate the structure and control of in-service education provision;

develop the problem-solving and consultancy-based approach;

examine, and if necessary encourage change in, timetabling and grouping of pupils and teachers in order that the role of the teacher as we now see it is duly recognized in his work pattern taken over the year;

evaluate and improve courses as a method of in-service education;

clarify and fulfil the roles of the local education authorities as employers in the in-service education of their teachers;

develop the special contributions which can be made by different providers and hence move towards a coherent pattern which will support the whole spectrum of situations and activities which featured in my first objective.

References

1. DEPARTMENT OF EDUCATION AND SCIENCE, *Teacher education and training* (the James Report), Her Majesty's Stationery Office, 1972.
2. CENTRAL ADVISORY COUNCIL FOR EDUCATION, *Children and their primary schools* (the Plowden Report), 2 vols. Her Majesty's Stationery Office, 1967.
3. *Education: a framework for expansion,* Cmnd. 5174, Her Majesty's Stationery Office, 1972.
4. THE UNIVERSITIES COUNCIL FOR THE EDUCATION OF TEACHERS, *The in-service education and training of teachers,* UCET, 3 Crawford Place, London, W1. 1973.
5. THE ASSOCIATION OF INSTITUTE AND SCHOOL OF EDUCATION IN-SERVICE TUTORS, *The universities and the in-service education of teachers,* mimeographed statement, Further Professional Training Division, University of Nottingham School of Education, 1973.
6. POTTER, F. W., *University involvement in the in-service education of teachers: some future possibilities,* mimeographed, Educational Studies Division, Adult Education Department, University of Surrey, 1973.
7. TAYLOR, J. K. and DALE, I. R., *A national survey of teachers in their first year of service,* 1971;
    BOLAM, R., *Induction programmes for probationary teachers,* 1973, Research Unit, University of Bristol School of Education.

8.   JOINT COUNCIL OF HEADS (Association of Headmistresses, the Headmasters' Association, The Headmasters' Conference, the National Association of Head Teachers), *The role and status of the professional tutor*, Maxwelton House, Boltro Road, Haywards Heath, Sussex, 1973.

9.   FIELKER, D. S., *Review of the first five years*, Feedback No.31, Abbey Wood Mathematics Centre, Eynsham Bridge, London SE2, June 1972.

10. JOINT MATHEMATICAL COUNCIL'S EDUCATION COMMITTEE, *Report on in-service training for teachers of mathematics*, 1965.

11. STURGESS, D., *The first six years of a mathematics advisory unit,* (1966-1972), University of Nottingham School of Education, 1972.

12. ERAUT, M., *In-service education for innovation*, Occasional Paper 4, National Council for Educational Technology, 10 Queen Anne Street, London, W1, 1972.

13. SNAPE, T. P., Changing management ideas and the time-table, in WALTON, J. (Ed.) *The secondary school time-table*, Ward Lock Educational, 1972.

CHAPTER 4

The Role of the Local Advisory Service in the In-service Education of Teachers

THE phrase "in-service training" in most people's minds conjures up a picture of teachers attending courses. Most people would also see the major role of the local inspectorate as that of course provision — either running the course or getting others to do so. This has been a fairly typical role during recent years, but the picture is now changing with the growth of teachers' centres and may change very radically in the future, if the recommendations of the White Paper *Education: a framework for expansion* come to be implemented. In any case, this has always been a somewhat limited view which does not describe adequately the part played by many of the most successful inspectors and advisers in the professional development of teachers in their area. The phrase "in-service training" itself already seems too limited to describe the ways in which a teacher's development may be supported.

A serving teacher is open to many influences. He brings ideas and assumptions as well as knowledge and skill from his initial training. He will be influenced by his colleagues in his own school and elsewhere. Advice from those senior to him and from peers and staff room discussion will help him to evolve his own ways of working. If he is able to watch experienced teachers in action and work with them, he will select from what he sees and use his colleagues as models, trying out various kinds of teaching behaviour in the process of discovering his own teaching style. His personal reading and study will influence him and will interact with his experience to contribute to his development. The children he teaches will add to his knowledge. Consultants from outside the school may help him and he may select from what is on offer his own amalgam of courses and conferences and discussions and workshops, according to the way he sees his own needs. A good teacher goes on with this process throughout life, learning a bit here, developing a skill there, refining and modifying practice in the light of experience and continually attempting to sort out what he is doing and trying to do it better.

Professional development is therefore a business of continuous growth. In one sense it is something each teacher must do for himself. At the same time it is clear that other people can do a great deal to help the individual teacher to grow professionally.

This paper is therefore concerned with four questions.

A. What are the ways in which teachers need to grow professionally?

B. How does such growth come about?

C. What part can the local education authority's advisory service play in this professional development?

D. What are the implications of this for the local education authority?

We can examine each of these questions in detail.

A. *The nature of professional growth in teachers*

We choose, as a society, to hand over an important part of the education of our young to specially trained professionals and as a society, we have certain expectations of our schools. We want our teachers to be good human beings, balanced and educated people who will set a good example to our children, and to have the knowledge and skill to guide them surely.

The teacher needs to know himself as a person. He also needs to know something about his own style as a teacher — his strengths and weaknesses and his most effective modes of operation. As a professional teacher too he needs to know where he is going, to see his goals for his own work in the overall context of the goals of education in his own school and more widely, and he needs to see this as part of the whole process by which society prepares the young for the future. He must be sensitive to change and able to assess what is likely to be valuable in the new and what part of the old is important and should be preserved.

A teacher needs knowledge and there appear to be four major areas in which he needs to know. He must know about children. The younger the child, the more apparent is the need for knowledge of child development, but in fact it is knowledge teachers in schools for all age groups ignore at their peril. He must also know something of how people learn and how they behave in groups if he is to teach effectively and be in control of the situation. He must also know the material he has to teach and must keep up with developments in his subject or subjects.

In addition to knowledge, the teacher needs skills. Perhaps the most important of these is the ability to observe and interpret human behaviour and to respond to it. Everyone has this skill in some degree. Life would be imposssible without it. A person whose job depends on understanding others needs to develop this skill to a high level and for a wide range of different people. A teacher in school needs to develop it in relation to children who may be unable to express themselves very clearly in language. Teachers of very young children and children who are handicapped intellectually or socially have a special need to interpret, but those who teach older and very able children also need to be skilled interpreters of behaviour if they are not to be misled by what the pupil may say.

Observation of behaviour should lead to the ability to evaluate the performance of children and to the teacher's ability to evaluate his own performance. The teacher needs to know how to sample behaviour and how to use tests, both to evaluate and to diagnose problems.

The knowledge of the children the teacher gains through his observation has to be translated into classroom activity which leads to certain kinds of learning. The teacher must therefore also be skilled as an organizer. He must be able to control children in groups and yet remain aware of individuals; to create situations in which children learn; to know how to select appropriate ways of teaching and learning for particular situations and gradually help his pupils to become independent of him. He must be able to use resources to good advantage; to plan ahead and yet keep a measure of flexibility. He needs to have strategies for identifying and solving problems.

The teacher also needs skills in making relationships. Part of this is concerned with communication. The good teacher needs to be able to explain and present material in a variety of ways; elicit response from pupils and interpret it, lead discussion, modify practice in the light of response and select or make material which teaches.

He also needs skill in establishing good relationships with individual children. Somehow he has to make each pupil feel that he matters; that he is accepted as the person he is. At the same time he needs to create the kind of tension which demands the best from children and somehow enables them to do better than they throught they could.

Skill in creating and maintaining good relationships with colleagues and parents is also important. Colleagues can do much to support a teacher in his work and can help him to learn. The teacher who can work with a child's parents for the good of the child is likely to increase what he is able to do to help the child.

Much of this makes up an identifiable body of knowledge and skills which a teacher can build up and which others can help him to develop. Some of this learning is part of his initial training, but it must develop and go on developing with experience.

Experience and training mix with the teacher's personality to produce in him a set of attitudes which will to some extent govern his professional development. He will develop attitudes to the process of education; to colleagues, children and their parents, to the local education authority which employs him and to many other aspects of his work. His attitudes may make it easy for him to develop and learn or they may prevent him from using a number of sources of help and information.

One important set of attitudes are those concerned with what it means to be professional. This is an area in which relationships with the local education authority can be tender and advisers in particular need to consider whether they are according the teachers they work with the right level of professional status.

Professional status and professional behaviour are difficult terms to define. While they have some relationship to salary and conditions of service, they probably have more relationship to attitudes to work.

A. N. Whitehead observed that a professional person's activity in his job differs from the activity of other workers in being governed to some extent by theory in the worker's own mind. Professional behaviour would also seem to include commitment and detachment. Commitment involves putting the work first on many occasions and it is noticeable that teachers taking various kinds of industrial action will usually stress that it is in the longer term interests of their pupils that they do it.

A measure of detachment is also needed by a good teacher. This is not to suggest that he should stand back from his pupils so far that he does not appear to care for them, but that he is not so close to them that he is unable to see their needs clearly. There is an analogy here with the work of the doctor or nurse, who must care for the patient without identifying with him so closely that he/she is unable to help him.

We might also hope for some other attitudes in teachers. The good teacher produces a positive reaction to problems. It is only too easy to blame others when children do not learn, to blame society, parents, the previous teacher, the local education authority or the children themselves, without accepting that there is a problem concerned with particular children in a particular school, which can be solved by professional expertise and hard work.

Teachers who have developed problem-solving skills often manage to solve problems which teachers with less throughtful attitudes have declared insoluble.

This kind of attitude brings with it a set of attitudes to children and to teaching. The good teacher usually believes in the abilities of those he teaches, and is able to raise them above their normal level by his encouragement and confidence in them as well as by good teaching. He also accepts and enjoys his pupils as they are here and now and is not continually wishing them to be something different, although he may hope to change some aspects of their behaviour.

Along with the attitudes, the knowledge and the skills, we hope that the teacher will have personal vision, so that children catch from him a sense of enjoyment and enthusiasm for what they are learning. At senior levels in the profession we hope for an ability to co-ordinate vision, to get excited about the vision of others as well as one's own, and to weave it all into a coherent whole.

The knowledge, skills and attitudes we have so far been considering are needed throughout the teacher's professional life. They come down to the solution of particular problems however. Each group of children will bring problems peculiar to them, requiring specific solutions. If the problems of a group or a child are entirely unfamiliar to the teacher, he needs to know how best to set about discovering how to solve them.

In theory we might expect the professional teacher to be able to teach anything within his capacity to almost anyone. Part of his skill lies in knowing how to set about tackling the particular problems of the particular situation. In practice a teacher needs a good many resources behind him if he is to be more than an instructor for a limited curriculum. He needs to be able to draw on the experience of others, to have some material and ideas sifted and sorted for him, because he has not time to do all the sifting and sorting he needs for himself. He therefore needs various kinds of consultancy service, some of which should be provided by his employers.

We have so far been considering the professional development of the classroom teacher. Senior staff in schools — heads, deputy heads, senior teachers and heads of departments — also have needs. They have greater need of the skills of dealing with adults and they need further skills of organization and management. They also need knowledge of possible patterns of organization and administration so that they can select appropriately. They need the ability to define and solve problems on a larger scale than the classroom teacher. They need considerable ability to analyse problems and to synthesize a collection of evidence and ideas to arrive at a solution.

These skills are more difficult to acquire but they are still fairly identifiable and we are gradually learning how people acquire them. The present problem is that this is a comparatively new area of professional learning which has come into being with the advent of larger schools, although it has applications in schools of all sizes. Very few teachers now in senior posts and very few heads have had much in the way of specific training for the job they do. Most acquire the skills of administration and management on the job. In a school where there is much discussion among the staff, they will learn a great deal from colleagues, but at all levels and particularly at the top, there is a need for a consultancy service, for someone to turn to, whose experience is wider, who can be seen as a peer to be talked with on level terms. This again, ought to be provided by the employer.

B. *How does professional growth take place?*

We have seen that professional growth is a continuous process in which many elements come together. Different teachers will have different ways of learning. One will learn largely alone, through personal reading and observation of pupils. Another will learn largely by attending courses. Most need a mixture of opportunities.

All teachers will learn individually to some extent. Most learn a certain amount through personal reading. Almost all learn by experience and experiment in the classroom or more broadly within the school or department. Many learn through opportunities to talk over ideas with colleagues. Some are fortunate enough to see and learn from other teachers at work or to work with experienced colleagues in a teaching team. Some have the opportunity to see themselves at work on video-tape.

Professional growth will also take place within the school. Discussion in the staff room or on the job will help the teacher to sort out his ideas and improve his skills. Group problem solving and team work will do this even better. Some teachers will grow professionally and develop their work through some form of management by objectives, in which senior teachers help less experienced teachers to define objectives, consider how to achieve them and evaluate progress towards them.

There should also be some professional growth outside the school. Some of this will come from living a full and interesting life, from more general reading, talking with others, travelling and observing, listening to the radio and watching television; but some will also come from different forms of in-service training, from lectures and seminars, and workshops and simulations. Some growth will come from work in groups with particular tasks, perhaps in relation to curriculum development.

Growth will also come from visiting other schools and talking with other teachers. This offers similar benefits to those coming from good staff-room discussion but extends it into another environment and brings experience of another set of problems.

Each of these ways of learning may be fostered or helped by an agency or a consultant. The degree to which any agency or consultant can contribute to the development of any particular teacher will, of course, depend on the attitudes and expectations of the teacher concerned.

C. *What part can the local education authority's advisory service play in the professional development of teachers?*

The adviser is likely to influence the development of teachers in a number of ways. Perhaps the greatest point of influence is within the school itself, where the discussion is usually centred on particular problems. Outside the school, an adviser may work on particular or more general problems with groups of teachers from a number of schools. He may arrange visits for them or he may run workshops, simulations and straightforward courses. He may provide publications of various kind to help teachers. he may offer course notes and booklists; he may provide material for distribution to a number of schools. He may develop collections of learning materials which teachers can use without him, or provide exhibitions of work or books and equipment which may be helpful.

Advisory services are still at an early stage of development. The body of skills and knowledge needed by an adviser is ill defined compared with that of the teacher and there is still much to be learned about how best to be effective in visiting schools and what it is necessary to sample in order to get an adequate picture. We saw that the teacher learns from his own experience and from discussion. The adviser should be able to offer help to a teacher by observing him at work, discovering through talking what his ideas are and then drawing out from these experiences points which seem to be important and relevant for the teacher's growth. The adviser reflects for the teacher some parts of his own teaching behaviour and helps him to interpret them and put them into context, ready for building on. He can do this because he has analysed the work of many teachers and has worked out what seems to be important. He may also be able to put the teacher in touch with other teachers doing similar work, suggest visits, reading or courses or offer written suggestions of various kinds. He should know more than most teachers about the range of ways of teaching in some areas of work because of his opportunities to see a wider vista. He may need to support and reassure some teachers. On a few other occasions he may want to disturb complacency.

Some work of this kind will be with inexperienced teachers, some with teachers in their probationary year. Most people in advisory work have a permanently guilty conscience about probationers. The probationer may be given a great deal of help within the school or he may not. If the local adviser is unable to spend enough time with each probationer, some may get into difficulties which could have been avoided. No doubt the induction programmes hoped for as a result of the White Paper *Education: a framework for expansion* will help, but at present the majority of advisory services are unable to support probationers to the extent that their members believe desirable. In many cases it is probably better for an adviser to concentrate attention on those probationers who are in real difficulty and upon working with heads and senior staff to help them to help inexperienced teachers. The idea that the school has a responsibility for staff development is a fairly new one, which seems likely to develop as a result of plans for induction and in-service training.

This leads to a consideration of what an adviser can do to help the head and senior staff in a school to arrive at a satisfactory kind of management which provides an effective organization for the life and work of the school and supports the teachers. This must also include encouragement for teachers to grow professionally.

With the development of large secondary schools, there has been a growing consideration of the managerial roles of head and senior staff. This has perhaps highlighted the need to think about what is involved in good management at all levels. As a society we are moving away from hierarchical structures towards more democratic ways of working. Many schools still work in paternalistic ways and while this may be quite effective so far as the learning of the pupils is concerned, it does little to help the teachers to grow professionally and in the long term this affects the pupils.

Part of the task of the senior members of an advisory service is to help individual heads and senior teachers to set up management structures which are more democratic and which provide for the professional growth of teachers. This probably means that some decision making must be delegated so that teachers feel a genuine involvement in the processes of planning, development and evaluation.

Such a move demands a great deal of a head. He is being asked to delegate a great deal and yet to remain responsible. He has to discover which decisions need to be made by a group in order to create involvement and commitment and which are best made by individuals. He is asked to do this more or less in isolation, perhaps with no personal experience of the possible outcome, and yet he has to answer to parents and to the authority for the results of the changes he makes.

The adviser should be able to help here. In the first instance he should be able to act as a sounding-board for the head contemplating change. He may be able to put the individual head in touch with other schools with comparable experience and from his own wider experience may be able to help head and staff to foresee some of the results of their actions. He may be able to warn of dangers and difficulties and help those concerned to see their objectives more clearly and to consider how they will evaluate what they are doing. At a later stage he may be able to help in the evaluation of the change. He may also provide encouragement and support for those concerned.

In all these ways he is contributing to the professional growth of the senior staff. He may be doing this in the way he guides them towards certain forms of organization rather than others, and he needs to be clear about his own criteria in offering advice.

In addition to examining whether an organization provides well for the education of the pupils he needs to examine with the head and senior staff questions such as the following:

1. Does this organization provide opportunities and encouragement for the teachers to talk through ideas in small groups, so that they learn from each other and constantly refine their own thinking?
2. Are there enough opportunities for ideas to come up from the bottom as well as down from the top? Will ideas be welcomed and, if possible, used, wherever they come from?
3. Have the decisions which have been delegated provided the necessary involvement or could they have been made by an individual with no loss?

Democratic ways of working which provide for the professional development of teachers are more time consuming than authoritarian patterns. A head and staff will need to be convinced that this time is well spent. During a period when a school is moving from authoritarian to democratic ways of working, it is likely that a great deal of discussion time will be wasted while people learn how to operate in this way. There will probably be a number of teachers who resent this and prefer situations where they are told what to do. The adviser's help and support is needed here, both for those who are convinced of the value of what they are doing and for those who think it a waste of time. If he has experience of the value of what is being done, he can tell of this and so help a school through a difficult period of transition.

The adviser also provides for the development of teachers outside the school. One way of doing this is to gather together groups of teachers with particular interests to discuss problems or to work at a task. There are a good many different ways of working with groups of this kind and some are more effective than others.

In planning this work the adviser needs to start by looking at the motivation which will make teachers join the group and remain with it. No group will continue in being unless those concerned find it helpful.

A group may be concerned with problem solving. This can be concern about a specific problem or problems and may include staff from one or two schools only. The task of the group is then to try to define the problem and to look together for solutions which can be tried out by members. The group then evaluates the result.

This is an opportunity for professional development which is probably under-used at present. An adviser frequently acts as consultant in schools suggesting solutions to problems or helping individual teachers to discover them, but it is not yet very common for him to act as leader of a group looking at a specific problem. This way of working has the advantage that the teachers themselves are likely to be highly motivated. It also has the advantage that an attitude and an approach to problem solving is likely to be developed by the group and this may enable the teachers concerned to build on from the immediate exercise.

Sometimes the problems may be a bit more general. The members of the group may come from a wider range of schools and each may contribute problems for others to consider. A common practice at secondary level is for specialist advisers to run regular meetings of specialist teachers to look at common problems. A good many groups have also come into being to look together at various curriculum development projects or to work together at a place of research or seek to develop ideas which all members in the group can use. One such group, for example, worked over a period of about 2 years on religious education in the primary school. The group worked by first talking out their ideas on a particular theme. Then each member put forward ways in which he or she would explore the theme with children and the results of this exploration were brought for others to see at the next meeting.

The function of the adviser in this group was very much that of discussion leader although she was sometimes able to make suggestions from a wider knowledge of the subject and a wider experience of schools.

Another area in which there has been a good deal of work with small groups is in the training of heads and senior staff in management. Much of the work in groups here has been at least partly concerned with the way people interact with each other, although it has also included simulations, discussion of day-to-day problems and many other topics. Heads in particular need opportunities to talk with their peers. An adviser often serves this purpose in visiting a school, but there is also a need for heads to talk out problems with colleagues from other schools.

Very often groups set up within an authority to look at questions such as the provision of equipment, work with the adviser in choosing and evaluating equipment for the authority. Some groups at all levels may be formed for this kind of purpose and although the immediate task appears to benefit the schools generally rather than the particular teachers taking part, in practice there is often considerable benefit to the members of the group from the consideration of wide issues.

In one authority, for example, when an improved building brief for primary schools was needed, teachers' groups were set up in various areas of the county each considering overall aims and some particular sections of the brief. The work was coordinated by the advisory staff working with teacher representatives. The function of the advisers here was to set up the organiza-tion and plan the work of each group. Each group also had an adviser as chairman, so that there was some on-going coordination. In the process of doing this, teachers not only had the opportunity to talk through ideas with their colleagues, but also the opportunity to visit and see other schools in ac-tion and to discuss what they saw. Obviously this kind of exercise benefits the members of the group in differing degrees, but it will be a rare teacher who gains nothing for himself from it. The authority also gains from the advice and support of a wide range of teachers, as well as from its own advisory staff.

In addition to work of this kind, the advisory service of a local authority usually plans more formal kinds of in-service training for teachers. This will include courses to provide additional knowledge and to develop particular skills and will include various modes of learning and teaching — lectures, seminars, working groups, films, discovery learning, programmed learning and so on.

Another area in which an adviser can work effectively is in providing the right kinds of publication for teachers on topics of immediate concern. Many advisers provide book lists and course notes which may well have a wide circulation, but if an adviser can produce practical material in the right kind of format, he may succeed in reaching a very wide audience.

It is, of course, difficult to generalize about what may be valuable. Undoubtedly different groups of teachers have different needs and different interests, but effective material probably needs to satisfy the following criteria:

1. It must be "bite" sized. A good criterion is to ask how much a teacher could get from a given publication during the morning break. This is not to suggest that teachers are unready to read longer material, but that this is already well provided.
2. The layout must be such that the message is quickly seen. Illustrations may help, but it is mainly a matter of well-spaced paragraphs and a good use of headings.
3. It must be seen as practical, but at the same time needs to be more than a "how-to-do-it". One of the best ways of assembling such material is to list the questions which a teacher needs to examine on a given topic and to set beside them a range of the possible answers, so that the reader can choose from them.

Material of this kind can be compiled by groups of teachers and assembled by an adviser. This has all the advantages of the group project described above and would seem a very good way of helping teachers to help each other. It also avoids the problem which worries some advisers who fear that if they set pen to paper, some teachers will use the suggestions given in unsatisfactory ways or for long after they are relevant. The counter question to this is "what are such teachers using anyway?".

In one authority, for example, infant schools were asked for specific information about the reading schemes they used. This was made into a booklet by an adviser working with a group of teachers. Relevant details about each scheme were given, together with users' comment and a list of schools using the scheme where teachers would be happy to answer questions about their scheme from others contemplating buying it.

Another kind of material which can be built up by an advisory service can be the outcome of preparing a course. Many groups of teachers, in individual staff rooms and at teachers' centres, are prepared to come together to listen to a short tape, accompanied by slides or overhead projector transparencies. This material is not difficult to produce and spreads ideas further.

Exhibitions and collections of children's work are also effective ways of showing some things. One of the many advantages of local teachers' centres is that they offer a venue for exhibitions of various kinds.

The advisory service of a local authority is only one of a number of agencies contributing to the professional development of teachers. One of the difficult questions for any advisory service is how the contribution they might make fits in with contributions being made by other agencies, such as teachers' centres, colleges of education, universities, the Department of Education and others. This has for many years been an area of confusion and it is still difficult to see how the parts can fit together so that an individual teacher can choose from a wide range of opportunities, those which for him will add up to a satisfactory whole. The answers are not made easier by the variety of provision in different parts of the country, so that in one area there are several providers and teachers will be spoilt for choice and in another there will be few providers and an inadequate programme.

What therefore is the particular province of the local authority advisory service? Advisers are firstly, like the teachers, employees of the local authority and as such must be concerned with implementing the authority's policies. It would seem also to be the task of the advisory service, together with teachers and the administration, to weave the various policies agreed by committees into an educational whole.

In many places, for example, a decision has been taken to reorganize primary education into first and middle schools, and secondary education into one of the forms of comprehensive school. This decision has usually been preceded and followed by a great deal of thought and study and observation by administrators, advisers and teachers, in order to arrive at a concept of the kinds of schools the new policy might create. This in turn has given rise to a programme of in-service training specifically geared to the needs of teachers in the schools of that particular authority at that particular point in time.

The second area which would seem to some extent peculiar to the local authority advisers is the provision of a consultancy service within the school. Of course, others also act as consultants, notably Her Majesty's inspectors, but it ought to be possible for the local authority adviser to be a more frequent visitor than other consultants. He also has an important link with the administration and may be in a better position to help individual teachers and schools because of this.

Providing a consultancy service within the school also suggests providing the kind of problem centred in-service training described earlier. Work with certain kinds of small teachers, gróups would therefore seem to be mainly a matter for local authority advisers perhaps together with the staff of teachers' centres although others may contribute.

Another area in which the local authority adviser must be expected to contribute is in training for work in projects where the authority has provided special finance. The adviser may simply be the agent through whom the training is arranged here, or he may be personally involved.

Most of the other kinds of courses in which local authority advisers now take part are also provided by other agencies. It would seem that at present the decisions about which agency does what, can come about only through local consultation.

No doubt this will gradually be sorted out as new plans for in-service education develop, but the local education authority to some extent will monitor the opportunities available to its teachers. It does this in various ways. It will make it easy or difficult for a teacher to attend a long or short course run by one of the other agencies by its policies in financing this and the generosity with which policies are applied. Information about a good many courses and meetings reaches teachers because local authority officers put it in the bulletin or pass it on to schools through the advisers. Keen teachers will overcome problems caused by poor communication systems about courses, and inadequate financial support, but the majority are dependent, to some extent, on the good will of the authority. The adviser has a very real responsibility to see that the opportunities reach the teachers.

A rather different aspect of the influence of the adviser on the work of the teacher lies in his relationship with the administration. The local education authority creates situations in which its heads and teachers may or may not be encouraged to think things out for themselves. In many authorities, for example, a large share of the spending on new and existing schools is outside the control of the individual head. The officers and sometimes the members decide on whether or not they will let a school have a kiln or an additional sewing-machine or tape-recorder. As the money available is usually considerably less than the demands made by schools an individual school may ask for something year after year, never being in a position to plan towards it or to say "this year we'll go without something in order to buy the major item we need". Similarly, heads of new schools may be given very little choice in purchasing furniture and equipment.

This kind of practice is administratively convenient and appears to save money through bulk purchasing, but it does not encourage schools to make long-term plans or to weigh up the needs of one area of curriculum against another. It probably does little to save money, because it gives the school no encouragement to find the cheapest ways of doing something and they may well be provided with a piece of equipment which is better and more costly than they actually need. Much the same can be said about the practice of insisting that money cannot be carried over the end of the financial year. There are also other administrative practices which take autonomy from the school often in the interests of public expenditure, but in doing this operate against the development of thinking schools. The adviser is the person most likely to be aware of this and most likely to be in a position to encourage changes in policy.

The local authority adviser, because of his relationship with the administration and education committee, is in a rather particular position in relation to the teacher. He is firstly the representative of the teacher's employer — someone from "the office", who could be dangerous, who very often has some sort of key to additional money and resources and is frequently also concerned with promotion. These are all reasons why the advice of the local authority adviser may be viewed with caution. It does not make much difference whether he is called inspector, adviser or organizer. His role is *much* the same and he is in a position which requires a great deal of tact and integrity.

D. *What kind of an advisory service does a local education authority need?*

British education is unique in the freedom given to individual schools and teachers to devise their own curriculum and plan their own work. In practice a variety of social pressures operate to create a fair amount of similarity between different schools, but nevertheless, each school has its own flavour and each local authority has its own way of looking at education, reflected in the areas of spending in which it is generous or mean. The local authority view of what is important is likely to be a mixture of the views of its elected members, its senior officers, and its advisers, but it is the adviser who helps to translate the policies into action in the schools and mainly the adviser who feeds back the views of the schools to the administration and members. Each adviser is likely to contribute to the development of the teachers he serves in the light of his own enthusiasm and interests. In an authority where there is no attempt to evolve a coherent view of education on the part of senior officers and advisory staff, where each adviser does his own thing without reference to the other advisers who are also doing their own things, it is easy for the contribution made by advisers to the professional development of teachers to be somewhat incoherent and idiosyncratic.

The most satisfactory situation is undoubtedly one where the officers of the authority and particularly the advisory staff have talked through to a measure of common vision, in which specialists see their work as part of a coherent whole and where there is agreement that the task is one of helping to create thinking schools where teachers also enjoy a measure of common vision and are able to grow professionally.

A great many local authorities now try to provide a consultancy and advisory service for their schools and an advisory service for members and administrators, by employing a team of inspectors or advisers which has within it people who can offer expertise on every aspect of education, who have substantial teaching experience and broad knowledge and understanding of educational issues.

A teacher should be able to ask any question about his work and know that someone in the advisory service can offer an adequate answer. Such a service is difficult to provide unless the team is fairly large. Larger teams bring other problems, particularly problems of coordination. Each member of the team needs to see himself as part of a total picture, knowing where his own knowledge and skills fit in, in terms of providing a balanced curriculum at different stages of education and in terms of a local pattern.

To cater for this, the local education authority needs to provide both for coordination on an area basis and coordination on subject and age-group bases. If the authority is large, it will probably be necessary to form a local team to serve each area. Subject specialists and specialists in the education of different age-groups will need to work across the areas, coordinating what is happening. This should certainly be organized to prevent a situation where a number of people go separately to the same school, unknown to each other, offering sometimes the same advice and sometimes advice which is conflicting.

If there is to be coordination it needs to be someone's task to see that it happens. An authority probably needs to have advisers in coordinating roles in local areas, across stages of education and across areas of curriculum. There will also be a need for overall coordination.

In a similar way coordination is needed in seeing that the programme of in-service training offers teachers what they need and bears some relationship to the agreed aims of the advisory team. It is also necessary to see that there is an adequate relationship between the programme provided by the local authority advisory service and that provided by teachers' centres and other agencies.

The team also needs to offer support to its members and provide for their professional development in a similar way to the staff team in a school. Very little has been done so far to train advisers for advisory work and, like heads, they have had to pick up the job as they went along, often with even less chance than a head of seeing a professional colleague at work and learning from him. This is to some extent changing as more advisers are appointed, but there is a long way to go at present and induction and training programmes are needed.

In considering the contribution a local authority advisory service might make to the professional development of teachers, we need to consider the qualities and skills needed by the adviser.

We have already seen that he is in a somewhat difficult position because of his involvement in the promotion of teachers and because he is a representative of the employer, who has a function as an inspector, whatever he is called in practice. The desirable situation is one in which teachers and advisers work together at problems, a situation in which the adviser is seen as a friend coming into the school to help.

If he is to be a welcome friend, however, the adviser must convince teachers that he has something to offer them. What should he have to offer? The individual adviser must be able to bring additional experience to the head or the teacher. He must be able to offer advice on a given problem from experience of one kind or another gained personally or through observing the solution of similar problems in another school.

But that is not enough. The old image of the inspector picking up something in one school and passing it on in the next is inadequate although it has a measure of truth in it. The first thing a local authority adviser needs is a personally thought-out philosophy of education against which he can measure changes and developments. He needs this whether or not he is part of a team with a common vision or policy. His philosophy must be more than a collection of prejudices; more even than a collection of examples of good practice. He must have a clear idea of what the needs of education might be and be aware that there are many ways of achieving them. This involves a good deal of conscious and continuous effort on his part. He not only needs to get his basic thinking clear. He also needs to study and evaluate new developments in the light of it. Only then will he have a frame of reference against which to consider particular problems.

The adviser not only needs knowledge. He also needs a body of skills, which includes those of the good teacher and the good head, and also includes further skills of observation.

He needs to be expert at observing teachers and the way they work and interact with children. Over the years he will build up experience of different types of teacher and different teaching styles, which should help him to match his advice to the individual teacher and school. He needs also to be expert at observing what is actually happening as distinct from what seems to be happening; at distinguishing work which is teacher directed to the point where the children have learnt very little from that which is teacher directed but offers the children a lot, and at distinguishing both of these from that which is truly children's work.

He needs to be able to assess groups of children and their work and to try to discover whether the teacher who knows them far better than he does is getting all they have to give. He needs to be able to read school and classroom atmosphere and assess the hidden curriculum.

An adviser also needs the skills of the salesman. He often needs to be persuasive, although he must guard against persuading people to fall in with his own prejudices. He has to be able to judge the right amount of suggestion and persuasion. He needs to give teachers the kind of positive help that enables them to think on for themselves. In visiting schools he has to know when to press questions and create discussion and when to praise and encourage and when to leave things alone.

A good deal of advisory work involves discussion, sometimes with individuals and sometimes with groups. The adviser needs to be a skilled leader in discussion, knowing how to make people feel at ease, how to invite, welcome and use contributions to help the work of the group. He needs to be good at spotting the shy member and helping him to contribute, and equally good at helping the group to contain its more dominant members. He must be able to draw contributions together, to sum up and help the group to arrive at conclusions through its own thinking. He also often is in the rather subtle role of being more than just a chairman. The group may well expect him to know more than they do in some areas and he has the difficult job of deciding when to draw the contributions from the group and when to make his own contribution. If he comes in with his ideas too early, he may take others faster than their own thinking is going and prevent their own working out of problems. If he never contributes, however, the group may well be losing the value of his wider experience.

We looked earlier at the need for teachers and heads to be men and women of vision. This is even more true of the adviser, whose vision must be strong enough to withstand the frustrations of being part of a service in which movement has to be slow, strong enough to accept misunderstanding and misinterpretation of his ideas, strong enough to enable him to persist and above all strong enough to enable him to go on supporting and stimulating others. He needs to be an optimist, believing in progress, believing that the weakest teacher can grow with help.

Sometimes he will help a school or a group of teachers to grow by the help he gives. Sometimes he can offer the experience or the encouragement which will enable them to move forward. Sometimes he will sow the seed from which new development grows and keep it alive by his interest.

The adviser needs to be an enthusiast, a source of inspiration to teachers, finding good things in unlikely places, stirring, stimulating and enlarging the experience of each teacher and so helping him to grow and achieve his full potential.*

---

*Local authorities have a variety of titles for those doing advisory work, of which inspector, adviser and organizer are probably the most common. The titles given are largely a matter of history, although in some authorities the title inspector is used for the more senior posts. Whatever the title, the actual job is largely the same, and must include elements of inspection and advice, since it is not possible to advise in any satisfactory way without first "inspecting" to assess the problem, and inspection without advice seems a somewhat pointless activity. Throughout this paper I have used the words "adviser" and "advisory service" because these appear to be the terms most used. What I have to say applies to all local authority officers doing work of this kind.

CHAPTER 5

The In-service Education of Teachers and the Colleges of Education

Introduction

THE main focus of this book is on the in-service education of teachers and teachers' centres as established over recent years. This chapter, however, argues for a complementary development of professional centres based upon institutions of higher education as an important alternative and extension of the concept of teachers' centres. The emphasis throughout will be upon the colleges of education, but it is important to note that the colleges themselves are undergoing a period of massive reorganization and change, and within a decade few of them will be recognizable as the monotechnic institutions so familiar to most teachers. Thus, the arguments advanced in this chapter for professional centres based upon colleges could be applied in a large part to other major institutions of higher education in the public sector. As will be indicated in various stages, the departments of education within universities can offer valuable additional resources to teachers, and universities should certainly see the provision of courses for teachers as part of their continuing responsibilities to public education.

The thrust for the current national review of in-service education was provided by the report of the James Committee in 1972([1]) in which it was argued that "the best education and training of teachers is that which is built upon and illuminated by a growing maturity and experience. In-service training comprehends the whole range of activities on which teachers can extend their personal education, develop their professional competence and improve their understanding of educational principles and techniques."

Teachers' centres organized outside the colleges of education can, of course, make a major contribution to this provision. It is, however, vital that those agencies providing initial training of teachers should also play a central part in in-service education. This again was perceived as central by the James Committee:

> All our proposals (for initial training) depend for their force upon what is argued and recommended for in-service training. The proposals regarding initial training assume an established pattern of continuing education and training of teachers, and take the twin objectives of initial training as being to equip the student to be as effective a teacher as possible in the first assignment, and to provide him with a basis upon which his in-service training can be methodically built. Equally they assume that the student has, in the formal sense, "completed" his initial higher education and is now sharply motivated towards teaching.

Following the publication of the report, in-service training has become detached in public argument from the question of initial training and the development of professionalism in teachers. However, if such a view predominates and in-service training is separated firmly from initial training, it will fail to realize its full potential. The main argument for seeing that colleges of education and other training bodies (polytechnics, departments and universities) have a continuing role in induction and in-service work is based upon their continuing responsibilities for initial training of the nation's teachers. It would be unsatisfactory for such institutions to carry out initial training unless in their professional work they are also entrusted with some responsibility for the continuing education of teachers. How else will they be able to assess the value of their training for the "early concerns" of the teachers, and have a base for continuous review and reappraisal of the higher education and professional training courses offered to teachers at the initial stage?

Colleges of education

It is extremely difficult to generalize about 150 institutions varying widely in size, location and character. Colleges will shortly be designated as further education institutions, and various forms of diversification will follow. A small number will merge with polytechnics, and one at least with a university. Others will merge with colleges of technology, and some remain independent but with additional courses in fields other than teacher training. The reference groups for the colleges will be more diverse, and they will be less dependent upon links with a university. In in-service training the regional authority will be a consortium of interests, in which the university and college will be only a part, with teachers and local education authorities playing a substantial role.

For the purpose of this chapter, however, it is assumed that the institutions of which we are thinking have a significant higher education role, with a central core of teacher education and substantial in-service responsibilities. This would be true whether the colleges are acting independently or within the context of a much more generalized further education provision — normally of an advanced kind.

The professional centre

It is hoped that all higher education institutions with a major concern with in-service training will establish a professional centre. In a limited number of cases it is possible that a small college may, in fact, become a professional centre concerned solely with in-service education and training. In most institutions, however, work with qualified teachers will be a part only of the purpose of the college. Indeed, any institution concerned solely with in-service training will be able to provide only a part of what a teacher essentially needs as a fully professional person for whom continuing opportunity for personal education is also of significance. However, in-service education with the scope now proposed cannot be sustained by the part-time — and frankly peripheral — attention which many colleges give to it. It is essential to concentrate staff, resources and organization to serve the special and continuing needs of practising teachers. One way of ensuring this concentration is through the establishment of a professional centre which is the responsibility of a senior member of staff, with its own board representative of the various interests in the field of in-service education. If a college has a series of schools or faculties, then such a professional centre should have equivalent powers, a substantial budget and a well-articulated policy which has been agreed by the college's academic board, governors and local education authority. It should have power to respond to requests, as well as to initiate major programmes; it should be given responsibility also for research and inquiry in what is the most critical field of development in the whole of teacher education. Such a structure would enable the colleges to make a substantial contribution to induction, in-service and innovation.

Induction

The induction period is the essential bridge between training and teaching, and much of the quality of the profession and the response to future in-service opportunities are dependent upon what is done in the first year of teaching. It is also a key stage in the professionalization of the teacher. As the White Paper([2]) points out, "induction should offer a systematic programme for professional initiation, guided experience and further study. To do so, teachers must be released for not less than one-fifth of their time for in-service training." The whole direction of courses and guided experience should be to support and help the new teacher to become more skilled and adequate as he works his way through the various stages of his most concentrated and decisive professional experience. Central to the entire development will be the role of the professional tutor. The colleges have an important role to play, although from the beginning it must be clear that this should in no way be prescriptive. It is neither possible nor desirable to sit down and plan a 1 day a week course for the 200 inductees who may take up appointments within easy travelling distance of a college. It is necessary to be familiar with the schools in which the new teacher will be working and to have close liaison with the professional tutors, the advisers and headteachers. The programmes of support and guidance should be closely related to the individual needs of the different teachers, with group seminars, access to resources, and introductory sessions common to all working within particular kinds of school. Much else will be individual and group work, done sometimes in the college, sometimes in a teachers' centre, and often in school.

One approach would be to have an "assigned tutor" who would establish and maintain a working relationship with a group of schools. The tutor would assist with in-service programmes for such schools, make a contribution to teaching in the school and hope to gain the confidence and respect of the head and his staff. In co-operation with the professional tutor he should meet the new teacher at the very beginning of his year and, if possible, before he has actually taken up his appointment. The need for more students to be appointed to specific schools and to know about them well before they take up their jobs in September is urgent if one really wants teachers to feel some commitment to the schools and children with whom they are working and to feel that they are being treated as properly professional people. Any new teacher faces problems and one task of the assigned tutor is to try to link the teacher's induction period study both to his classroom difficulties and to whatever kind of initial training he received. While the "assigned tutor" should be seen to be closely identified and actively co-operating with the professional tutor, he should also provide opportunity for contact outside the context of the school, and provide a listening ear for the young teacher without being identified with the status system either within the school or within the local authority. The college could provide a social base for the young teacher, as well as full and free access to the library and to audio-visual and other resources. The new teachers should be given the opportunity also to help trainees by talking to them about the ways in which they are tackling the problems which arise in the first year. This is one extremely important way in which a college role in induction has particular value for initial training.

The "assigned tutors" from the college should be active professionals working also in a school of professional studies concerned with initial training. They will be mainly field-based tutors working more outside the college and in the schools than inside the college itself; they will be closely identified with professional tutors, teachers' centre wardens and practising teachers. Indeed, they should form part of a wider professional group which plays a role in both initial and in-service training. This, of course, will only be possible if the college regards initial training and induction as part of one continuous process. The core of such an approach is the day-to-day professional experience for the practising teacher. This accepts the need for early concerns, the need to understand the way in which particular children learn, why teachers have certain attitudes, what resources are most appropriate for children of different ages and abilities, the effects of home background, the attitudes of parents, an understanding of the questions which children ask, and the ways in which answers can be articulated or discoveries made. New teachers will need help in recognizing the qualities which are most valuable in particular situations: the usefulness of particular kinds of knowledge and understanding gained from higher education, the value of critical analysis, using such techniques as simulation and micro-teaching, and the consideration of the values implicit in certain forms of the curriculum, and ways of assessing the success of teachers and of children. Young teachers more than their elders are very alive to such issues, but impatient of an approach which is too highly theoretical — at least at the beginning.

A seminar and tutorial approach must be the one adopted for the induction year. This will involve the young teacher in a sharing of experiences and a slow realization of ways in which it is possible to be critical but constructive about one's own performance. It will also help in resolving some of the problems of individual children and of groups by suggesting strategies for using resources, for pacing one's output, and for keeping one's sincerity as well as one's sanity. It would also be the responsibility of the "assigned tutor" and the professional tutor together to help the young teacher to see the way in which he is developing and changing, so that he is able to assess for himself ways in which he is failing and succeeding so that each year he makes progress or seeks out those who can help him to find areas of work which enable him to achieve greater success. This is the essential challenge of the induction year.

In-service

The professional centre at the college should cater first of all for the individual needs of the teachers in the region as a resource centre, and secondly as a centre for various kinds of courses. The major thing to emphasize, however, is the role of the centre as a resource. The centre will need to be a place with good facilities, an educational technology area, spaces to make things, to experiment with materials and see examples of work done by children and of publications and apparatus for use in schools. There should be a major social area, common-rooms, a cafeteria and accessible parking areas. In addition, all parts of the college should be open: library, studios where available, laboratories, access to computers, further social facilities such as sports and bar, etc. For the use of the more obviously social facilities some fee may well be charged. It will certainly be necessary to finance from the authority the kind of materials bank which would be involved, and the additional pressure which will be put upon the library and other resources. Initially the major use will be made by teachers, but it is essential from the beginning that the needs of social workers, youth and community workers, and others working in the area should be recognized: indeed, it is important that in-service education should not be organized separately from other services to the community. Teachers will lose out if their continuing education is seen as separate from the improvements of public provision in higher education generally. Also the opportunities for various professions to get together both socially and professionally should be seized. This may begin with a common concern for children, and then extend to the linked problems which affect families in the area, as well as the various services which are provided. It would however, be preferable if colleges offering interprofessional opportunities were also able to train such workers at the initial stage, as the same advantages which would accrue for teacher trainers being involved with in-service would also affect the initial training of social workers and others. Above all, it is now important to work out a realistic budget for such activities, to relate the various agencies together, and to determine the priorities in terms of development.

In-service courses

The modern approach to course design advocated by the White Paper is for the use of units or modules which enable courses of various lengths and patterns to relate to each other and to lead eventually to substantial awards. Thus, although there will always be a need for specific and concentrated courses in limited areas, it is no longer necessary to assume that these are the only kinds of courses that will deal with the urgent and relevant concerns of teachers, whereas the longer, high-level courses are assumed somehow to escape the need to be relevant and appropriate. The overwhelming desire indicated by Brian Cane[3] and H. E. R. Townsend[4] is clearly for in-service Bachelor of Education degree courses available both part-time and full-time A critical problem is, however, to ensure that the new B.Eds. are much more professionally relevant and flexible than those which exist at the moment. The flexibility should be established not only to fit in with the needs of teachers in professional terms, but also in relation to the opportunities they have for leave and for part-time study. Thus, teachers should be able to obtain qualifications by a wide variety of means: by one-year, full-time study, one-term, full-time interlocking with part-time study, as well as entirely by part-time study. The use of vacations and weekends should be exploited, as should one-day and half-day release. Tutorial supervision in schools related to curriculum development, and emphasis upon independent study should all free the teachers to tackle urgent professional questions at a good intellectual level. The fact that teachers will be members of the boards responsible for planning courses of in-service training should lend in-service programmes greater relevance to the teaching situation.

A professional centre would enable teachers to have access to higher education courses and to read for a Bachelor of Arts degree as well as for a B.Ed. However, in the main the degree normally offered would be the B.Ed. whilst the approach to main subjects, for example, English, might pay particular attention to the needs of teachers working in educational priority area schools, or to the problem of language and communication at a very practical and specific level. On the other hand, a study of areas of literature might lead the students to question the approach of Dr. Halsey and his team in their volume on educational priority,([5]) that is that the curriculum in educational priority area schools should be aimed primarily at the critical and constructive *adaptation* of children to the actual environment in which they live and that the balance of the curricular diet should change from "academic" to "social" with reality-based themes forming the staple intake. Again, an English department might pay particular attention to reinforcing the teaching of English to the immigrant child. There are many practical questions to be answered, although experienced teachers will undoubtedly see, as June Derrick did,([6]) that the teaching of English is only one part of the cultural growth of an immigrant in a new environment. Thus, short and highly specific courses on a subject basis will inevitably lead to more substantial and deep considerations of the role of the teacher and the purpose of the school.

Innovation

One of the major considerations which led the James Committee to put in-service training at the top of their priority list was the impossibility of preparing a teacher at the beginning of his career for all the responsibilities he is going to face in a world of rapidly developing social and cultural change. The current inability of so many schools and teachers to cope with the rapidity of change in curriculum, methods of teaching, and the changing motivations and attitudes of children is a powerful argument for a national system of continuing education for teachers. Attempts to maintain a sabre-toothed curriculum or to return to a traditional relationship with children are both doomed to failure when one comes to analyse the present pace of change in school organization, in social demands, in learning content and teaching methods. However, it must be said that a large number of brilliantly innovative programmes developed by the Schools Council and independent foundations have failed to make any effective impact on the children for whom they were intended. It is, therefore, essential that professional centres should aid the vital task of establishing curriculum change in schools, and thus crucially affect the standard of education which children receive. This thesis has been well argued by Hoyle,([7]) who has written persuasively on the strategies of curriculum change.

By curriculum change is meant changing methods, materials, hardware, school organization and educational principles, i.e. virtually any sort of innovation at the school level. It also accepts that the fundamental aim is to improve schools and the educational experiences of children. In-service training of teachers is one way of achieving this objective. The current patterns of curriculum change rely upon diffusion, research and development and finally problem-solving.

Unfortunately diffusion, which is relatively unstructured, is extremely patchy and uncertain in operation. The research and development approach has had very limited success mainly because of the distorting effects of adaptation, which often means completely transforming the innovation in order to bring it into line with prevailing beliefs and procedures — thereby robbing it of its innovative character. There is also undoubtedly a lack of congruence between the rational, systematic and intellectualized research and development strategy, and the idiosyncratic, intuitive and individualistic approach of many teachers. Finally, the problem-solving model is concerned with the perspective of the school itself, as indicated by the interesting series of lectures by the Dean of the Teachers' College of Columbia[8] where the school is itself a learning system concerned with trying to establish innovation within its own environment. The difficulty here is that such innovation may often be ad hoc and chancy, and it tends to make unwarranted assumptions about the level of expertise and permanency of the staff in a school. This then underlines the need for a professional centre strategy of the kind advocated by Hoyle. The basic premise here is that there is a need for an institution intermediate between the school and the agencies of curriculum change.

A professional centre strategy would reinforce existing agencies. For this purpose the base is assumed to be a college of education. Its functions might be linkage, support, consultancy and in-service training. Thus, the linkage function would be to act as an intermediary institution between national agencies of curriculum development and innovating schools. Currently the Humanities Curriculum Development Centres established at the Berkshire College and Bishop Lonsdale College, Derby, show how colleges can act on behalf of major project teams, and at the same time give close support to schools within an area.

Thus, the centre would collect, exhibit and make available resources of various kinds, act as a centre of information for what is happening in the locality, link colleges, schools and other institutions, and create awareness of current innovation in schools. Its work would supplement that of local authority advisers and Her Majesty's inspectors. A second function would be to provide continuous support for projects in participating schools after the withdrawal of the development team, and for non-participating schools which would like help and guidance in the adoption and institutionalization of an innovation. A third function would be to provide a base for a permanent group of consultants and act as an agency for people from the appropriate departments of colleges, polytechnics, universities and other institutions who might be able to make a contribution towards assisting change. towards assisting change.

Here the two main targets of change are the curriculum and the social system of the school. The consultant would work together with the school staff or part of it as a group, provide theory, analysis, research and support. His interests would include perspectives of the school, the relationships between teachers and pupils, and the organization of the school. A great deal would depend upon the degree of involvement of the schools themselves in the management and development of the centre, so that consultants could be fully accepted.

Professional centre strategy could particularly help in working with groups of teachers. Much of current in-service training is aimed at individuals rather than the functioning group. The problem of individuals returning with personal enthusiasm is that it is often hard to sell the innovation to their less-committed colleagues who have not attended the course. However, for a school contemplating a major innovation — such as introducing mixed ability groups — the professional centre could help to prepare staff in a number of ways: firstly, by providing a setting, a support programme and the attachment of staff on a part-time basis with a specific expertise. Thus, the professional centre could provide much of the support for innovative activity, and give a base for in-service training linked to school programmes of innovation involving functioning groups of teachers rather than individuals.

Research is obviously an important element in innovation. In the National Foundation for Educational Research survey 75 per cent or more of the teachers said that they would like to join working groups of teachers with the definite objective of exploring subjects or topics in terms of classroom teaching which involved participants in practical trials and experimentation with methods, materials and ideas. A cogent argument for such an action programme as opposed merely to developing "taught courses" is the paucity of research findings which can be used to provide an adequate base for professional decisions (including the evaluation of curriculum development) – this in spite of the fact that expenditure on educational research and development has gone from some £200,000 in 1961 to well over £3,000,000 in 1973.

Major professional centres should be strongly supported as bases for relevant research. It is to be hoped that the Advisory Council on the Training and Supply of Teachers, and the new Regional Committees will encourage research in professional centres conducted both by teachers and by full-time researchers. The atmosphere of a centre developing the kinds of programmes indicated above may be a more appropriate base for genuinely useful educational research than units which are loosely attached to certain existing centres of higher education.

Conclusion

The argument of this chapter is that there is a need for a number of major centres of professional activity concentrating upon the continuing education of teachers. The number and scope of such centres is clearly a matter for debate and must be linked to other priorities in the field of higher education and teacher preparation. However, there will shortly be nearly half a million teachers with responsibility for educating the young members of our society during their most impressionable years. In view of the dramatic and far-reaching problems which are currently facing this country and the world, it seems common prudence to ensure that teachers should be assisted in shouldering such responsibilities by the provision of major centres which can be personally sustaining and professionally relevant.

References

1. DEPARTMENT OF EDUCATION AND SCIENCE, *Teacher education and training* (the James Report), Her Majesty's Stationery Office, 1972.
2. *Education: a frame work for expansion,* Cmnd. 5174. Her Majesty's Stationery Office, 1972.
3. CANE, B., *In-service training: a study of teachers' views and preferences,* National Foundation for Educational Research, 1969.
4. TOWNSEND, H. E. R. in Department of Education and Science, *Statistics of education, Special Series no. 2: In-service training courses for teachers,* 1967, Her Majesty's Stationery Office, 1970.

5. HALSEY, A. H. (Ed.), *Educational Priority*, Vol. 1. *E.P.A. problems and policies*, Her Majesty's Stationery Office, 1972.
6. DERRICK, J., *Teaching English to immigrants*, Longmans, 1966.
7. HOYLE, E., in WATKINS, ROGER (Ed.), *In-service training: structure and content*, Ward Lock Educational, 1973.
8. SCHAEFER, R. J., *A school as a centre of inquiry*, Harper & Row, 1967.

CHAPTER 6

School-based Curriculum Development and the Task of In-service Education

CURRICULUM development is an activity that has been the vogue amongst educational reformers in Britain for more than 10 years. The most conspicuous form of curriculum development has been the material-producing national project team. Like many of the educational preoccupations of recent times the project team approach had its immediate origins in the United States where, in the 1950s, academic and public dissatisfaction with secondary education culminated in the national crisis of confidence which followed the launching of Sputnik 1. This one traumatic event was taken by many commentators at the time to signify the superiority of Soviet scientific and technical education over American life-adjustment education. Life adjustment was a form of secondary education which gave greater emphasis to socially adaptive skills and to what some critics designated a "fun culture" than to attainment in the academic disciplines. The basic objective in life-adjustment education was to equip the mass of pupils in secondary schools with knowledge and skills deemed appropriate to living in contemporary adult society. This objective, according to its exponents, was not best achieved through the submersion of youth in the discrete disciplines of knowledge.

The American critics of life-adjustment approaches in secondary education, like the history professor Arthur Bestor and the nuclear submarine admiral Hyman Rickover, were joined by a generally right-wing press whose leaders managed to combine an envious admiration of Soviet science and engineering with a vociferous denunciation of any leftist tendencies in American educational theory. During the fifties, John Dewey's thought was still a powerful influence in the U.S.A. and it was not uncommon to find hysterical critics linking Dewey both with left-wing politics and intellectually undemanding schooling. Whether this distinctively American climate, compounded of hostility to theory, denunciation of the social goals of schooling, insecurity in the face of Soviet strength, and the academics' zeal to seize control of the schools, largely explains the different direction curriculum development subsequently took in America from what has occurred in Britain is a matter of speculation. There is, in the Black Paper ideology, a strident British parallel to the attack in America on life-adjustment schooling, and on other aspects of progressivism, but there is, as yet, scant evidence of the impact of this kind of reactionary thinking either directly on the work of the schools, or on the curriculum development movement as it has emerged in Britain. There are signs, however, of looming reaction against some of the newer approaches, e.g. in science, language and mathematics teaching. It is clear that progressively during the sixties British practice has followed its own paths. The American origin of the team-based curriculum development movement is now a matter merely of historical interest, although there is a continuing influence of American theory on college and university courses in curriculum studies, the most prominent examples being the Open University courses in curriculum.

American influences do not, of course, fully explain the origin of the curriculum development movement which in many respects is not a recent growth at all. Two main forms of curriculum development in Britain may be detected. First, school-based activity, depending on the skill, interest and resourcefulness of individual teachers or small groups working within schools or in informal project teams through local teachers' centres. Second, the sponsored, national projects initially funded by the Nuffield Foundation and then by the Schools Council, which since its founding in 1963 has rapidly become the chief patron of curriculum development in Britain. These movements converge at various points, for example in trial schools and in teachers' centres, but they may be distinguished both conceptually and in practice.

The first movement, which for convenience in this paper I shall designate either school-based or teacher-centred, is by no means a recent innovation although it has been discovered recently by foreign admirers for whom it is one of the greatest strengths of the British system especially at the primary stage. There is a tendency to attribute school-based curriculum development in the primary school to the insights and enthusiasms of teachers which are themselves left unexplained. It owes more debts than have been acknowledged to reformers occupying positions of influence. These were more often than not working in the Froebelian tradition of child development and included such figures as the McMillan sisters, Susan Isaacs, some of the principals of the early training colleges, a neglected band of pioneers, and the principals and staffs of the independent progressive schools.

After a period of submergence, school-based development is beginning to undergo a major revival. The visible exponents of this approach are the primary school teachers, many of whom, it should not be forgotten, have been trained in colleges where until very recently Froebel, Dewey and other upholders of the tradition of child study and education for growth have been highly influential. The college culture has communicated an educational ideology which has exercised a powerful influence on teachers' perception of the scope and nature of their role.

Since the relationships between curriculum development and teacher education is the theme of this paper, I want at the outset to draw attention to the traditions and practices in teacher education from the analysis of which the practising teacher, particularly in the primary school, has formed his judgements, sharpened his skills and developed his understanding of the tasks of teaching. Teacher education, the object of a great deal of criticism throughout the sixties, has not received its due as one of the principal formative influences in both the school-based and project team approaches to curriculum development.

The second, and highly publicized, form that curriculum development has taken in Britain is the activity of refurbishing teaching-learning materials through the research and development activities of national project teams. These teams, funded on an unprecedented scale through the Schools Council, are drawn mainly from school teachers and college and university lecturers, and their work covers all principal subjects taught from lower primary to upper secondary school. Further education and tertiary education have been relatively neglected; the former remains so, while the latter (for example, those institutions being studied by the Nuffield Project on university teaching methods) is showing a vitality and flexibility which may surprise some of the outside critics of university conservatism.

The Schools Council, for which there is no parallel in the United States of America — or in any other country — is primarily a sponsoring agency with a developing interest in questions of global policy and support systems. It is not comparable to a national educational development centre, although the matters touched upon by many of the projects would seem to indicate the need, if not for an institutional centre, then at least for a greater coordination of policy than has been achieved so far. Despite the structure of central, regional and local centres, and 10 years of funded development, it cannot be said that Britain has a policy for curriculum development — piecemeal reform is the prevailing mode, whether school or project team-based. This, of course, is entirely consistent with the empirical tradition in British life and thought and in mentioning some of its shortcomings I do not wish to overlook its inherent strengths such as flexibility and cultural pluralism.

These two main thrusts of curriculum development — school-based and project-centred — derive from different strands of educational thought and practice, but the shortcomings of each in recent years have shown the desirability of their being brought closer together, by conscious, deliberate action. However, it is not my purpose in this paper to discuss the manner in which a blending might be achieved. Instead, I want to draw attention to some of the possibilities for supporting and strengthening curriculum development within the school and at the local level.

One important lesson that has been learnt from the project-based movement is that the role of the teacher in curriculum development is of central importance and is not peripheral, as some enthusiasts for so-called "teacher-proof" materials at one time assumed. Furthermore, the role of the teacher is recognizably important from a much earlier stage in the process of curriculum renewal than exponents of the concept of research-development-diffusion have been prepared to admit. This is not to deny that many teachers effectively abrogate this role especially those who abandon the analytic and diagnostic tasks of teaching by accepting a predefined syllabus and its attendant texts. My point is, rather, that where development is proposed or under way, teacher awareness, understanding and skill play a central part in effecting an innovation. Hence successful innovation is generally dependent on the teacher to a degree that is still commonly underestimated.

The research-development-diffusion attitude to educational progress diminishes the role of the teacher. Despite its utopian critics, some of whom appear to wish it out of existence where their arguments fail to demonstrate its inevitable demise, the school remains the locus of educational effort, and the teacher is the key to curriculum development as to any other major aspect of educational reform. By "teacher", of course, I am not intending a narrow professionalism. Also, emphasis on teachers should not lead us to overlook the role of pupils and parents whose interests, needs and rights in this matter are still widely neglected. The research-development-diffusion approach assigns to experts outside the classroom all the decisive roles in curriculum development until the stage of adoption has been reached. Thus experts conduct research, including research on teachers, treating them for this purpose as objects of inquiry. Experts prepare the objectives which teachers and pupils are to pursue, they design and undertake the development of new teaching materials, drawing upon schools and teachers for use in trial runs. Only at the stage where materials are to be "diffused" do the classroom practitioners become important.

It should cause no surprise that outside the examination régime neither teachers nor pupils have displayed great alacrity in adopting materials and methodologies to whose development they made no effective contribution. Education is not a process of buying and consuming gaily packaged goods and educational development should not be equated with commercial production and salesmanship. The research-development-diffusion approach is derived from diverse non-educational fields of practical application such as agriculture, engineering and drug production. It is a central part of the industrialized society's need to produce, advertise and sell. It has the unfortunate characteristics of treating teachers and pupils as objects in need of manipulation or redirection rather than as participants in an activity which they have chosen, of tending to disregard the complex, inter-personal context of teaching, and of overlooking the institutional frame, the school community, which decisively affects the manner in which educational decisions are made in our society. Thus, curriculum is isolated and abstracted, deprived of its concreteness in a real world of relationships, and reduced to content and methodology, themselves schematized as so many steps in the developer's work programme.

This has led to a neglect of an alternative view of curriculum, one which treats it as both a constituent and a function of the relationships of teacher and pupil in a distinctive institutional setting. These relationships are, or should be, structured by educational criteria, which it is the responsibility of the teacher to disclose to the pupil through the learning situations he devises. Furthermore, this alternative view of curriculum treats it as transactional and adaptive, a function of the school's interactions with its environment.

The organic, individualistic nature of a school and the distinctive qualities of the culture it establishes for itself and expresses through its apparatus of symbolic, ritualistic and other modes of communication are entirely misconceived by approaches to curriculum development that presuppose a homogeneous system of identical units and determinate processes. What are of importance, in this transactional approach which I am proposing, are relationships and contexts, and it is to the analysis, the articulation and the reconstruction of these that the curriculum developer should turn. This will require him to operate at the local level or, more precisely, this is a conception which requires the average or ordinary teachers at school to see themselves as active participants in the development process. For this to happen, different approaches from those now commonly found will be needed in teacher education, both pre-service and in-service.

In the mounting wave of dissatisfaction with the research-development-diffusion approach to curriculum development, however, the very real achievements of this approach should not be overlooked. Not the least of these achievements has been to conceptualize curriculum as problematic, as susceptible to analysis and reframing, and as needing a substantial investment from the funds available for education, too small a proportion of which has ever gone into research and development. Furthermore, the engagement of distinguished scholars and skilled research workers in curriculum development has brought to school education an infusion of knowledge and expertise which it has not always had in the past. These have helped to rescue schooling from the cultural isolationism and dependence to which it is prone and have facilitated informed public interest in and scrutiny of educational practices, a matter of great importance in democratic societies. These achievements can be capitalized in the next stage, which should include a close analysis of the problems and processes of school-based development.

The project-based movement has brought with it considerable incidental advantages in addition to its central achievement of having transformed subject content which is available for use by schools. It is, regrettably, necessary to use the qualifier "available for use", since the actual impact of projects on the practice of schooling is very patchy indeed, partly for reasons to which I have alluded. These advantages need to be borne in mind in considering the shift towards more local and school-based approaches to curriculum development.

I have drawn attention to the peculiar weakness of the research-development-diffusion approach, which is its failure to grasp the central significance of teacher and pupil initiatives, teacher and pupil understanding, teacher and pupil motivation and teacher-pupil relationship in the context of the school as a living institution. The inter-personal context and nature of learning, again long appreciated within one of the progressive traditions in education, has been treated as a secondary consideration, subsidiary to the production of materials which embody the models, metaphors, concepts, methodologies and idiosyncracies of communities of scholars — or, even more narrowly, of the particular project team which generates the materials, and the trial schools. These schools, in the course of the project, become something of an expressive ideological network within which the developers function.

It is time for the policies by which the project team approach is sustained, to be assessed in a more radical way. There is little evidence of this radical appraisal, but many indications are emerging of interest in alternatives. The Schools Council, for all its achievements, is a ponderous bureaucracy which recurrently reflects the survival and power needs of its financial supporters and effectively reconciles their demands for a "voice" in educational decision-making. It lacks flexibility, in particular the flexibility needed to undertake self-criticism directed at its fundamental strategies as distinct from its survival mechanisms. Its opportunities for influencing the factors and forces that change the curriculum are limited, not only by its brief, its structure, its budget and its initial commitment to the national project approach, but also by the complex ramifications of curriculum. These, as I have already noted, go well beyond the traditional static components of "content" and "method", into the dynamic fields of relationships, institutional contexts and policy.

It may be, indeed, that by starting with a view of content to be up-dated, and seeking to apply to its development the process of research, development and diffusion we are ensuring, not development in the sense of continuing growth, but a temporary lurch forward followed by a massive consolidation of the status quo. The new materials are regarded as an investment. Once produced, they must justify themselves in use, and become almost an impediment — so much obsolescing stuff which must be used until it "wears out". Progressive up-dating is, like the manufacturers' modification to a successful car, a means of keeping it in production longer whether or not it is serving other utilities than that of production. If the product is engendering all kinds of undesirable side-effects, or failing to meet basic needs, these will be kept in the background, in case they should interfere with the manufacturer's intentions. At a time that suits him best, he will tool up to produce the new model, and go again through the whole process. The Schools Council ought not to be in this business but, having got itself in, it will not easily get out, not least because of the narrow professionalism that dominates its policies and procedures.

If we think of the curriculum, not in terms primarily of content to be produced, disseminated and assimilated, but of activities which characterize situations, we need to ask what kinds of activities, what sorts of situations, and how these activities and situations can be sustained and strengthened? The production and dissemination of materials, hardware and methodologies *may* be the appropriate answer, sometimes, to these questions. It is not always so. We need a policy, and structures to sustain it; one that encourages the asking of these questions, facilitates the answering of them, and directs resources accordingly. The Schools Council and the conception of the project team have served their purpose in this respect; they are no longer adequate.

At first sight, school-based curriculum development sounds an attractive alternative since it posits a direct local activity which expresses the needs of the school. However, simply to assign all responsibility for the curriculum to individual schools would not solve all the problems to which I have pointed and it would create new difficulties. An effort to produce and disseminate materials at the local level may be just an inefficient and cumbersome way of repeating national level mistakes; local definitions of policy may half-heartedly attempt what is better done at the national level.

Part of the task of analysis is to distinguish those tasks, such as global policy-making and strategic planning, which are best carried out nationally, from those which it is appropriate and desirable to undertake locally. At the local level, the task is to find ways of strengthening and supporting the school and the teacher as agents of development in their own situations. If we make the school the object of our inquiry rather than a distant element in the diffusion process, we may get what is required.

It should not be overlooked that "school" is a generic term, referring to institutions of higher learning as well as to the primary and secondary schools. Control of their own curriculum, of course, has in the Anglo-Saxon tradition of higher education long been vested in the universities whose autonomy in this respect may be regarded as vital. The universities are pioneers of school-based curriculum development with long experience of the possibilities and pitfalls. They are also the object of jealousy and suspicion not merely because of their success and strength but also because their independence and initiative in the cultural sphere represent a fundamental challenge to upholders of monolithic politics and to the enemies of liberal thought. Primary and secondary schools, if they were to attain this measure of freedom and power, would doubtless attract similar hostility.

The school is the place where direct curriculum exchanges occur: the classroom is the interface where, despite such innovations as open plan, team-teaching, school-without-walls, etc., the transactions between learners and teachers occur. The curriculum as mediated through teachers and experienced by pupils is a classroom function. Schools and classrooms remain the setting for the educational enterprise, and they justify and warrant the elaborate super-structure of which administration and teacher education are two of the most conspicuous components. Conversely, if the school ceases to function as an effective educational agency, its claim on support services and resources would have to be justified, if at all, on the other grounds, e.g. custodial, or protecting the labour market, etc.

Curriculum development is, accordingly, appropriately a matter for schools to involve themselves in although not to the exclusion of other agencies and institutions which have a legitimate interest. It could be argued, of course, that involvement need consist of no more than helping in defining needs, and receiving the resources, human and material, required to satisfy these needs. There is, however, already sufficient evidence that this is not an effective way for the school to change itself. For the school to play a more active part in analysing its needs, defining its purpose, devising its own work style and teaching-learning strategies, and assessing the results of its efforts, a much more carefully thought-out policy and support structure is needed than is available at present. The definition of the teacher's role would have to change, as would the length and structure of the working day and year. Furthermore, since teachers are neither trained nor supported as curriculum developers and would in fact experience the utmost difficulty if faced with the prospect of developing the curriculum as an ongoing task, in-service re-training on a massive scale would be required. Teacher education and curriculum development are in fact two aspects of a single process. Some years ago this was partially recognized by the introduction of in-service programmes as part of project implementation. What is really needed is the education of teachers as developers — not training them to use a package developed elsewhere.

Of course, the point I am making presupposes a certain view of curriculum. As the term is now widely understood, curriculum refers to the whole complex of learning experiences mediated through the school and legitimated through the school's subscription to such public domain considerations as examinations, vocational requirements, parental pressure, local authority influences, and so forth. Alternatively, the curriculum consists of those school-mediated learning experiences which are justified by the objectives to which, when challenged, teachers refer. Thus curriculum can be given either a social or a technical meaning, according to which dimension is invoked in its explanation and defence. This is not to deny a multiplicity of other meanings; for example, those of pupils, their parents, specific groups of teachers, and other sub-groups within society. But I am not concerned with these at present.

As I have defined it, curriculum might be thought of as static or re-capitulative. In fact, the curriculum of the schools has always been in a fluid condition if only because the mediating processes of learning necessarily involve shifts and modifications of meaning. However, the changes which curriculum has undergone may be broadly divided into two kinds. Firstly, those changes which are a function of extra school factors, for example, changes in the composition of the school population, or in the content of the disciplines which, in some form, it is one of the tasks of the school to transmit or, more precisely, to mediate. Secondly, changes occur in the curriculum which are a result of the deliberations and choices of the participants in these processes. I grant that this difference is not always clear cut, since the deliberations of participants may be over possibilities which are made available through or pressures which result from, for example, population changes or the growth of knowledge.

Nevertheless, there is an important distinction to be made between changes by which participants in a situation reconstruct that situation for their own satisfaction and changes of which they become the objects. There is a further distinction to which I wish to draw attention before returning to the concept of curriculum development as a series of stages in an action programme. This is the distinction between changes which function to maintain and stabilize situations by absorbing and assimilating new elements, and those which are of a more disruptive and comprehensive kind. This distinction is sometimes defined as the difference between non-innovatory and innovatory change. Whether the innovatory change is a consequence of some indigenous principle of growth in the individual organism or institution, on the one hand, or of their reactions to external events is not important for my argument, although in a wider consideration of change processes it would be.

These two distinctions may be expressed in a simple diagram which I shall refer to in contrasting curriculum development with more haphazard changes in education:

Change

Haphazard   Planned

Innovatory   Non-innovatory

Curriculum development is a planned, not a haphazard change, and it may be either innovatory or non-innovatory. Presumably it is one justification of project-based, heavily-funded curriculum development that it is so planned as to stimulate innovatory change; instead of relying on the natural and possibly haphazard processes of reaction, assimilation and accretion, a decisive effort is made to transform a system. Is the project team approach the only or even the best method of achieving such changes supposing them to be needed? Putting this question another way, what would be required to equip schools as agencies of planned, innovatory change? Would it make sense to conceive of this kind of curriculum development taking place through the thousands of individual schools? This is a question that, in the present state of knowledge, can hardly be answered. What is needed, though, is a careful appraisal of the issue.

If we consider each of the major stages in a process of curriculum development we might better appreciate the complexity of this issue. Curriculum development starts with a teaching-learning situation which is to be transformed. This situation is, for some reason or other, thought to be unsatisfactory. A common cause of dissatisfaction in the earlier years of the current movement was the impoverished or outmoded knowledge content of teaching. This is something that might reasonably be inferred from textbooks, and examination questions and answers, and these would disclose a national situation. However, other expressed dissatisfactions with the curriculum are not so readily demonstrated and require a more detailed observation and appraisal of learning situations than is possible even for the best funded research. We begin to unearth here a problem whose solution probably lies not in funding observational research projects but in equipping teachers to play a more effective role in diagnosing learning situations.

The theoretical knowledge gained by teachers during their initial training should contribute to their diagnostic capacity when faced with learning situations. However, it can hardly be maintained that present arrangements for training are adequate in this regard. The explanation for this does not lie wholly in the crowded nature of the college curriculum, or in the limited time given in most courses to practical problem-solving exercises in school situations. There are more fundamental problems of a social and an intellectual kind.

The social problem is that of the institutional separateness of schools on the one hand and colleges and universities on the other. The natural and easy access to schools which would seem to be required to facilitate students' development of diagnostic skills is inhibited by this institutional separateness and by the different career structures available to teachers working in different parts of the system. The close co-operation between school teachers and college teachers required for the student to acquire practical diagnostic skills is much more difficult to engineer, in present circumstances, than critics of teacher education imagine.

The intellectual difficulty to which I referred is a consequence of the opaqueness of learning situations. This may be readily demonstrated.

The task of situational analysis is one of daunting complexity given our lack of diagnostic tools and the difficulty of defining parameters. These difficulties may be indicated by a brief outline:

(a) External	(i)	cultural and social changes and expectations including parental expectations, employer requirements, community assumptions and values, changing relationships (e.g. between adults and children), ideology;
	(ii)	educational system requirements and challenges, e.g. policy statements, examinations, local authority, expectations or demands or pressures, curriculum projects, educational research;
	(iii)	the changing nature of the subject matter to be taught;
	(iv)	the potential contribution of teacher support systems, e.g. teacher training colleges, research institutes, etc;
	(v)	the flow of resources into the school;
(b) Internal	(i)	the aptitudes, abilities and defined educational needs of pupils;
	(ii)	the teachers; their values, attitudes, skills, knowledge, experience, special strengths and weaknesses, roles;
	(iii)	the school ethos and political structure: common assumptions and expectations including traditions power distribution, authority relationships, methods of achieving conformity to norms and dealing with deviance;
	(iv)	the material resources including plant, equipment and potential for enhancing these;

(v)   the perceived and felt problems
        and shortcomings in existing
        curriculum.

In an institution, such as a school, a learning situation is a compound of political, economic and psychological factors. For a teacher to diagnose a learning need in a concrete fashion requires knowledge not only of the academic history and performance of the pupil in question, but also of the social interactions in which he engages in the classroom, the cognitive possibilities of the subject matter in which he is or has been immersed and the socio-political structure of the school within which knowledge resources and indeed power are mediated and distributed through a variety of mechanisms. It is impossible, during a preliminary course of training, and lacking a reality bearing which involvement in classrooms provides, for the average young teacher to acquire the kind of competence which is needed if he is effectively to diagnose learning situations. It is doubtful whether many mature and experienced teachers have the practical ability or the resources to cope with these demands. Yet the individuality of learning situations requires that support should be brought to the classroom, in the form of specialist advisers and consultants, material resources, and skills and understandings which the teacher himself must acquire.

For each step or stage in curriculum development it is probable that similar needs must be satisfied. Initial training, combined with what is often of necessity an indiscriminate kind of classroom experience in the early years of teaching, is insufficient as a means of preparing the teacher to:

define learning situations;

think concretely about learning objectives;

devise teaching materials;

implement learning strategies;

test pupil performances and assess the overall effectiveness of the learning designs he has created.

It is not surprising, as research has shown, that teachers in practice plan their courses in a much more mundane fashion, by addressing themselves directly towards topics, themes, materials and modes of learning. They neither engage in elaborate diagnostic exercises nor spend time in defining objectives. How far it is appropriate to do so is indeed a matter for debate. In all the scholastic niceties of this debate about the intellectual legitimacy of setting out to define objectives and legislate means whereby they might be pursued, some simple questions remain: is the teacher interested in self-criticism; does he intend to evaluate pupil performances; what criteria govern assessments of self and others? It is through the analysis of these criteria that we disclose the objectives or the intentions that articulate the teachers' own thinking and work. Defining objectives is a matter of making these intentions specific, clear, and public.

I have suggested that in each stage of curriculum development conceived as a rationally ordered process, the classroom practioner needs various kinds of support. It would not be sufficient and may not be necessary or even desirable to provide this support by way of national project teams themselves going through each of these stages and then seeking to disseminate the results of their work to the teaching fraternity. We have sufficient experience of this approach to know that as a national strategy of educational development it will not work. However, I have also suggested that there are problems in the teacher attempting to do this work aided only by his professional knowledge and experience of classrooms and the relatively modest flow of resources for teaching which public education authorities have been able to sustain. There are further difficulties of grass-roots approaches, which I shall not discuss — for example, the diverse, miscellaneous nature of programmes, the waste of resources, the over-dependence of curriculum on the individual and unevenly distributed talents of the teacher, and the insularity and parochialism of exclusively localized initiatives. It is clear that the emerging strategy of school-based curriculum development needs to be well thought out in relation to national and regional strategies and that various support structures, outside the school, will be needed.

Some of these support structures may now be considered. I shall divide them according to a simple scheme of local, regional and national provision and control.

There is in British education partial provision in respect of each of these three levels, but there are also serious gaps and lack of overall co-ordination of policy, and indeed conflict over some aspects of control. At the local level, most conspicuous are teachers' centres which are themselves remarkably diverse. Less visible but, for purposes of school-based curriculum development, no less important are the informal networks and communications systems which the centres were in part designed to achieve. The specific needs of a particular school or group of schools are local matters which cannot be adequately determined or satisfied without a comprehensive local support system. There should be no schools which are out of frequent contact with other schools in local areas, which presupposes either a complete network of teachers' centres, or a comprehensive and well-financed advisory service, or both.

To make the best of local characteristics and opportunities whilst avoiding parochialism, a great deal more of structural in-filling is required, including the universal adoption of the principle of substituting for teachers participating in courses and workshops. This in-filling is essentially for the purposes of facilitating exchange of experience, and it can take effect through small project teams, and the mutual support that can be achieved through constructive work on common problems. Structures and resources are not enough, however, since teachers will need to learn to work in small groups on problem-solving exercises. From long hours spent in group workshops in several different national systems I am convinced that much more effort needs to go into the preparation of teachers for group interactions. The tradition in secondary teacher training of subject specialization, based on the assumption of single subject teaching in a teacher-controlled classroom, is no longer adequate for the kinds of tasks teachers are performing at the local level of curriculum development.

At the regional level, there is need for more experience and specialist support services for other types of curriculum development work. For example, in urban areas of 100,000 population, and rural areas of rather less, we should be thinking more of regional support structures. The expertise that can be made available through consultancy, the production of materials, the involvement of colleges of education and other institutions of higher education — these all fall within the ambit of regional support. Regional centres are places which should be within the comfortable reach of teachers on half-day release, for school vacation conferences, and for the long promised sabbatical term programmes of in-service education. It is only at the regional level, if at all, that it will be possible to provide comprehensive resource centres and to install the extremely costly mechanical and electronic equipment upon which the retrieval and analysis of information in education will increasingly depend in the future. Funding for regional level activities will be more demanding than regional resources alone can sustain and should become a national responsibility. One implication of this is that a considerable amount of national control and development activity can and should be transferred to regional centres whose long-term programme planning might be co-ordinated in a more federal way than is possible at present. Such changes would have implications for the Schools Council, in particular turning it from its present monolithic to a much looser structure.

The national level activities in curriculum development, according to my analysis, should be substantially diminished, so far as the creation of materials and the exercise of control are concerned. Policy formation, which is a decided weakness in British education, is a national function with clear political overtones, and it is essentially this which needs to be strengthened at the national level. The disbursement of funds in support of well-organized regional and local activities is increasingly being undertaken and could be greatly extended. Examinations, in practice one of the greatest obstacles in secondary as they have been in the past for primary school innovation, are a national-type institution which in their present form should be dismantled. They are a major impediment to serious educational advance specially in the individualization of learning, and they continue to deaden the processes of teaching and learning.

As Britain moves fumblingly and haltingly towards a more defensible system of higher education the cumbersome machinery of examination boards will become even less justifiable than it is now. Universities and primary schools alike enjoy a measure of autonomy in curriculum development which secondary schools feel is denied them because of examination pressures. The establishment of a certificate of secondary education, awarded by schools which, like universities, might be chartered or recognized for the purpose, and subject to the moderation exercise of mode III in the present certificate of secondary education, would be a national level function which should not be confused with the established devices of a national level construction of syllabuses and marking of scripts. Whereas there is evidence of a growing interest in the local and regional initiatives to which I have referred, the laborious efforts in recent years to produce a structure of secondary examining suited to all parties have as yet yielded a relatively impoverished return. The school is still not recognized as the educational unit whose responsibilities include designing and implementing its own procedures for pupil assessment.

For each level of activity which I have adumbrated, different forms of teacher education and training would be appropriate. Through the emerging system of universal in-service education for teachers it will eventually become possible to equip the average professional teacher as a school-based developer in the manner I have outlined. He will need to possess certain skills, to have his own ideas and be receptive to the thinking and initiative of agencies and institutions at the regional and national levels. The co-ordination of on-the-job, off-the-job, shorter and more sustained training programmes which are needed at the local and the regional levels is a task that cannot be adequately managed at the local level, although the provision of content of courses should reflect local needs. A very close connection could readily be established between curriculum development at the school level and in-service training.

Regional centres, including colleges, polytechnics and universities, have a part to play in supporting local initiatives and many of them have had a profound influence on curriculum change through the frequently unacknowledged efforts of individual departments and members of staff. However, both for the individual teacher and for the institution in question other roles are important, too. At the in-service as well as the pre-service stage it is important not to overlook the right of the individual to undertake self-chosen studies and to qualify himself in ways that do not necessarily coincide with the needs of the schools. Traditionally, academic qualifications have been extremely individualistic in the sense that the actual or prospective employers of the teacher have not played a large part in determining the content or the availability of these courses. By contrast, on-the-job training, the provision of short courses, and other forms of local in-service work are very much orientated towards system needs as distinct from those of the individual teacher.

In addition to providing courses and qualification for classroom teachers, regional centres can make an effective contribution through advice and consultancy, and they can provide a venue for the courses and conferences increasingly needed by other members of the education services if they are to continue to play a significant part in supporting local efforts by teachers. For example, the specialist training, mainly through in-service courses, of members of the inspectorate, advisory services, school management committees, school principals and other members of the central and supervisory systems are badly needed. It is a gratuitous assumption that only the teachers will benefit from the opportunity for in-service education. The concept of life-long or recurrent education has its most immediate applications in courses, conferences and workshops for responsible professionals, at all levels, preferably working in groups where they do not encounter only their own kind.

I have not, in this paper, attempted to examine in detail the manner in which the structures I have outlined might be articulated. Nor have I discussed the content of teacher education courses, either pre-service or in-service, that might be thought to make an effective contribution in preparing teachers as curriculum developers. Articulation is something to which a great deal of attention must be given, and it is a task for national level consideration. Curriculum development, to be effective, must become much more an activity to be performed by teachers, but the structures needed to sustain and ramify throughout the educational system are not a matter about which classroom teachers should be expected to speak with authority.

The content of courses in curriculum theory and development is likewise not merely a local matter even though one obvious need at present is for more problem – and practice – centred work which relates directly to the issues which are uppermost in the minds of classroom teachers, while not becoming submerged in the purely practical and possibly ephemeral needs of the moment. There is a danger, in a problem-orientated teaching strategy in teacher education, that distinctions will be blurred between what local practitioners recognize as a problem in their experience and one of the fundamental purposes of education which is to disclose entirely new possibilities and to demonstrate the inadequacies of currently popular categories and frames of reference. In curriculum theory, problems and issues of profound cultural significance may not be always readily translatable into practical issues for the classroom. Teachers at the pre-service as well as at the in-service stage would be deprived of one of the staples of their own education if the problem-centred mode were to drive out all others. Perhaps the separate modes should be clearly indicated: for example

a mode of problem – and practice – centred inquiry designed to illuminate issues and map out problem-solving procedures;

a mode of disciplined knowledge, based on interpretations and applications of established bodies of knowledge which have a discernible relationship to curriculum decisions;

a mode of category reappraisal and frame-of-reference analysis in which different disciplines and forms of experience are utilized in the analysis of policy questions and intellectual puzzles which lie behind issues of practice.

For each of these modes different courses and course combinations are appropriate. From the foregoing, it will be apparent that I would give high priority to programmes which aim to develop in teachers greater initiative and capacity for co-operative action in local curriculum development.

The field of curriculum studies in Britain, greatly enriched and stimulated by the practical activity of 10 years of sustained development, has not yet been articulated into a set of discrete branches of study. This may be no bad thing, but what would be unfortunate is settling for a narrow range of practical studies to support school-based development in the mistaken view that it is a purely local affair of no theoretical significance. The tasks of teacher education for curriculum development, as I have tried to show, require a comprehensive provision of workshops, conferences and courses at the local, regional and national levels. This provision will need to include interpretations and applications across a wide field of human knowledge, together with the opportunity for teachers to learn more about themselves and their relationship with others in intensive group work situations.

CHAPTER 7

The Professional Teacher

ALTHOUGH the in-service education programmes and the other activities at teachers' centres are developments of high promise, their complete fulfilment may yet depend upon the progress the teachers themselves make, and have said they want to make, towards an enhanced professional status. An elaboration of this point is the purpose of this chapter. We shall be considering something of what this progress would imply, and towards the end we shall offer a tentative proposal as to the form it could take. For the moment, we baldly assert that if the teachers are to gain this enhancement, they must first come to grips with what "profession" is usually taken to mean. Furthermore, until there is more of the right kind of empirical evidence available as a basis for future programmes and policies, the progress of teachers in this direction is very likely to remain pedestrian. In saying this, we neither overlook the existing empirical studies which bear usefully upon the problem, nor ignore the descriptive and analytical ones which also make their essential contribution. We *do* however, claim that a core factor has not yet attracted the careful attention it merits, namely the nature of the conceptions that teachers have (or indeed may not have) about "professional" and "professional status".

The legitimacy of "profession" as a sociological category, and its moral status as a social one, are matters of profound challenge to both sociologist and social philosopher, and will therefore not engage us. We merely say that professions plainly exist in our society. Whether teaching should become a major profession, or remain that quasi one it undoubtedly is at the moment, or whether as an alternative it could conceivably become a major profession and yet differ in significant respects from the existing ones, are matters which the teachers themselves must decide. But if such crucial decisions are to be at all clear-eyed and rational, they can be made only *after* the teachers have gained considerable insight into the meaning and implication of "profession", not before. If they then take action to accomplish their designs, its quality and effectiveness will again depend upon this insight as a critical factor.

115

The inherent complexities of the problem are distressingly obvious; for example, the sheer size of the teaching force, its consequent wide spectrum of ability and commitment, the difficulties of determining what constitutes teacher-competence, the conflicting interests of teachers in the different sectors of the total system. The list seems endless, and the difficulties infinite. But daunting as the problem is, the spur to resolve it should be not only the injustice the teachers presently and patently suffer, but the sharper one of the adverse social forces this releases. The need can no longer be one for palliatives, but for a resolution as enduring as we can devise. Although his context is Australian, Webb's observations on this point surely constitute a principle, within which the particular case should be easy to locate:

> Teachers' dissatisfaction with status is a social reality of some importance. It means that in a greater or less degree teachers are at odds with the community, and that is something which is bound to affect adversely their work, the social groups with which they are most in contact and probably also recruitment. It is therefore important to get into the minds of teachers and discover the sources of their status grievances.[1] .

His remark about recruitment is clearly one of momentous significance. We merely add in general that a "getting down into the minds" is a little too ambitious. An equally effective mode would be to examine, at the everyday conscious level, the extent to which the teachers themselves may be compounding their own problem, and doing so because they are as yet unclear about what their status claims imply. And to be thoroughly (though we hope not unreasonably) optimistic, such an inquiry may well reveal an underlying unitary and conceivably causal factor.

The literature

This is so vast and variegated as almost to defy attempts to bring it into some kind of reasonable order, and clearly a short chapter is hardly the appropriate place in which to attempt even a minimally adequate survey. But as possible useful preliminary, and in order to glance at some of its more obvious deficiencies, we make three very rough and ready distinctions. There is, firstly, the literature of the teachers themselves, and that of their organizations. This in itself is sufficiently sprawling and amorphous as to make any kind of succinct appraisal extremely difficult, though Inglis seems to have his finger on its pulse: "Twentieth century literature on teaching as a profession is mainly a literature of frustration and vague aspiration."[2] We see it also as one of strange and motley array, where rhetoric and assumption jostle uneasily with assertion and anxiety. Secondly, there is the smaller literature of the descriptive study, exemplified by the 1953 Yearbook[3] and also by the accounts of the 1966 UNESCO conference.[4] Here there seems to be considerably more economy, and some interesting attempts at diagnosis; but equally noteworthy are its moments of quite unwarranted euphoria. For example, in his comments on this conference, Thomas writes: "If public opinion realises the paramount importance of the teaching profession for the future of education, of the rising generation and of society as a whole, a just solution is certain to be found, either now or in the future, to the problem of the status of teachers."[5] While such a statement might well serve as a stirring conference crescendo, and while it also reveals an impressive or even touching faith, distinctly less acceptable is its readiness to dub teaching a "profession" when it is the very elusiveness of that status which constitutes the vexed core of the problem. There is also its unhappy implication that time is of little account; that the "just" solution will somewhere, somehow and at some time be stumbled upon. Thirdly, there are the lithe and questing academic studies, to be found for example in the writings of Wilson[6] and Hoyle.[7] These have been relatively few, though always analytical, frequently elegant, and occasionally written with considerable insight. Regrettably, and despite the illumination they could undoubtedly bring to the hard practicalities of the problem, they seem only rarely to have slipped their peaceful moorings in the quiet and respectable academic journals, where they find their rightful though somewhat comfortably insulated place.

Though it would be quite wrong to see this literature in total as having had little effect on raising teachers' status, its achievement in this regard has fallen far behind its volume. The need now is not for yet more literature of the existing kind, but for a different form of investigation. In the teachers' literature, demands have been more evident than viable and constructive proposals, and its tenor has understandably (though perhaps not very usefully) become one of grievance and frustration. But in having exhausted its point, there is now surely little new left for it to say. The descriptive literature has been thorough and wide-ranging, but its recommendations have seemed too often to be prescriptions, though ones made prematurely and without the benefit of prior and careful diagnosis on which prescriptions ought always to be based. In the case of the academic study, diagnosis has rested more securely upon careful analysis (usually sociological), but with a shortfall of empirical evidence about what teachers themselves think about its proposals, whether these be stated or implied. A rare exception is the recent inquiry by Grace,[8] who with a very small and restricted sample of English secondary school teachers examined the role conflicts with special reference to the Wilson study mentioned earlier. The role studies as such have been prolific, but of rather uneven quality. Few, however, seem to have given careful attention to a theoretical though highly relevant point.

If Linton's concept[9] of a role-status nexus has validity ("Role and status are quite inseparable, and the distinction between them is of only academic interest. There are no roles without statuses or statuses without roles"), then an alteration in the role must to some extent or other affect the associated status, and vice versa. To labour the point, if the teacher (assuming his competence) is ever to give even adequate implementation to some of the roles suggested in these studies, he must first have the appropriate status. If a man is expected to direct, he cannot do so without being recognized as director. Inversely, the burden of what sociologists so aptly call "role inflation" already finds teachers with too few of the relevant skills. The Jack of all trades derives little status from any.

Despite the distinctive and necessary contribution made by each of these categories, they seem nevertheless to have a collective deficiency, partly because they make too few suggestions about *how* changes might be wrought, and partly because they do not *fully* account for the present unhappy situation. We have urged that this arises substantially because empirical evidence about many of the factors involved is insufficient or even non-existent. In having become self-evident, the global contention that teachers need "a better deal" has now outlived its usefulness. Nor can suggestions (already abundant) about this betterment retain their purchase if they neglect to examine *how* this can be achieved. An integral part of this would be to unearth those factors which are likely to *impede* the particular betterment being proposed.

"Teachers should have better professional status" is a particularly good example of the global and invincible proposition we mention. However, inquiry into what teachers in general understand by "profession", and furthermore the extent to which variables such as sex, qualifications and experience bear on this understanding, may well produce some highly differentiated results, and enable us to discern what the impediments are and where they mainly lie. While we cannot anticipate the findings, we can at the outset say that if their concepts turn out to be vague, teachers can neither appreciate the nature of the obstacles which confront them, nor as a consequence be clear about how these might be surmounted. This would be critical, for in modern industrial society (as the kind which concerns us here) it is clear that professional status is to be attained only as a result of intelligently directed self-conscious effort.([10,11]) If conceptual deficiences do in fact exist, if, for example, teachers fail to recognize that the attainment of professional status implies professional obligations of a quite specific kind, then their self-consciousness would seem to relate more to the evident injustice of their present plight than to what steps *they themselves* might take to improve it. In other words, "We want status" can at best indicate a rationally based programme of clear and informed intent, or at worst reveal an attitude which is merely querulous.

Some existing impediments

We differ from some writers in that of the five impediments we discuss, we regard two — the inappropriate use of the word "profession" and the nature of the existing career structure — as being more serious than the remaining three — size, the preponderance of women teachers, and the bureaucratic setting. There is certainly a sixth, concerning formal qualifications and length of training. This is also serious, but one about which we prefer our views to emerge by implication, rather than explicitly through the inevitable tedium of a detailed and comparative discussion invoking the major professions.

1. The inappropriate use of "profession"

When the reference is to teachers in particular, an indiscriminate or even inadvertent use of the word "profession" creates much more of an impediment to their professional advancement than would first appear. This has been well put by Lieberman, and although the context this time is American, his remarks have no less a generality than Webb's:

> The vast bulk of the writing on professional education assumes that education is already a profession. The assumption is seldom questioned or seriously criticized. It is sometimes necessary to "upgrade the profession", but rarely is education referred to as anything but a profession. Partially as a result of this attitude, the problems of professionalizing education are typically accorded superficial treatment or are ignored altogether in the writing on education as an occupation.([12])

We should note that he wrote this nearly 20 years ago, and deplore that his admonition has not since been heeded. We should also note that he uses "education" to mean "teaching". His "professionalizing" has a much more intense and calculating connotation than we would accept — a difference which we hope will become clear as we proceed.

Lieberman's impediment is perhaps the overarching one, but there are related ones also of no slight account. Possibly the most subtle and insidious has its roots in the deference which "profession" continues to command. "What is your profession?" still survives as a more tactful and indeed more flattering formula than "What is your job?" or even "What is your occupation?" No doubt many teachers feel that they have had to endure this kind of patronage for far too long. But more to our immediate point is the likelihood that the reiterative ascription (perhaps made in particular by teachers' own organizations) causes many teachers to assume uncritically that their occupation does in fact have major professional status. Some Australian evidence on this point — and one suspects it might well obtain elsewhere — shows that the less discerning teachers claim that teaching is a profession already, but lacks sufficient public recognition of the "fact": others more cautious concede that teaching is not yet a profession, but is making progress towards that end.([13]) However, their grounds for this latter claim are far indeed from being substantial, in that the teachers are neither clear about the nature of the progress, nor about its rate. Perhaps this was the kind of situation Inglis had in mind when he spoke of the literature as being one of frustration and vague aspiration.

But the luckless teachers are also losers on another count. Although the general public defers in unruffled times to teachers as being a body of professional people, the same public is quick to censure them for acting in an unbecoming manner whenever they take militant or even reasonable and vigorous action to improve their professional lot: "Professional people do not behave in such unseemly ways." And among the teachers themselves appear to be those who, because of their delusion about "profession", echo precisely the same sentiments, and in their imagined superiority stand aloof. Lieberman's admonition indeed merits the most careful attention and consideration. Not only does it apply to the writing he mentions, it also bears on the associated problems we have sketched. A more neutral term like "teaching force" would seem to deprive the teachers only of the difficulties which "teaching profession" so clearly generates.

"Profession" itself is no doubt as vulnerable as any other sociological category to the forces which continually make for societal change. In this sense we may see all categories as being more or less impermanent. But whatever modification to "profession" may ensue, it seems most unlikely to lose its identity entirely,[14] and even less likely that we can ever come to ascribe the term arbitrarily and without regard to the characteristics of whatever occupation is in question. These characteristics are in themselves a basis for a classification of occupations, and these in turn one for a rational and appropriate division of labour. For the time being at least (and most probably for a very long time to come), if an occupation is to fulfil its claim to be a profession, and to be seen as able to do so not only by its members but more importantly by those outside, it needs to have a number of distinctive attributes, of which some at least must be open to an empirical verification of one kind or other. It appears that criticism of "profession" as a category rest in substantial part upon an implication that one kind of occupation is more socially valuable than another — for example, that neurology is more worthy than plumbing. Comparisons on this kind of basis are clearly repugnant, but it is surely possible and useful to distinguish one occupation from another on less emotive and more instrumental grounds. It is also certainly the case that "profession" has attracted much empty rhetoric, which regrettably and reprehensibly the major professional bodies themselves have taken at best only feeble steps to refute, still less to rectify. But whatever the arguments for or against the continuance of "profession" as a category, the fact remains that it is the one within which the teachers are seeking a secure place. There are few if any signs that they wish to belong to one so radically different as not to be recognizable as a major profession at all.

2. The present career structure

If there must as yet be some uncertainty about the extent to which teachers' notions of "profession" may constitute an impediment, there need be little about the existence of a major impediment within the career structure itself. We claim this not only because we see the pivot of the entire educational enterprise as being the interaction in the classroom between teacher and pupil, but also because this interaction needs a more direct and obvious support, and indeed a better recognition, than it receives now. The administration of the education system, the research and other innovative activities connected with it, and indeed any other non-classroom activity one cares to envisage, need obviously to be excellent in themselves. But they also need to bear directly and with expedition upon the classroom practitioner, who as the instigator of this interaction becomes the key figure upon whom the ultimate quality of the entire educational provision depends. In other words, he is the person not merely to be talked *at* or *about* but essentially talked *to* and *with*. Administrators and researchers would no doubt accept this simple and rather obvious point, and already make commendable efforts to forge this kind of communication. Their efforts might, however, be more effective, and of more immediate benefit to practitioners, if the target had a sharper focus than the general body of teachers "out there" in the field. The development of this point we leave until later. Here we simply say that within the teaching force in general, there needs to emerge as part of the career structure a group of practitioners forming the focus we mention, and whose role would be a vital one. This is the first of two aspects of that career structure we wish to emphasize.

The second concerns its present incapacity. If the classroom practitioner has the importance we claim, then there is clearly something seriously at fault with a system which in effect encourages able and committed practitioners to seek advancement in places other than the classroom. Under existing arrangements, if such practitioners wish to fulfil what amounts to no more than a reasonable ambition to further their careers, they must try to relinquish their classrooms (where they would really wish to be, and where their skills and talents would be the most appropriately employed) to become headmasters, lecturers, inspectors, or whatever. Moreover, in doing so they not only become better paid (and contrary to some popular belief, practitioners in the major professions are by no means careless about their financial standing) but are also seen as having enhanced their status. Movement of this kind occurs within a society, of which of course teachers are a part, which is achievement oriented, and Hoyle interestingly relates this to the stratification pattern within society itself. But in particular relation to this incompatability between career-line and role-commitment, Wilson is graphic indeed: "There is an inducement" (for the teachers) "in this situation to make right impressions on significant people rather than significant impressions on the right people — the children."([15])

Hoyle also indicates that the more "cosmopolitan" a teacher becomes (a term borrowed from Gouldner([16]) which, very roughly speaking, implies a heightened alertness to and taste for theory and principles), the more likely he is to develop career aspirations whose fulfilment can under present arrangements only encourage him to forsake the classroom. This raises a number of highly important issues, one in particular of which has seemingly saddled the teachers for years, and about which there still seems to be a great deal of misunderstanding and confusion. Although a teacher should, and a good teacher does, have considerable personal regard or even affection for most children, this should not be regarded as his major, even less his sole, attribute. If it *is* so regarded, we have what we might call the tea and sympathy syndrome,[17] in which the feelings of both teacher and pupil are indulged, but the educational needs of the pupils rank only second, or even lower.

The teacher best serves his pupils through his knowledge of and skilful use of psychological, sociological and other factors which bear upon their learning processes, their social and intellectual development and so on. In short, his usefulness to them is directly proportional to his awareness of their educational needs and his knowledge of how these might best be served. There is of course some gradation in this, in that younger children no doubt need a more overt affective support than older ones, but in principle at least, the kind of usefulness we speak of extends over the whole age and academic ability range.

Of the knowledge itself, we claim that it needs to be further and deeper than it is ever possible to provide in a pre-service course, however good. Further study is essential, and it is in the pursuit of this that the teachers concerned are likely to pick up a cosmopolitan orientation, which as Hoyle says, needs a wider context than the classroom can fulfil. But this happens precisely because there is little in the present career structure which offers a sufficiently tangible reward to the teachers who develop this kind of orientation. In becoming cosmopolitan, he is likely to find more scope for these interests and more status (and it should also be mentioned, better conditions and pay) outside the classroom.

Furthermore, it is still likely that among the teachers themselves, there are those who, with the public generally, regard the pastoral role as being of first importance. We are certainly not suggesting that the teacher-pupil relationship should become affectionless and one of clinical detachment, but we do maintain that teacher-competence is in its substantial part a matter of striking a balance between pastoral care and pedagogical need. There is a parallel here, which we can deal with only very briefly, between the teachers as would-be professional persons and the members of the well-recognized professions. Patients and clients would fare ill if in the former case diagnosis and treatment rested only on sympathy and compassion, and in the latter if the legal case were similarly based. Both doctor and lawyer would be in gross dereliction of professional duty if instead of sound medical or legal advice and management, they were to offer only kindness and personal concern.

Children and pupils do, of course, differ in many significant respects from patients and clients, but we believe that the principle still holds. In particular, as far as career structure is concerned, it is important to note that in order to rise to the top of his profession, neither doctor nor lawyer (or indeed any other professional person) need relinquish his professional practice and become a non-practitioner. Yet within the educational complex, recognition and status seem to increase exponentially with one's distance from the classroom.

3. The size of the teaching force

For the more prestigious professions, control of entry has long been a factor of central importance. Restriction on recruitment results in a relatively small number of well-qualified practitioners, ensuring on the one hand no erosion of the high professional status already gained (maybe hard-won), but on the other assuring the public of a service of generally high quality. This matter is clearly a much more contentious one than our terse statement reveals, but it is nevertheless a principle within which the teachers as aspirants to a better professional status may well have to manoeuvre, and one which they must at least take into account. A small number of practitioners seems, then, an essential to the attainment and retention of high professional status. But state provision for compulsory education brings teaching forces which are not only large, but enormous — of the order, for example, of 400,000 in the United Kingdom and 100,000 in Australia — and inevitably such forces must encompass a vast range of ability, motivation and commitment. Yet ironically, in their continuing press for small classes (hence more teachers) the teachers are both seeking to enlarge these already enormous forces, and thereby possibly even extending the range we mention. Notions such as "quality", "expert" and "efficiency" thus become highly relevant, the more so as they are the very attributes usually ascribed to and claimed by the professions with which the teachers are seeking to be favourably compared.

As a round assertion, we say that the pre-service courses at colleges and departments are able even at best to give students no more than a general orientation, an exposure to some of the more important educational issues, and a modicum of practical classroom experience within a sheltered and supervised setting. But this is a matter about which the teachers themselves seem to be in some confusion. The minimally qualified teachers should be seen as a device on the part of the State to provide its compulsorily educated children with "safe practitioners", and as such is one to serve the children's interests. It is *not* a device to protect the interests of the teachers, though it would often seem that in their rightful insistence that the unqualified be excluded, this is exactly what many teachers see it as being.

The "safe practitioner" should be regarded as a kind of base-line above which the thoroughly desirable "quality" we have spoken of begins to emerge. A much-boasted 20 years' experience can at worst be little more than nine repetitions of the first two, without further study, without attendance at courses or centres, or without attempts to up-date or reappraise existing knowledge or concepts. At best, it can approach the quality we have in mind, and become something finely textured, where the salt of experience is the vitalizing agent brought to the activities we have just mentioned.

Rising above the base-line should be a voluntary matter, and no doubt for good reasons there will be many teachers who will not wish to be other than the "safe practitioner". But if sheer size is not to remain the massive impediment it is in principle, some differentiation among teachers must somehow emerge. Ideally, this would be a matter for the teachers themselves to organize and supervize, and we offer some suggestions in the final section. At this point we conclude that although size may be gargantuan and tyrannous, it need not be seen as invincible.

4. The preponderance of women teachers

As with total size, the preponderance of women teachers would at first sight appear to be an almost insurmountable obstacle. Supporting "evidence" for this appears to be plentiful. The major professions have but a small minority of women practitioners, whereas in teaching recent figures show that in the United States of America 72 per cent of teachers are women, in Australia 64 per cent and in Britain 58 per cent. (Are, then, British teachers of higher professional status than their American and Australian counterparts?) There are writers[18] who claim that women are more submissive to bureaucratic control than men, and that teaching can at best become only a semi-profession such as nursing, librarianship or social work where women again predominate to the professional disadvantage of these occupations. Other writers[19] point out that entry to teaching is relatively easy, that hours and conditions are uniquely suited to married women with family commitments, that re-entry to the force after raising a family presents little if any difficulty, and finally that because women teachers already have a higher professional status than most other women, their motivation to increase it is minimal. And, incredibly, "the job can be made either an excellent training for marriage, or a means of satisfying the maternal feelings of those who are less fortunate".[20]

It would be idle to deny that teaching does in fact offer many women advantages of a kind virtually absent from other occupations. But it would be equally idle to parade this as "evidence" that women teachers are, as far as an enhanced status is concerned, necessarily a gross and permanent liability. Historical antecedents, and the position of women in society generally, make the preponderance a much more complicated matter than total size, but a similar principle would seen nevertheless to apply. As long as women are referred to and seen as an undifferentiated whole, the "evidence" we have cited could possibly just totter to its feet. But the counter-evidence seems much more robust.

Studies in Australia,[21] Canada[22] and the United States[23] clearly show the foolishness of trying to argue that as far as professional tasks in general are concerned, women are less capable than men. Nerrer home, we might note that it was the drive and discernment of Elizabetn Adams, as a general inspector, that brought into being a vigorous and effective Surrey Schools Council, with its notable pioneering work in the area of teachers' professional development, and hence their progress towards a better status.

As we said in relation to the size of the teaching force, if a teacher (man or woman) wishes to become something more than a safe practitioner, if he or she wishes to extend and deepen his or her professional knowledge, if he or she wishes to play an innovative and developmental role within the teaching force as a whole, and is seen as doing so efficiently by male and female peers, it is difficult to see, either on logical or empirical grounds, how sex can be a significant variable. The significance is surely in the degree of commitment to career of the person (male or female) concerned.

Some recent British evidence[24] on this point is interesting. In effect, it shows that although married women with or without children found more satisfaction in family than in career, there was a distinct tendency for this to apply also to the men. Of the married men without children, 42 per cent found greater satisfaction with family, but an equal 42 per cent found it in career. But of the married men with children, 50 per cent found greater satisfaction with family, and only 29 per cent with career. Of the single men, 53 per cent found greater satisfaction with career, compared with 42 per cent of the single women — hardly an enormous difference.

These figures were for graduates, but in view of what we have said about further qualifications, and in view also of what we shall say in our concluding section, evidence such as this can hardly be said to support any assumption that because women teachers preponderate, those who wished to rise above the base-line would vastly outnumber the men, and on that account arrest the progress of the teaching force as a whole. And referring once more to the major professions, their status has been achieved through the positive development of the attributes we shall discuss under "profession as a concept", and *not* negatively because of the relative absence of women from their ranks.

5. The bureaucratic setting

As employees of their local education authorities, teachers may be said to work within a bureaucratic setting, and in some respects (though not all) resemble the professional practitioners, for example lawyers and chartered accountants, employed by large public or private organizations or corporations. With the professional autonomy of the practitioner as a cornerstone of professional life, the relatively new phenomenon of the salaried professional has not surprisingly attracted the attention of the sociologists. Some[25] see it as an inevitable source of strain, not so much between practitioner and organization, but essentially because profession and bureaucracy are two irreconcilable systems. Others obviate the difficulty theoretically by posting an "ascriptive professional",[26] for example the army doctor or municipal treasurer, where the practitioner derives his basic status from his qualifying association, but whose current status and duties are determined to a very considerable extent by his employing organization.

It is perhaps easy to see where the strain might originate, making the relationship between practitioner and administrator potentially abrasive. The very nature of professional work causes practitioners to regard administrative "tidiness" as quite ancillary to the actual execution of the professional task: a supremely well-administered hospital, for example, would be nevertheless deficient if its medical and surgical services were only mediocre. But it would be churlish and insensitive not to concede that sound administration is supportive of good professional practice. Moreover, the technical and administrative facilities provided by a large organization are almost certain to have been a factor in the practitioner's decision voluntarily to join that organization in the first place.

There is much which we could say about this situation in general, for example that because an organization employs the professional as the expert who will best accomplish its particular tasks, it would be counter-productive if its administrative procedures so restrained him as to cause a deterioration in his services. More specifically, there are studies[27, 28] to show that organizations and bureaucracies have become increasingly sensitive to the forces involved, and are now considerably more enlightened than they once were. But the point which concerns us in particular has been made by Goode,[29] for whom the crucial matter is not the simple one of whether or not professional practitioners work within a bureaucracy, but whether or not they control its essential work.

The relevance of this to teaching is clear, and relates to the career structure we have already discussed and to the opinion we hold that it is the classroom practitioner who is the lynch-pin of the entire educational enterprise. In this context, Goole's "essential work" is the teaching itself, and in many respects, especially in Britain, teachers already have a very large measure of control over what happens in their classrooms. But this is normally an individual affair, and not the collective one of the teachers as a body controlling the educational practice within a given geographical area, say, of city, county or state.

Furthermore, if a teacher does move into an administrative post as such, for example at a county hall or even into the headship of a large school (where administrative work is likely to claim most of his time), this is seen not as the translation we would claim it ought to be seen as being, but promotion. However, there is a highly important factor which bears closely upon this, and one which has its parallel in the qualifying association to which the salaried professional owes a substantial part of his allegiance. If the teachers are to win control, they must have (and be seen to have) as close a relationship with the academic educationists, as the "qualifiers", as the salaried professionals have with their qualifying associations. This again invokes the notion of "quality" which we referred to earlier in our discussion of size, and which we shall raise again in our concluding section.

State-employed teachers may be compared with the British doctors who work within the National Health Service. The doctors' early and vociferous misgivings about the erosion of their professional autonomy[30] has considerably lessened with their realization that their continuing clinical freedom constitutes a powerful control over the essentials of the service. It must, of course, be conceded that prior to the advent of the service, medicine was a well-established profession already, and therefore astutely aware of the issues. But as far as this general principle concerns the teachers, the winning of what we might call pedagogical control would make the context, bureaucratic or otherwise, irrelevant.

"Profession" as a concept

Teachers' perusal of definitions is likely to be of severely limited usefulness. Attempts to define "profession" are legion, ranging from the merely fatuous[31] to the positively fearsome,[32] and all extremely vulnerable to personal interpretation. In applying to almost any occupation, the fatuous offer no differentia, while in their implication that professional practitioners should be saints or heroes, the fearsome are grossly misleading. In providing but a general orientation, even the better of the definitions – for instance that of Cogan[33] – fall far short of fostering the insight which only a careful *analysis* of the concept can bring.

A perspective is important. Much of the earlier writing on the professions was certainly fulsome, and did a very great deal to conceal their true nature. The professions were said to be the wholesome and necessary counter to the rampant materialistic excesses of a rapidly developing capitalist society, though this view did not go entirely unchallenged. Laski's impassioned indictment[34] was of the professions' degenerate aspects, while Parsons[35] saw the motives of professional practitioners as being little different from those of the ambitious entrepreneur. Adverse criticism continues today, though in a somewhat different form[36, 37] but this in turn is challenged by some well-informed and discerning defenders from outside the professions' actual ranks.[38, 39]

The reticence of Carr-Saunders and Wilson,[40] whose early study is still widely regarded as authoritative, is noteworthy – "Indeed, the drawing of a boundary line would be an arbitrary procedure, and we shall not offer, either now or later, a definition of professionalism". At least two distinguished contemporary writers would substantially agree.[41, 42] But on their next page Carr-Saunders and Wilson remark, with much significance, "Nevertheless, when we have completed our survey, it will emerge that the typical profession exhibits a complex of characteristics, and that other vocations approach this condition more or less closely, owning to the possibility of some of these characteristics fully or partially developed".

This implies, commendably, that many occupations have attributes highly similar to those had by the well-recognized professions, and for that reason can be regarded as being on the same occupational continuum. Thus far, we seem to escape the league table within which odious comparisons between occupations have for so long been made. However, there is also an implication that along this continuum exists a segment within which the established professions like law and medicine find their secure place. The moral and social issues here are profound and complicated, best left as we have said to the deliberations of the pundits concerned. On the lesser and pragmatic level, we merely try to say that it is not so much a question of whether an occupation is a "profession" or a "non-profession", but more one of the *extent* to which its existing professional attributes can be further developed. It is, moreover, a matter of the motivation its memebrs have to bring about this extension in an effective and fruitful way. On this basis we might, for example, accept that the differences between, say, midwives and obstetricians, or motor mechanics and chartered automobile engineers, are real and not apparent. The need for members of an aspirant occupation, such as teaching, to discern the nature of and extent to which certain attributes are possessed by the already recognized professions, and then to compare this with what currently obtains within their own work, becomes an imperative first step. A consensus of opinion about these attributes among sociologists and political scientists would be useful in this regard, and this we now briefly consider.

Separate surveys of the literature have been made by Millerson[10] and Kleingartner,[43] and although their terminologies are slightly different, the following attributes of "profession" emerge as the most significant:

> organization
> adherence to a code of ethics
> skill based on theoretical knowledge
> education and training
> competence tested
> altruistic service

To be regarded as a profession, an occupation must have at least these attributes, each developed to a considerable extent. A necessary refinement and extension is made by another writer (Hall) who sees "profession" as having structural and attitudinal components:[44]

Structural	Attitudinal
the professional association	the professional association
the establishment of a training school	as the practitioner's major referent
a code of ethics	belief in public service
professional autonomy	a sense of calling and vocation
	autonomy through self-regulation

The highly important factor of autonomy (which should concern the aspirant teachers to a marked degree) is structural in the sense that it is the formally constituted professional association which excludes the unqualified, and attitudinal in that practitioners accept that only their practising colleagues are capable of assessing their competence. Again in relation to teachers, it is interesting to note (as a sign of an increasing professional awareness, or merely from a sense of injustice?) that many Australian teachers now implacably refuse to be "inspected", while in many parts of England, the local inspector has quietly withdrawn to reappear as an adviser.

An exploration and elaboration of all these attributes would demand an entire and lengthy chapter. Our intention here is merely to mention some factors which the teachers need to consider carefully if they are to come to grips with what "profession" usually means; but by way of some explication we say a little about two — the professional association and the professional (miscalled ethical) codes. The major professional associations do from time to time, and in ways scarcely to their credit, indulge in the protective activities which mainly characterize trade unions. Less dramatically, and less publicly, their more usual and continuing function concerns matters such as the oversight of professional education and training, in-service courses, peer evaluation of professional competence, the policing of the professional code, to mention only some.

An important point is that these routine-like activities are of ultimate benefit to the laity as well as being of immediate benefit to the practitioners themselves. If teachers' associations are to compare, they too will have to assume similar responsibilities, including those concerning the needs of the children. Teachers should therefore be considering what role their associations currently play in the provision of in-service courses, the policing of ethical codes, the appraisal of teaching competence, and so on. It is possible that, given a close enough study of the roles of the associations of the major professions, teachers would come to appreciate that a professional association is very much more than a congregation of people with similar occupational interests, and that such a congregation does not become a professional association simply because the individuals concerned decide to give it that title.

Codes, in the general sense of the word, are shorthand devices understood only by the initiated. More particularly, professional codes seek to bring about an "understood" behaviour in and between practitioners which is protective both of their interests and also the interests of their clients. In this respect they far exceed a mere formal reiteration of the courtesies which ought anyway to exist between one practitioner and another. (It is curious that some teachers' codes find it necessary to remind teachers not to make adverse comments about each other in the hearing of parents or children!) With truth, though somewhat unkindly, one writer[45] has said of some Australian teachers' codes:— "the most that can be said about the ethical codes of teachers' unions is that they are on the records and have been peacefully there for years" — which hardly suggest their viability.

The function of professional codes has much to do with the altruism which we claim is mistakenly ascribed to professional persons. There are logical as well as empirical grounds for *not* making a diffuse ascription of altruism to a body of people in general. A gracious state of altruism may be unattainable, but it is by no means impossible to devise codes which practitioners can be expected to follow dutifully and conscientiously, and in so doing act *as if* they were behaving altruistically. This would depend upon the content and status of the codes, which would need to be effectively policed by the professional association concerned. On this principle, teachers ought to be as accountable to their professional associations as were the struck-off doctors, the disbarred lawyers, and the cashiered officer to theirs. The question of the number of occasions on which teachers' associations have actually recommended the dismissal or suspension of a teacher for incompetence or unprofessional behaviour is an intriguing one, the more so if we agree that children are much more defenceless in the face of professional malpractice than are adults.

We have been able to say nothing about the other important professional attributes, but we hope that even in this brief sketch we have managed to indicate the kind of study teachers need to make if they are to come to appreciate what "profession" means, and to understand some of the implications of their quest for better professional status. The empirical inquiries which we have claimed are needed, could include something about the provision currently made (or possibly not made) for teachers, either during their pre-service courses or later, to examine the concept of "profession" in this way. Indeed, it seems necessary to make this provision somewhere, and it would very probably benefit from being on a formal or organized basis. If it emerged that teachers had to pick up the concept as best they could, this could in itself be seen as an impediment.

Ideally perhaps, and largely because so much of the nuance of "profession" is caught from continuing contact with fellow experienced practitioners (assuming of course that these themselves are well informed), teachers' own associations might be the main agents, but at least something might with great advantage be done in a preparatory way within the pre-service institutions themselves.

The empirical inquiry

The main purpose of this would be to determine the *extent* to which teachers understood "profession", but it would be of obvious advantage also to see whether this was significantly affected by such variables as length of teaching experience, sex, type of formal qualification and level of responsibility, to mention only some. There would be many ways in which such an inquiry could be designed and implemented, and therefore our suggestions and comments here will be general, except for the specific point we now make. Theoretical questions or items would be distinctly less useful than ones which placed the teachers in the educational or teaching situation with which they are, of course, already thoroughly familiar. For example, their reactions to "The professional association is the practitioners' major referent" may well be a massive "don't know", whereas (assuming their membership of a teachers' organization) "The censure I would feel most keenly would be that of my professional association", or "Details of my qualifications and experience should be kept by my professional association" or "It is not the business of a professional association to propose educational reforms" would not only be more readily understood, but also accommodate a wider variety of response along a "strongly agree — strongly disagree" continuum. While the theoretical items might be appropriate for teachers with a good grip on the concept already, they could hardly envelope those whose grip was less sure, and would therefore not expose the extent of the understanding which we see as being basically important.

Considerable advantage would be gained from using Hall's schema, with its inclusion of the attitudinal factors, rather than the consensus of Millerson or Kleingartner, where the emphasis is mainly on the structural. On the attitudinal side the teachers may be already well equipped, and therefore have a more extensive understanding of the concept than might first appear. If so, then we shall at least have gained some firm evidence to replace the existing assumption, albeit a reasonably safe one, that many teachers have a notable degree of commitment, perhaps dedication. Attempts to sensitize teachers to "profession" on the basis of attitude only (and these do seem to have been over-abundant) would be largely unnecessary; a concentration on the structural would then seem to be the more profitable.

It should be possible to write items and questions covering the structural and attitudinal aspects, and then to use them in combination to form a scale which measured a teacher's "professional score". The technical details of this need not detain us, except to say that the instrument thus fashioned would need to have a construct validity, and one probably established with the aid of a factor analysis.[46] If the variables we mentioned at the beginning of this section are to emerge as significant or otherwise, either singly or in some kind of interaction, the sample of teachers drawn would need to be stratified accordingly.

This would bring many advantages. It might, for instance, be the case that women graduates with several years' teaching experience gained a better score than, say, younger non-graduate men. The gross assumption at present seems to be that men are more professionally orientated than women, but that because of the women's preponderance, the men's efforts to gain better professional status are continually frustrated. More accurate evidence on this point (as indeed but one among many) is sorely needed. The scale we refer to may well be a means of showing that the men's orientation is in fact towards the protective activities which are more characteristic of a trade union than of a professional association. Again, the stratified sample may be necessary to show that an understanding of "profession" may not relate to length of teaching experience at all, in which case an assumption that older and more experienced teachers are able in this respect to advise and guide their younger colleagues becomes invalid. Or as another possibility, this variable may have no significant effect mainly because opportunities for a consideration of "profession" are too few for *all* teachers, regardless of their length of experience.

Apart from the professional score we envisage, the instrument could be designed to elicit other relevant information. For example, items such as "I have little opportunity to observe my colleagues actually teaching" or "I would object to regular observation of my teaching by my colleagues" may receive wide endorsement. If so, the peer evaluation of professional competence would be something about which teachers would have to think very carefully if their claims for professional autonomy were to be seen as something different from a mere disinclination to be appraised by anyone, colleagues or not. It would be interesting to see too whether high scores on the professional scale were to relate in any significant way to membership of a teachers' organization, and likewise to regular reading of a teachers' journal.

Perhaps also a rather more oblique approach could find a place. Teachers could, for instance, be asked to consider a list of factors likely to affect the *professional* efficiency of the teaching force as a whole, and then to rank these in order of importance. The rank given for example to "Quality of school buildings" *vis-à-vis* "Opportunities for in-service training" would surely be indicative, as would "Opportunity to meet parents" *vis-à-vis* "Consultation between teachers in different types of schools", as an example of a more finely poised choice.

The inquiry could take many forms, and what little we have managed to say here in no way amounts to a research programme. We have suggested but one possible frame of reference. But whatever the form, it should aim to reveal where deficiencies lie, and to say something about their extent. The necessity or otherwise for appropriate and remedial action could then be a consideration for the teachers themselves.

Conclusion

In attracting public attention, a generally improved education service could bring teachers some enhancement of their professional status. But one clearly discerned by the public as having been improved by the teachers themselves, would be likely to compel it.

A point we see as being of paramount importance for teachers concerns the high quality of the service the major professions, at their best, offer society. As we briefly indicated in our outline of the consensus, professional work is essentially guided by principles, these in turn deriving from theoretical knowledge and inquiry, and its articulation is with respect to the practical affairs of society. There is a strong element of apprenticeship in courses at professional schools, but equally there is no lack of emphasis on the learning of principles. Significantly, the recruits to the major professions are nowadays regarded as bona fide students, and not the apprentices they once were. Herein lies the source of the quality we mention, and if teaching is to offer a comparable service, the interplay of theory and practice must likewise become a matter of fundamental importance. But as far as the study of education is concerned, this interplay is at the centre of some sharp debate, though it is with respect to this very fact that we try to justify our point.

The arguments on both sides are subtle and sophisticated, with O'Connor and Hirst[47] as perhaps the principal proponents. We offer no rehearsal of them here, but instead relate them to a hypothetical situation concerning two teachers. The first teacher is keenly aware of the nature of theoretical issues in education, but the second regards educational theory as at best of doubtful value, and hence chooses to ignore it.

The first teacher is critical of educational theory, and therefore vigilant as to its use, *precisely because* he has read his Hirst and his O'Connor. He neither sees theory as a lot of high falutin' irrelevance, nor deludes himself that it can necessarily inform and enlighten *all* his classroom procedures. In fact he regards theory with some suspicion. But the reaction of the second teacher to theory is not merely one of suspicion, it is openly hostile. In probably not having understood the nature of theory in the first place, and in having been "let down" by it so often in the second place, he repudiates it and proceeds intuitively by the seat of his proverbial pants. The point is that both teachers may be said to have arrived at very roughly the same destination, though by different routes and for very different reasons. However, the significant distinction lies in the discernment and flexibility of the first teacher, as compared with the dogmatism, rigidity and ignorance of the second. And we find it most difficult to see how the quality we have repeatedly mentioned can in any way arise from or be based upon these latter three attributes.

In developing this point a little further, we refer especially to the part of educational theory which is so often though mistakenly seen to be the most remote and effete, namely the philosophy of education. Seemingly by sharp contrast, curriculum development and design appears to be highly relevant to the actual practice of teaching, which of course it is. But in meeting questions about what should be included in a school curriculum, further questions concerning usefulness and value are never very far away; nor is the fact that the various emphases teachers bring to the different parts of their work reflect the values these teachers hold themselves.

If these latter factors are explored, as they surely ought to be, they lead directly to considerations, for example of "good" and "valuable", which have engaged moral philosophers for so long. Indeed, so many of the arguments which go on in staffrooms everywhere about "freedom", "individuality", "authority", "discipline", "punishment" and so on are philosophical at root, but rarely seem to get beyond assertion and counter-assertion simply because the protagonists there are hardly aware of the philosophical issues involved. More specifically, notions such as "learning by discovery",[48] "the open classroom", and "creativity" are so often claimed as panaceas mainly because their most fervent advocates are unacquainted with the conceptual analysis which could bring the notions into a more critical focus, and thus ensure their more judicious and appropriate use — to the benefit of the pupils. Unless teachers themselves are clear about such matters, and are always able to explain and justify their own procedures in the classroom to intelligent and inquiring parents, it is unlikely that teachers will ever be able to hold their own with the practitioners in the established professions, for whose knowledge the same parents doubtless have a very considerable measure of respect. Indeed, in the face of parents' not inconsiderable knowledge about children already, the necessity for the teachers in this regard becomes the greater.

We leave the similar considerations which would apply to psychology and sociology, and come directly to our central and final point.[49] Goode's principle of control would certainly seem to be the one to adopt, though the radical changes it implies should not be made at the cost of a ruinous upheaval of the present system. With this in mind, the necessity is one for a more capacious career structure, one where a new element is welded to the present infrastructure of classroom practitioners and also the superstructure of what we conveniently call educationists — academics, researchers, administrators, advisers and the like. In other words, there needs to emerge from among the classroom practitioners a group of teachers whose members were able to talk with confidence *and competence* to people in *both* structures.

Obviously, in the case of fellow practitioners, this would come without difficulty because of the extensive and successful teaching experience of the members themselves; they would already have an intimate knowledge of work at the coal face. But the essential question to be answered concerns the source of this confidence and competence when the members were in

continuing contact, as we envisage, with the educationists. Quite emphatic-
ally, the relationship here must *not* be of the doctor-patient or lawyer-client
kind. It would need to be one in which the practitioners were able to talk to
the educationists in the latter's own terms, and at something which approached (though never actually equalled) the latter's own level of competence.

As things are at the moment, we believe that few teachers would be equal
to this. But if special facilities existed for such experienced practitioners to
undertake studies themselves in education at the universities, *at no less than
doctoral level*, the competence (and hence the confidence) would accrue. This
would not, of course, mean that each member should study all the con-
tributory disciplines, but that *collectively* the group would exhibit a knowledge of most or all of these.

As to how many practitioners would or could be admitted to the group,
we can only be tentative. But bearing in mind the considerations we
examined earlier under size, perhaps 10 per cent of the total force would be
appropriate, each teacher with a minimum of about 7 or 8 years' successful
(and preferably varied) continuous classroom experience. This experience
could be in *any* sector of the system (certainly to include the primary sector)
and with the quality of the experience assessed in the main by fellow practitioners. The major criterion for membership would be an *interaction* of
practical and academic ability or potential (one without the other would be
insufficient), with age, sex, seniority, and present location in the system as
being almost certainly irrelevant. The universities may, of course, demur on
grounds of entrance qualifications, but one hopes that they could be per-
suaded that, for example, neither the University of Sussex in England, nor La
Trobe University in Melbourne regrets its enlightened admission of some
highly successful and intensely motivated, though "unqualified", under-
graduates.

With regard to the duties and responsibilities of this group, we refer again
to Goode's dictum of control. The group would have oversight and control
over the actual educational practice within a given area – city, county, state,
or whatever. Towards this end its activities could include the staffing and
supervision of in-service courses, oversight of the newly qualified, participation at colleges and elsewhere in pre-service course, leadership of teachers'
study groups, educational innovation, local "action" research (and through its
liaison with the professional researchers, the instigation of more ambitious
research programmes), and the development and further encouragement of
closer and more viable relationships between schools and staffs in different

sectors of the system. No doubt other activities would come with local exigencies, but *essentially* the group would need to have a close and continuing relationship with the educationists, and so form a focus of communication to replace the present rather tenuous line.

The discharge of such duties would mean that while the members of the group would *remain classroom practitioners*, they would need time away from their classrooms. The arrangements for this would again be a matter for local decision. However, it should be remembered that arrangements are already in force for the release of teachers for in-service courses. More generally, if teachers are to conduct their own affairs, and thus move towards an enhanced status, some sort of concession must be made, and it would be most unrealistic to expect those most closely concerned to exercise an effective measure of control, and at the same time not to be relieved of some of their day-to-day classroom duties. The (different) control exercised by full-time officials of teachers' organizations is a parallel case.

The other highly important matter concerns pay. In view of the tasks and the *responsibilities* of this group, and having regard both to the high quality of the experience and formal qualifications its members would have, it is by no means unrealistic to suggest that their pay should match that of senior educationists. This would still be a bargain, for at relatively little total cost the best teachers would be retained as practitioners, and the very existence of the group would most probably have a favourable effect on recruitment to the teaching force in general.

An enhancement of professional status is something the teachers need and deserve, but it is hard to see how merely tactical moves could ever bring it about. The moves need to be bold and strategic, and in line with what "profession" as a concept implies. As a first step, we need to know just how familiar or otherwise the teachers are with this concept. With this as a basis, a strategy could be devised, ideally by the teachers themselves and evolving possibly along the lines we have very roughly sketched. But whatever the strategy, it must aim at bringing practioner and educationist into an equal partnership, wherein each values and openly acknowledges the indispensable contribution of the other.

References

1.   WEBB, L. C., The teaching profession, *Australian Journal of Education,* 7 (1963).

2. INGLIS, W. B., The General Teaching Council for Scotland, *British Journal of Educational Studies*. **18**, Feb. 1970.
3. *Yearbook of Education, The status and position of teachers*, Evans Bros., 1953.
4. UNESCO, *Special intergovernmental conference on the status of teachers*, Paris, 1966.
5. THOMAS, J., *Teachers for schools of tomorrow*, UNESCO, 1968.
6. WILSON, B. R., The teacher's role: a sociological analysis, *British Journal of Sociology*, **13** (1962).
7. HOYLE, E., Professional stratification and anomie in the teaching profession, *Paedogogica Europaea*, **5**, 1969.
8. GRACE, G. R., *Role conflict and the teacher*, Routledge & Kegan Paul, 1972.
9. LINTON, R., *The study of man*, pp. 113—14, Appleton Century, 1933.
10. MILLERSON, G., *The qualifying associations*, Routledge & Kegan Paul, 1964, esp. Chapter 1.
11. READER, W. G., *Professional men*, Weidenfeld and Nicolson, 1966, esp. Chapter 10.
12. LIEBERMAN, M., *Education as a profession*, Prentice Hall, 1956.
13. GOODMAN, R., Teachers' status in Australia, unpublished doctoral dissertation, Australian National University, Canberra, 1955.
14. PARSONS, T., Professions, *International encyclopaedia of the social sciences*, Macmillan and the Free Press, 1968.
15. WILSON, B. R., *op.cit.*, p. 30.
16. GOULDNER, A., Cosmopolitans and locals: towards an analysis of latent social roles, *Administrative Science Quarterly*, **2**, 1957 and **2**, 1958.
17. LETT, W. R., Teacher games and the problem of control, in D'URSO, S. (Ed.) *Critical writings on Australian education*, Wiley (Sydney), 1971.
18. SIMPSON, R. L. and SIMPSON, I. H., Women and bureaucracy in the semi-professions, in ETZIONI, A. (Ed.); *The semi-professions and their organisation*, The Free Press, 1969.
19. LEGGATT, T., Teaching as a profession, in JACKSON, J. A. (Ed.), *Professions and professionalisation*, Cambridge University Press, 1970.
20. LEWIS, R. and MAUDE, A., *Professional people*, Phoenix House, 1952.
21. ARMSTRONG, S., Women working — limitations?, in *Employment opportunities for women*, University of New South Wales, Sydney, 1965.
22. ARCHIBALD, K., *Sex and the public service*, Queen's Printer, Ottawa, 1970.
23. EPSTEIN, C. F., *Woman's place*, University of California, 1971.
24. FOGARTY, M. P., RAPOPORT, R., and RAPOPORT, R. N., *Sex, career and family*, Allen & Unwin, 1971.
25. HARRIES-JENKINS, G., Professionals in organizations, in JACKSON, J. A. (Ed.), *op.cit.* (see 19, above).
26. FELD, M. D., Professionalism, nationalism, and the alienation of the military, in VAN DOORN, J. (Ed.), *Armed forces and society*, The Hague, 1968.
27. BENNIS, W. B., Post bureaucratic leadership, *Transaction* **6**, 1969.
28. ENGEL, G. V., *Professional authority and bureaucratic organization*, paper read to the American Sociological Association, San Francisco, 1969.
29. GOODE, W. J., The theoretical limits of professionalism, in ETZIONI, A. (Ed.), *op.cit.* (see 18 above).
30. ECKSTEIN, H. H., The politics of the British Medical Association, *Political Science Quarterly*, **26**, 1954.
31. TAEUSCH, C. E., *Professional and business ethics*, Holt, 1926.

32. RODDENBERRY, E. W., Achieving professionalism, *Journal of Criminal Law, Criminology and Police Science,* xliv, 1953.

33. COGAN, M. L., Towards a definition of profession, *Harvard Educational Review,* 23, 1953.

34. LASKI, H., The decline of the professions, *Harper's Magazine* 171, Nov. 1935.

35. PARSONS, T., The professions and social structure, in *Essays in sociological theory,* pp. 34-50, The Free Press, 1958.

36. JOHNSON, T. J., *Professions and power,* Macmillan, 1972.

37. Professions under Examination (anon.), *The Economist,* 4 Feb. 1967.

38. RAISON, T., In defence of the professions, *New Society,* 8, 18 Aug. 1966.

39. PARSONS, T., *op.cit.,* see note 14, p.546.

40. CARR-SAUNDERS, A. M. and WILSON, P. A., *The professions,* Clarendon Press, 1933.

41. BECKER, H., The nature of a profession, in *Education for the professions,* 61, Part 2, National Society for the Study of Education Yearbook, Chicago, 1962.

42. HUGHES, E. C., Professions, *Daedalus,* 92, 1963.

43. KLEINGARTNER, A., *Professionalism and salaried worker organisations,* Industrial Relations Research Institute, University of Wisconsin, 1967.

44. HALL, R. H., Professionalisation and bureaucratisation, *American Sociological Review,* 33, 1968.

45. GOODMAN, R. G., *op.cit.,* p. 229.

46. NUNALLY, J., *Psychometric theory,* McGraw Hill, 1967.

47. O'CONNOR, D. J. and HIRST, P. H., see their respective chapters in LONGFORD, G. and O'CONNOR D. J. (Eds.), *New essays in the philosophy of education,* Routledge & Kegan Paul, 1973.

48. DEARDEN, R. F., Instruction and learning by discovery, in PETERS, R. S. (Ed.), *The concept of education,* Routledge & Kegan Paul, 1967.

49. DUCKERS, A. S., The education graduates, *Education for Teaching,* 77, Autumn 1968.

CHAPTER 8

The Role of Teachers' Centres in the In-service Education of Teachers

Introduction

INITIALLY it is necessary to establish what the term "teachers' centre" can mean so that one can gain a perspective on such an organization's possible role in the provision of in-service education opportunities for teachers. Then one is better equipped to understand the main body of the chapter which constitutes a review of the extensive range of factors which determine the manner of functioning and potential effectiveness of teachers' centre activity. As the process of communication forms a major part of the centre warden's work, a detailed examination of the communication problem will enable the reader to identify the range of different individuals and bodies within the education service with whom it is necessary for him to liaise. It will also demonstrate the dilemmas posed in determining the appropriate means of contact for a specific situation. In this way, as well as by considering some of the problems of the newly appointed centre warden, it is hoped to convey a realization of how delicate and subtle the process of communication can be in this field of work. Finally, programmes of activity in teachers' centres are analysed to show developing trends, whilst different levels of teacher involvement in centre activity are examined as a means of reflecting the range and degree of teacher response to the opportunities available in the teachers' centre.

What is a teachers' centre?

Basically a teachers' centre can be thought of as a meeting-place for teachers. Such centres are also normally frequented by other workers in the education service, including local education authority advisers, school ancillary workers and college of education staff, to name but a few, although the main emphasis is placed on the involvement of practising teachers as the name suggests.

The programme of activity will vary in direct relation to the policy of the local authority within which the teachers' centre is situated, the nature of the leadership and the geographical characteristics of the area concerned.([1]) However, in view of the fact that these variables are discussed at a later juncture, it is sufficient now to say that when everything has been taken into consideration, one can expect to find a fairly comprehensive programme of activity on-going in the majority of teachers' centres.

Courses for practising teachers, staffed by their colleagues, local authority advisers and college of education staff, provide teachers with an opportunity to explore new techniques, improvise equipment for the classroom and exchange ideas in workshop situations. Study groups are formed to enable teachers to meet and discuss such topics as recent educational developments, subject specialisms, important publications or television and radio series for school use. Similarly, working parties are set up to consider problems and new challenges as they arise. In addition opportunities are frequently provided for teachers to participate in national and local curriculum development projects.

Social functions are treated with varying degrees of priority, some centres possessing their own licensed premises, whereas in other cases, the preference is for the occasional social or cheese and wine party. Certainly every teachers' centre endeavours to provide tea and coffee facilities and a lounge of some kind, for it has been found that such accommodation almost invariably becomes the hub of centre activity.

Persons in charge of a teachers' centre can have many titles, among them "Curriculum Development Officer", "Head of Teachers' Centre" and "Principal", but in most cases the term "Warden" is used. Normally the actual job does not carry the residential commitment which in other contexts one usually associates with the title "Warden".

The building provision for teachers' centres is extremely varied. A minority of centres is purpose-built, the tendency being rather to utilize old school buildings, disused mansions and prefabricated rooms. In some cases there is an arrangement where the premises are shared with a school, a college of education or even a college of further education. In these circumstances, it is more than likely that the situation will provide more problems than benefits in the long run. It is common experience for wardens of teachers' centres to find the lack of sufficient space a major problem, as on the one hand, the really small centres are unable to do much in the way of display, which is acknowledged as an important aspect of teachers' centre activity, while the large centres find that the same problem tends to hinder any expansion they might contemplate in their activity and resource provision. The extent of the problem naturally varies according to the attitude and policy of the local authority concerned.

The geographical factor

The location is obviously an important factor in determining the nature of the teachers' centre's functioning. However, it is important to stress that a seemingly poorly located centre, coupled with successful leadership, appears to work in many unlikely situations. The urban situation springs to mind, primarily because this has been found by many wardens to be as near to an ideal setting as they are likely to inherit, with a likelihood that the centre itself will be housed in a converted old school building. Such a centre would obviously benefit from possessing adequate car-parking facilities. It is also desirable that the centre should be sensibly situated in relation to its catchment area. The number of schools served might be anything ranging from forty to 150, although situations where there are too many or too few schools in a catchment area present their own peculiar problems. The warden is generally thought to be fortunate if the centre has a conveniently central location and public transport facilities readily available. Paradoxically, teachers' centres situated in cities suffer transport difficulties as a direct result of the volume of traffic. It has also been found that teachers working in cities frequently choose to live away from their schools in well-defined dormitory zones and for this reason are often reluctant to stay on in the city to attend centre activities of any kind.

In a sprawling metropolis such as London, there has been a tendency for centre provision to harvest the benefits accruing from a combination of relatively small centres and reasonably compact catchment areas, harnessed to vast resources which the Inner London Education Authority can and does provide. The undoubted success of this shrewd formula is particularly interesting when it is juxtaposed to the large-scale teachers' centre building provision in such areas as Birmingham, Sheffield and Liverpool. The main point to be noted here is that truly local provision is much more thorough and better serviced in the incredibly unwieldly Inner London authority than it is in many of our larger provincial cities.

The situation in clearly defined rural areas in terms of sheer distance between schools can be such that centre functioning as it exists in some urban areas is quite out of the question. In such circumstances some local authorities opt for mainly residential provision. Although it is difficult to generalize about the nature of activity in these situations, it would appear difficult for teacher-inspired patterns of activity to develop to the extent that is possible in a normal teachers' centre situation. Despite this an extensive pattern of actual rural teachers' centres does exist, where the centre warden has to be extremely mobile because of the scattered nature of the schools in the area. Unfortunately the tendency to appoint part-time wardens in such areas has more pronounced limiting effect on the potential functioning of a centre. Some centres, of course, combine an element of rural and urban in their make-up and consequently they experience the characteristics and problems of both.

The main aim in discussing the varying types of geographical location for teachers' centres is to establish that such a factor inevitably influences the way in which the in-service education process including curriculum development can be carried out, while differentiating between local authority residential centres and actual teachers' centres. It is also to suggest that the manner of operation in different types of area will vary, but that the basic objectives of the teachers' centres remain constant.

A key factor – the schools

The schools themselves are, of course, the most vital factor of all in determining the potential functioning of a teachers' centre. If there were one ultimate aim for a centre it would be to promote the growth and sharing of local curriculum innovations; and this could be achieved only with enthusiastic co-operation and participation from as many schools as possible within the area in question.([2]) This naturally leads on to the major "fly in the ointment": that is to say that whatever the outlook or provision of the local education authority and the geographical location of the centre, we are faced with the fact that the schools have the last word regarding in-service education activity. As one centre warden commented succinctly, "they vote with their feet" in describing the situation where, if teachers do not feel that an activity is worth while, they stop attending. Unfortunately, this is only part of the problem of stimulating active involvement in centre activities, for if any warden is honest he will readily admit that there are some headteachers and members of staff who seldom if ever grace any form of in-service activity with their presence. Basically this comes down to a fundamental problem of attitude and outlook towards professional commitment on the part of the teachers. Among those who display a concern for the way in which they carry out their professional responsibilities, there is a periodic questioning in their own minds as to what they attempt to do in the school situation and why. There are clearly others who feel self-sufficient and secure in the way they carry out their job and in all honesty it has to be admitted that in some but not all cases their overriding self-confidence seems justified.

In recent years the teaching profession has had to come to terms with the complex and countless implications of de-streaming, middle schools, comprehensive schools, open-plan schools, the changing character of family relationships, the growth in importance of an adolescent sub-culture and a tendency towards mounting aggression and violence in the community. It is confronted on the one hand by the arguments of the "élitists" and their defence of "standards" and "academic excellence" and on the other by the progressive school of thought that favours the education of the whole child in relation to his needs. In addition there has been an identifiable shift in the attitude of many teachers who no longer regard "teaching" as being some form of higher calling, but purely as an absorbing and challenging job. Equally, there are those who stubbornly take no account of change in education in any shape or form. Many of these are in the category of those who regard teaching as a "nine to four job", and that is the limited extent of their commitment.

Another factor that needs to be considered here is the type of school involved. From the in-service education standpoint, the large comprehensive school possesses both the physical numbers of teachers and the provision of resources to carry out its own programme to a great extent. Nevertheless even here, contact with other schools, whether they be feeder primary schools or secondary schools organized on different lines, can provide mutual benefits for all concerned.

The subject-oriented nature of much of the secondary curriculum, together with the staff commitments arising from a complex timetable and the demands of an examination-dominated system, tend to result in a situation where curriculum development is to a great extent fragmented. As a consequence, the release of secondary staff for local in-service activity becomes both limited and spasmodic. One might also argue that the pupil/teacher ratio and the demanding nature of the curriculum in the modern primary school militate equally against staff release for local in-service education purposes. It is a sad fact that teachers' centres in general tend to report a much more favourable and consistent response from teachers of children in the infant and junior school range than from the secondary sector. Regardless of their level of involvement, the attitudes and priorities of all teachers concerning their professional commitment, coupled with the attitude of headteachers toward the release of staff for local in-service education activities, constitute a major influence on the work of the centre warden.

Organizational innovations such as the development of the middle school have tended in some cases to blur the great divide between the primary and secondary stages of education, but the gap is still marked and taking measures to combat the situation constitutes a vital role for the teachers' centre.

The important contribution of the headteacher

Leadership in the school situation, the traditional role of the headteacher, is now subject to mounting pressure, but the warden of any teachers' centre must recognize the fact that the headteacher can still effectively block any attempt to communicate with members of the school staff if he or she feels so inclined. The circumstances under which such a state of affairs can arise are of course extreme, but the realization that this can happen means that the warden must be particularly careful in the way that he or she handles all forms of communication both with individuals and groups. The warden must endeavour to be positive in outlook and the headteacher should be viewed as a potential ally regardless of whether or not they share a similar educational philosophy. It is an established fact that enthusiastic and co-operative head-teachers are worth their weight in gold to the teachers' centre in their area. Furthermore, it is true to say that every teachers' centre is normally able to call on the services of many such individuals.

Who is the teachers' centre warden?

The process whereby the warden is selected for his appointment is directly related to the way in which the local education authority concerned sees the job. In 1974 the scale on which he or she is paid can be anything from Burnham Scale 1 Assistant Teacher to Burnham Scale 8 Headteacher. It should be added that the extent of responsibility does not necessarily relate directly to the scale of payment, another influence on the situation being the degree to which the warden controls the functioning of the teachers' centre. In some situations there is a danger of the centre warden being seen as "a glorified office boy" and in such circumstances it is unlikely that the centre policy will be democratic, teacher-oriented and teacher-inspired. The influence here is that adviser-run activities frequently tend to be somewhat authoritarian in their pattern and that this mode of working does not make for thoroughly effective and adequate in-service education provision, otherwise enough would have been happening prior to the arrival of the teachers' centre movement without having to create a new hybrid.

Generally it is accepted that wardens are appointed on a basis of previous successful experience in the classroom, possibly coupled with evidence of a pleasing personality, an apparent ability to make relationships and an identifiable leadership tendency.

In the foregoing outline an attempt has been made to enumerate various factors which can influence the life potential of a teachers' centre. This has been done because there appears to be no other way of showing the unique forces which have combined to create this comparatively recent form of in-service education agency. In summary it amounts to the fact that local authorities have been forced to recognize the emergence of the ordinary classroom teacher as the most potent unexplored factor in local curriculum development. The emphasis on the term "ordinary" is deliberate because in the past, as is well known, only certain outstanding classroom practitioners have been responsible for curriculum innovation. The vital difference lies in the relative numbers involved. Formerly innovation was the privilege of the fortunate few, whereas now numbers of practising teachers are actively involved in the making of curriculum decisions. The teachers' centre can be viewed as the appropriate agency for the promotion of this process and, therefore, it is now necessary to examine the anatomy of the teachers' centre in some detail so that its full potential as an innovation can be considered. To do this a description of such a centre must be provided in terms of its organization, its pattern of communications and its programme.

A teachers' centre – organization and the warden's contribution

Policy-making in a teachers' centre can be seen as a co-operative process. There is a tendency for centres to possess a representative committee of teachers who may have been selected in a variety of ways (such as by democratic vote or on a union basis or by a combination of methods). These committees normally include representation from the local authority apart from the warden (this is important in that the warden tries not to be seen as exclusively a local authority man). Normally too it is likely that local colleges of education will have some representation, although it is also possible and perhaps desirable that their voting powers should be limited. In some such committees all questions of major financial expenditure are their concern as are most of the important curriculum decisions, whereas in other situations much of the responsibility in matters of finance and policy is delegated to the warden. In any case it can be seen that the local classroom teachers in either set of circumstances have the opportunity to make their views and needs known. That is, of course, assuming that they choose to exercise their rights and thereby enhance their professional standing and the strength of the teachers' centre in the process.

Many teachers' centres nominate sub-committees to which matters such as future programme decisions are delegated. No one has yet been able to ascertain the extent to which these committees and sub-committees canvass local teacher opinion before putting forward their recommendations and suggestions, but the probable answer is that in some cases they do and in others they clearly do not: but here we may be moving into a communication problem which is reviewed in a later section. Many centre wardens are of the opinion that a situation which should be avoided if at all possible is the one where a centre committee can be described as "a rubber stamp", for such a statement implies a lack of involvement on the part of the teachers, which may or may not be their own fault.

The crucial point which needs stressing is that on the one hand, the representatives elected to serve on a teachers' centre committee should feel a clear-cut responsibility to put forward for consideration the views and aspirations of the teachers whom they represent. On the other hand, recognizing the often conflicting responsibilities of such committee members, constituent teachers should go out of their way to make their wishes and criticisms known to their representatives. In such a way classroom teacher opinion can make its impact on curriculum decisions.

The process of communication

On taking up his appointment, the teachers' centre warden inherits a major problem of communication. It is perhaps rather sad that poor contact and crumbling relationships are fast becoming a most significant feature of this, an affluent and communication conscious society. Nevertheless, a thorough examination of the communication problem and some possible solutions to it in the education field are central to the notion that the teachers' centre is at once the most significant and encouraging development in the battle to provide an education system that is thoroughly geared to the needs of life in the modern world.

Let us consider the activities of a new centre warden step by step.

The first step will be to establish relationships with every school in the area — and the nature and manner of the initial contact tends to establish the pattern for all future attempts to communicate. Thus if the warden is careful to make contact by telephone prior to making any intended visits, he will soon gain some measure of acceptance.

Ostensibly the visit is seen by the warden as a means of identifying potential contributors for the centre, discovering display sources, recognizing the needs of the teachers and discreetly advertising the activities and services to be found at the teachers' centre. Nevertheless he or she will soon discover that many a headteacher is keen to discuss what the school is doing and in the process may wish to take the warden on what can seem like a tour of inspection. If this does happen, then it is a clear indication that the warden in question is being given an opportunity to achieve all his own aims for the visit, whilst endeavouring to satisfy the headteacher's praiseworthy desire to secure an impartial view of the functioning of his or her school.

The question of school visits is frequently included as a topic for discussion when wardens of teachers' centres meet but there is not complete unanimity over their importance.([3]) Although one has to admit that the many duties that a centre warden may be called on to do can limit the extent and frequency with which a programme of school visits can be carried out, the composite experience of many wardens seems to suggest that regardless of the circumstances the centre warden should accord high priority to visiting schools.

The school visit can reflect some important facets of the in-service education role of the teachers' centre. First and foremost it is tangible evidence in itself of the local authority's interest in what the school is attempting to achieve. It can offer the occasional opportunity for one-to-one relationships where there is more likelihood of frankness in the shape of down-to-earth discussion, on what is and what is not happening in a situation. Again if we stand back we can see the warden as a sympathetic listener who nevertheless possesses the ability to recognize opportunities in terms of activities and services that the teachers' centre might provide.

After the initial contact has been made, subsequent visits encourage the emergence of positive feedback on the teachers' centre provision, whether in terms of resources or activities. As with communication as a whole, if visits do not follow a developmental pattern, with the centre warden acting as an acute and perceptive observer, then a vital opportunity to enhance and extend the validity of the teachers' centre may have been missed. Basically, the visit is irrefutable evidence that whatever the teachers' centre sets out to achieve will be attempted by means of a two-way process. It also means that teacher consultation actually within the class situation on developments in the curriculum will have become a reality on a much less limited scale.

Probably of equal importance, but more often than not treated as being even more so, the telephone symbolizes the centre warden's need for an immediate and convenient means of contact. The danger here is that conversation on a telephone tends at times to be misleading and in fact many wardens claim to have encountered more misunderstandings and upheavals as a direct result of misinterpreted telephone calls than from any other means of communication. However, this serves only to sound a note of warning about what can go wrong: it obviously should not detract from the undoubtedly indispensable value of the telephone to any centre warden. Certainly if an emergency of any kind crops up, the telephone has frequently proved to be a centre warden's salvation. When there is a choice between visiting and telephoning, however, it is advisable to choose the former.

The written medium can be at the same time the most time consuming and wasteful of all available means of contact. Many centre wardens are hard-pressed for clerical or secretarial assistance, but let us suppose that our new warden has part-time clerical assistance for 20 hours each week. In this situation he may well use the telephone to contact commercial concerns as well as schools, where the content of the message is such that the danger of its being misinterpreted is minimal. Thus it becomes possible to conserve the impact of the written communication by using it sparingly. Centre programmes have been found to be more effective if sent out to schools termly as opposed to weekly. This particular publication is a vital life-line between the centre warden and the teachers and for that reason it has to be planned and produced with the utmost care both in terms of content and presentation. Unfortunately some sincere attempts to communicate produce embarrassing situations and as such they constitute potential pitfalls. It is best to avoid using the programme as a medium for expressing the warden's own sentiments. Similarly it seems unwise to produce an elaborate and elegant programme if the activities described within it do not merit the treatment. Fundamentally it appears that programmes should be instantly recognizable as teachers' centre publications. They should also be sensible and practical in terms of size, shape and format.

Apart from the programme, teachers' centres are apt to find that as more groups and working parties become established, the need to produce various kinds of working paper tends to grow. Astute centre wardens ascertain beforehand what materials will be needed by group leaders and visiting contributors and try to ensure that duplicating or other preparation is done in good time. This "be-prepared" principle in fact provides an admirable golden rule for teachers' centre wardens in all matters of provision. Certainly it demonstrates a parallel which can be drawn between running a teachers' centre and a school, but only in the sense that the warden is in a position to set an example in terms of his organization of the available accommodation and resources.

The production of a working paper by a teachers' centre poses three important questions: is the production of such a document necessary; will it be of practical use; and even more to the point, will any one use it? Perhaps an appropriate yardstick to be employed here might be that the production of working papers should be contemplated only if in the eyes of the group members concerned they constitute a logical development from an on-going activity.

The subtle, complex pattern of desirable working relationships which the new teachers' centre warden is called upon to establish, is seen by many to be absolutely central to his potential effectiveness within the centre's immediate catchment area and for that matter the surrounding region as well. With the development of such a pattern of comparatively harmonious, genuine working relationships, the way is paved for a two-way channel of communications between curriculum exploration groups based on the teachers' centre in association with local schools, and the larger-scale operations of curriculum study groups based in universities, colleges of education or other curriculum review agencies within the education system. A closer analysis of this pattern of communication will perhaps serve a dual purpose in the sense that on the one hand it will illustrate what can be achieved by teachers' centres if the right provision is made by local education authorities in terms of staff, facilities and scope of functioning; while on the other it can pose some interesting questions regarding the situation as a whole in the in-service education field, and the unshouldered responsibilities of all concerned prior to the emergence of the teachers' centre movement.

The relationship between the local authority and the teachers' centre warden has already been considered to some extent, because the terms of the warden's contract and the facilities, services and physical assistance made available, tend to predetermine the basis of existing and future co-operation between the centre warden and his employers. Although it is obvious that the measure of autonomy afforded to a centre warden by the authority in question has a direct bearing on future attitudes, it is equally important that such considerations do not hinder the functioning of in-service education provision in the area.

In some situations there may be an attempt to carry out a dual function with an appointment as an adviser and as the warden of a teachers' centre. Anyone attempting a dual responsibility of this kind would appear to face similar disadvantages to those experienced by the teaching head. Such an appointment illustrates a misunderstanding of the teachers' centre warden's role in that it fails to take account of the way in which the warden is viewed by the teachers. This is, of course, not to say that teachers would not attend centre activities in these circumstances but that the nature of the activities and the reasons for teachers' attendance at them might be of a rather different, more limited and less teacher-inspired character. Fortunately the situation and organization just described are the exception rather than the rule. Generally the local authority possesses strengths and opportunities to exercise them, which can promote the functioning of a teachers' centre. In view of this fact, the centre warden needs to do all he can to maintain an atmosphere of mutual helpfulness and co-operation with his adviser colleagues. In this way the adviser's insight into the schools within the area can manifest itself in the shape of information regarding possible activities, potential contributors, new group leaders and feedback regarding the effectiveness of the teachers' centre as a whole. It would be less than realistic, however, to assume that all these potentially positive contributions from local advisory staff can be made in the practical situation, partly because many are already overworked and partly too because not all advisers understand or appreciate the nature and significance of the teachers' centre movement in terms of the aspirations of practising teachers.

An atmosphere of active co-operation between a college of education and a teachers' centre is clearly desirable, but the extent to which such an ideal arrangement can become a reality will depend on the attitudes and motives of those concerned on both sides. There is at least one centre where the warden is also a college of education lecturer. There appears to be no good reason why such a joint appointment should be viewed any differently from other dual commitments.

The teachers' centre does well to use the practical abilities of members of college of education staff as contributors to the programme. These staff are likely to come to a full appreciation of the aims and objectives of the centre if they also attend as group or course members. Co-operation between a centre and a college can lead to the involvement of student teachers in the activities of the centre. Such experiences whilst at college will probably facilitate subsequent contacts between new teachers and local centres during the induction year of service.

Much needed support for many teachers' centres, especially those in rural areas, is forthcoming not only from colleges of education, but from institutes, departments and schools of education in universities. As area training organizations, certain universities have responsibility for quality control of teacher education. The extent to which this has been exercised at the in-service stage varies greatly with different institutions, but they have made a great and varied contribution to the education of practising teachers throughout the post-war years. Before teachers' centres became widespread, the area training organizations were already establishing networks of contact with schools in some areas. The warden should acquaint himself fully with the situation regarding the area training organization in his area so that following local government reorganization and changes affecting institutions of higher education, contacts, services and resources built up over the years are husbanded by the centre.

A further link in the communication chain that requires a mention, however delicate, is the question of the teacher professional organizations. In some situations it is known that teachers' centres have been set up on a particular union basis. This can prove to be a retrograde step in that such circumstances must inevitably exclude some teachers from the functioning of the centres concerned. Ideally the teachers' centre provides a place where all teachers should be able to meet regardless of their union loyalties.

Finally in this review of the range of potential communication patterns which in one way or another can influence the functioning of a teachers' centre, it is perhaps appropriate to describe one individual who above all can develop enthusiasm and interest in a school, where other agencies and modes of communication come sadly unstuck — this is none other than the person in each school who has been given or has volunteered for the task of ensuring that everyone within the school is fully acquainted with all the patterns of on-going and forthcoming activities and services at the teachers' centre. In some situations the headteacher may decide to take on this responsibility himself, but the job is frequently delegated to a teacher who is known to possess a particular enthusiasm for centre activities. This job has been given various titles but probably the most common description in use is that of teachers' centre correspondent.

Many wardens would observe that it is not sufficient simply to set up a network of centre "agents" in the schools. Clearly the significance of a direct line of communication between the centre and the school is such that precautions need to be taken to make sure that this valuable contact is neither under-estimated in terms of utility nor misused. Thus the new warden may well be advised to show an active interest in teachers' centre correspondents, by discussing future policy with them and making it clear that their opinions and suggestions are of practical value.

There appears to be little doubt that the careful application of a teachers' centre correspondent system within an area can have a significant impact on the nature and degree of enthusiasm and participation in the in-service education process as a whole. At the same time this type of appointment offers the headteacher a further opportunity to delegate responsibility in such a way that the process of identifying candidates for potential leadership among the school staff becomes more widespread.

Characteristics of the teachers' centre warden

Interview committees frequently appear to experience difficulty in determining which questions and answers are likely to identify the potential centre warden, especially when it is taken into account that a whole variety of factors can influence the nature of the role which the warden can inherit. There are no easy formulas to apply especially when those who are making the appointments also create many of the limitations in the situation.

The newly appointed centre warden can, of course, make contact with a colleague either in the same area or within a different local authority in an attempt to secure guidance on the appropriate strategies to promote individual and group relationships. Whether or not the warden finds useful sources of information and advice, he alone has to deal with this complex pattern of groups and individuals. He may be an introvert or an extrovert: there is no evidence to suggest that either type of personality possesses advantages in a centre leadership situation.

The centre warden has also to learn to look at his own position with a frank and critical eye. He can feel some satisfaction if within the area served by his centre an increasing number of group leaders and practising teachers develop the kinds of qualities which the model warden aims to exhibit. At the same time he has to avoid making their commitment to the teachers' centre an end in itself for the teachers. Unless he holds fast to the avowed purposes of the centre and ensures the involvement of an ever-increasing number of teachers and groups, he may find that an inner circle or élite has grown up which soon has the effect of hampering the more general influence of the centre.

The knights of old would spend a night in vigil examining their attitudes and motives towards their calling. One would not wish to advocate anything quite so drastic for the aspiring teachers' centre warden. Nevertheless, many experienced wardens are critical of activities (carried on in some centres) which seem to them to be in the nature of ego-exercises. They are concerned to see that the teachers' centre movement is accepted for what it is. A majority of wardens look upon the centre as the most significant and dynamic development to date in the history of in-service education in this country. They are very wary of anyone viewing the centre warden's job as either a stepping-stone to better things or simply as that of a booking agent for centre facilities.

The new centre warden clearly has to be careful about the way in which relationships with the immediate centre staff are approached, because it is almost inevitable that everyone including the secretary, the caretaker, the cleaner, the warden (and if the centre is fortunate enough to have one – the deputy warden) will have to accept an exceptionally democratic exchange of functions and roles as situations develop. It is not surprising to find the caretaker or the cleaner answering the telephone or, for that matter, the centre warden washing up or making the tea. Here again there is a growing tendency for this democratic interchange of functions to spread to the teachers, the advisers, the college of education lecturers and in fact anyone who becomes connected with teachers' centre activity. Such patterns of shared responsibility seem to be breaking down long-established feelings and attitudes of isolation in teachers and in the process the way is being paved for more co-operative approaches to the solution of curriculum problems. Perhaps even more significantly the teachers' centre provides living proof that situations can create their own leadership and potential solutions.

Because of specialist knowledge in some aspect of the curriculum, some wardens set about providing activity and materials to satisfy developments in this particular field on behalf of a much larger catchment area than that covered by the normal teachers' centre. In this way a centre may become well known and may gain in status. There is the danger, however, of the warden's deep involvement in one sphere of interest working to the detriment of the rest of the centre programme. Even if a deputy warden or other leader were to maintain the momentum, there remains the risk of the warden's losing his overall perspective on the centre's functioning. Moreover, teachers in the vicinity whose immediate concern is unrelated to the area of the curriculum being explored in depth may well question the value of the teachers' centre to them. In general, it is unlikely that funds will be adequate to meet many other needs if one deep well has first to be filled. Although in the initial stages of setting up a centre it might be proper for the warden to participate in particular interests, he should identify headteachers, teachers and advisers to carry out such functioning as soon as possible, to leave himself free to concentrate on areas of the curriculum which need thought and provision. He should aim to involve teachers of all outlooks and dispositions rather than to identify himself with a particular subject or approach.

The warden — and others with responsibility for a centre — have to be able to give satisfactory answers to some crucial questions. Is the centre a teachers' centre or the warden's centre? Are the activities teacher inspired and led or do they all rely on the warden? Should the warden aspire to providing earth-shattering developments to attract teachers outside the centre's catchment area or should his first concern be the local teachers and their needs? Can personal specialisms and expertise be used within a balanced multi-purpose centre's programme?

The point that needs to be made here is that teachers' centres make their impact through the cumulative efforts of wardens throughout the country endeavouring to stimulate local teachers' interest in a review of their objectives in a teaching situation. The fact that some teachers' centre work may have been publicized by the press or embraced by the academics does not necessarily constitute a genuine value judgement.

The programme of the teachers' centre

Without a doubt the most important form of written communication devised and more often than not produced by the teachers' centre warden, is the centre programme. This document provides an excellent illustration of the range and diversity of in-service education aspirations, which have found a coherent means of expression as a result of the teachers' centre movement.[4]

Historically the first priority for the teachers' centre warden was to determine the nature of the contribution that the teachers' centre could make within the local education community. The earliest programmes tended to reflect this tentative approach to activity provision. Many of the courses put on in teachers' centres were of the lecture type with limited emphasis on practical or discussion work. This period was also characterized by the extensive provision of one-off lectures which attracted large groups of teachers but which were soon found to have limited influence.

Eventually study groups, workshops and working parties took up a major part of teachers' centre programmes and in the process the size of groups, their mobility, their roles and their leadership became the subject of close scrutiny by centre wardens. Immediately, it becomes apparent that a subtle new dimension had been added to the centre warden's role, for by now the wardens concerned were achieving a clearer perspective on group dynamics. They were gaining knowledge about the peculiar needs of their areas, and an awareness of the need to provide an activity programme, characterized by a variety of potential levels of involvement for the teachers.

More recently there has been a marked tendency for a shift in emphasis to resource-oriented activity patterns in teachers' centres and in the process implications have emerged for servicing-type activities (including among others, techniques with audio-visual equipment). Within this pattern, working parties have produced documents for distribution to practising teachers. Similarly project teams have devised schemes of work for various aspects and levels of the curriculum. These in turn have frequently been accompanied by directly related in-service education activities and necessary resources (such as written materials and audio visual software), so that teachers within the catchment area of the centre in question would have access to actual project materials as well as to guidance on their use in the classroom situation.

Activity provision for probationer teachers has been explored in a variety of ways that have included socials, courses, study groups, seminar situations with pastoral advisers and general information sessions. With the presentation of the report of the James Committee in December 1971([5]) it soon became apparent that a concerted attempt to formalize and extend the pattern of induction activities for probationer teachers was just around the corner. Virtually a year later, a government White Paper([6]) reinforced this notion and endorsed the recommendations of the James Committee regarding the situation of young teachers and the nature and extent of the help required by them. Unfortunately the corridors of education are littered with admirable documents and reports which are never implemented because of the sheer economics governing the situation. Nevertheless, the time may soon prove ripe for the government of the day to change its priorities and, in so doing, accord to education the funds and resources to make a reality of the recommendations in the James Report regarding newly qualified teachers.

During the same period, many centre wardens began to explore the possibility of patterns of location activity for teachers unable for one reason or another, to attend the main teachers' centre. This has proved to be an extremely interesting trend in the development of the in-service education role of the teachers' centre, in that it clearly demonstrates that activities and services can be tailored to the needs of a particular sub-area. In the same way, with such activities being held in different schools within the location area the teachers concerned are encouraged to share their ideas and resources. Thus co-operation can be fostered and the feelings of isolation often manifested in the outlying schools of a centre catchment area can be relieved. This, of course, can have formidable implications for the role of the centre warden and if anything, underlines the need to delegate group leadership where possible.

The nature of involvement in teachers' centre activity

Consideration of the nature and extent of the teaching population's involvement in centre activities can lead to the conclusion that teachers participate at three identifiable levels. Level 1 constitutes the body of teachers who have attended courses, visited exhibitions and gathered ideas. This is not to suggest that visits to the centre are necessarily infrequent, but that they can be described as surface involvement only. At level 2, teachers will have experienced level 1 activities but that their commitment is now deeper is indicated by their involvement in study groups, workshops, projects and working parties. At level 3, elements of the first and second levels will be present but the nature of the commitment is more complex. For some level 3 teachers the emphasis is on centre-based activities; for others, the focus of concern is back in the school. In practice, teachers reaching the third level are usually involved both at the centre and in their schools. At the centre they become group leaders, undertake experimental project work, develop new written materials or software and generally gain an awareness of the educational needs of a whole area. They identify themselves with the centre and some seek further opportunities, perhaps through secondment, for further study, group work or research. In their own schools such teachers provide a classroom example, improve the school's resources and give leadership in curriculum development, whilst at the same time providing liaison between the school and the centre.

Conclusion

I have attempted to establish that the teachers' centre can be a practical means of harnessing local teachers' aspirations to the present and future educational problems confronting society. This assumes that centres are democratically established and sensibly budgeted. As a result of centre activity there are indications that long existing barriers between primary and secondary teachers are beginning to crumble and this development has important implications.

The centre warden's role has emerged as a many-faceted and complex responsibility, while the work of every centre varies in relation to local circumstances. In total the teachers' centre movement possesses a high potential worthy of the support of the local education authorities and the Department of Education and Science.

References

1.   CANE, B., *In-service training,* National Foundation for Educational Research, 1969.

2. TOWNSEND, H. E. R., The in-service training of teachers in the City of Wakefield, unpublished M.Ed. thesis, Manchester University, 1968.
3. BRAND, J. H. B., The in-service education role of the teachers' centre, M.Phil. thesis (unpublished), Nottingham University, 1972.
4. ROSNER, B., *The British teacher centre: a report on its development, current operations, effects and applicability to teacher education in the U.S.,* mimeographed, Office of Teacher Education, City University of New York, 1972.
5. DEPARTMENT OF EDUCATION AND SCIENCE, *Teacher education and training* (the James report), Her Majesty's Stationery Office, 1972.
6. *Education a framework for expansion,* Cmnd. 5174, Her Majesty's Stationery Office, 1972.

CHAPTER 9

The Teacher Centre: Educational Change
Through Teacher Development *

ON 12–14 April 1972 the Policy Institute of Syracuse University Research Corporation and the School of Education of Syracuse University jointly sponsored a conference on "Teacher Centres", loosely defined as new organizational arrangements aimed at "providing local opportunities for teachers to exchange ideas, acquire new skills and further their own development". The Teacher Centre — a social invention distinct from university "refresher" courses, graduate education, "workshops", or other forms of in-service education — had developed with varying degrees of vigour in cultures as diverse as those of Great Britain, the Netherlands, Japan and the United States, and had been seen by its proponents as a practical way to develop teacher skills and knowledge, both in relation to general classroom operation and to the development and use of new curricular experiences and materials.

The conference itself was viewed as a diffusion strategy for "forefront" thinking in relation to the Teacher Centre, seen as a promising social invention aimed at educational change.

In the conference's opening session, Dean David Krathwohl of the School of Education of Syracuse University spoke of the conference as a means of bringing together a critical mass of persons concerned with the in-service education of teachers, with several purposes: to enable interaction and exchange among the participants; to create a readiness for and openness to the teacher-centre concept; to stimulate planning for the diffusion and extension of teacher centres in the United States, with the aid of United States Office of Education support; and (in furtherance of the above end) to display and discuss a diverse set of teacher-centre models.

Those persons invited to the conference ranged substantially outside of the present "invisible college" of persons interested in teacher centres; of the 120

*Adapted from the report of a conference, as described in Chapter 1. The spelling of such words as "centre" and "programme" has been made consistent with English usage.

or so persons present, six were directly involved with teacher centres as such, fourteen with public elementary or secondary educational systems; seven were from professional associations, seventy-nine from institutions of higher education concerned with teacher education (twenty-seven of these from Syracuse University's School of Education), nine from the Policy Institute of the Syracuse University Research Corporation, two from State Departments of Education, and one each from the Ford Foundation and the United States Office of Education. The make-up of the conference membership invites the inference that its organizers saw the main target as persons in the traditional teacher education establishment who might be crucial in decisions to adopt or extend the teacher-centre concept — perhaps more important as a target than teachers as an organized group, other local school district personnel, or State Departments of Education.

I was asked by the conference organizers to serve as "rapporteur" with approximately the following charge, according to Dean Krathwohl's opening remarks: "Consider the theories of change with which you are aware and write your report . . . in such a way that you think this will have some kind of maximum impact beyond this group . . . in such a way that the kinds of things that go on here can be related to theories of change." The conference report was seen as being more than a straightforward summary of the meetings, but as a discussion of the substance of the conference in the context of the literature on change theory, so as to promote meaningful dissemination of the teacher-centre concept to a broader audience.

This essay is the result. It constitutes a review, commentary and reflection on the issues and problems around teacher centres which surfaced at the conference, as seen by a social psychologist with a perennial interest in the processes of educational change.

The conference itself began with the presentation and discussion of several alternative models of a teacher centre, explored a series of questions relating to the promise (or lack of it) of teacher centres as a strategy for educational change, and worked in a series of smaller work groups on such topics as "What are teacher centres for?" and "The politics and economics of teacher centres."

In the remainder of this report, the first major section deals successively with the underlying need for which teacher centres are seen as a solution or remedy; the basic teacher-centre concept, with emphasis on the British version; a review of recent developments in teacher education, with emphasis on the role of the United States Office of Education; a review of the alternative models proposed and discussed at the conference; the highlights of the discussion centering around those alternatives and other, larger issues; and a brief summary of events relevant to teacher centres in the 10 months following the conference.

The second section of the essay constitutes the next chapter, dealing with a series of issues in educational change which either became apparent during the conference itself, or could be seen, on reflection, to have a bearing on the question of the usefulness, viability, and diffusion potential of the teacher-centre concept in American education. There are some concluding comments on the prospects for teacher centres' diffusion and spread in the immediate future.

Teacher Centres

The need

Those interested in this report do not need documentation on the state of affairs in American education. Words like "crisis" and "disaster" were frequently heard during the conference itself. In some sense, the optimism behind the large waves of curricular reform which began in the late fifties after the magical tour of Sputnik, and the giant efforts at educational improvement mounted in the days of the Great Society by large foundations and the United States Office, may be giving way to a sort of existential despair in the face of what seem to be nearly intractable problems in achieving anything like educational effectiveness. Stephen K. Bailey, then Chairman of the Policy Institute of the Syracuse University Research Corporation, said in his opening remarks:

> We have spent money and spent money and spent money; ideas have come up at a great rate; we've had scholars, teachers, and philosophers putting out pamphlets and articles — and somehow things seem to get worse. As a Regent of this State, I have had to face up to the patent failures of our educational system. In this state alone, a third of our young people are tragically behind levels of minimum competence in basic skills; this is particularly true in the inner cities. At the other end of the spectrum, there are literally thousands of gifted individuals, and millions of quite competent youngsters who are totally turned off by the system. At the eleventh and twelfth grade level there is pathological evidence of great inner stress as seen by violence and drug use. Even where there are evidences of success in terms of college entry or post-collegiate occupational and professional skills, we live in a generation filled with inner fears and anxieties, committing all kinds of outrages against each other. We continue with our propensity towards discrimination and prejudice and somehow short-circuit our capacity to move

toward any measure of joyousness in our ordinary lives. So, regardless of the successes one can point to in education, we are facing not only a dangerous but a tragic future unless we can do something responsibly about the condition of our educational system. The entire burden cannot be put on education, alone. It will take political leadership and a variety of shifts in social policy, but this does not absolve us from the responsibility of doing what we can to improve what we are doing, in order to hit hard at some of the things that are destroying us.

Another representative quote comes from a paper prepared prior to the conference by David Selden, President of the American Federation of Teachers, and David Darland, Associate Executive Secretary of the National Education Association:

> American education has now reached a crisis of near-catastrophic proportions. The crisis is not only the racial integration impasse, nor is it only the collapse of our system of school finance; our schools are simply not adequate to meet the demands of our time. The urgency of providing effective education for all Americans, particularly those blacks, browns, and other racial ethnic groups who have been largely excluded from our system, is extreme.

Few would argue with the proposition that the schools, along with most other major American institutions, are in serious difficulty, failing to minister alike to the poor and black, and the rich and white. What is perhaps new in the 1970s is the sense that we may not be able to bring it off — that man and social systems are somehow less improvable and malleable than we had thought — that the reforms discussed in (for example) Silberman's *Crisis in the classroom*([1]) may not only not be achievable in any serious sense — but may not even deal with the fundamental puzzles of educating children from all parts of our social structure for productive, happy lives in post-industrial society. That dark thread of doubt is never very far away in most discussions between educators I have been a party to recently.

The conference, however, can be seen as a conditionally optimistic effort to take another try at the difficulties in American education. Bailey spoke of the "unleashing of spirit and concern and of human regeneration" and suggested that the conference was "seeking to establish some agreement about the psychological truths having to do with human motivation, both student motivation and teacher motivation", and ended with a quotation from H. G. Wells' novel *The New Machiavelli* (1911):

> If humanity cannot develop an education far beyond anything that it now provides, if it cannot, collectively, invent devices and solve problems on a much richer and broader scale than it does at the present time, it cannot hope to achieve any very much finer order or any more general happiness than it now enjoys.

In essence, the teacher-centre concept takes as given the idea that educational reform, or at least educational improvement, can occur through a change in teachers — the operatives of the system, so to speak. Selden and Darland, for example, assert that:

> There is a growing realization that whatever else is needed for effective education, (1) schools cannot succeed without effective teachers, and (2) teachers cannot be effective unless they have confidence that what they are doing is right ... Good curricula, creative instructional materials, efficient organization and management, modern facilities and equipment — all of these contribute to the effectiveness of education, but all depend for their full realization upon the skill, the wisdom, and the commitment of teachers.

In this view, altering the skill, knowledge, and capability of the individual teacher is seen as a high-priority entry point into the improvement of the educational system. Many if not most persons involved in the education of teachers believe that pre-service preparation of teachers can only deal minimally with the skills and competences required. Thus, the core need is seen to be an upgrading or redesign of opportunities for in-service education.

Yet efforts to help practising teachers deal with their own needs for growth, development, and extension have apparently been too centrally focused on college and university courses which are more responsive to the interests and careers of college faculty members than to the actual problems of the redesign of teaching and learning. Alan Brownsword, a conference participant and a United States Office of Education official long involved in the improvement of teacher education efforts, asserts:

> For too long teacher education has been able to define its mission and prescribe its activities without involving in the planning and decision-making process the clients it serves. It has been an island of power, jealously preserving its turf against the encroachments of legislatures, certification departments and the rest of the higher education community. It has seldom gone to school administrators and supervisors, to teachers and students and to parents in the community for their sense of how teacher education can best serve them.

At the conference itself, William Wayson, of the School of Education at Ohio State, said:

> The professionalization of the schools and the colleges of education in America has placed increasing emphasis upon symbols that have no relation to productivity. It has moved the convenience and comfort of the servants into preeminence over the welfare of those they serve. It has corrupted an entire hierarchy of educational agencies into peripheral activities, such as the production of teacher-proof materials, which at best are nibbling at the problem and at worst

are sheer fraud; has raised blind obedience to be a virtue; and has contributed to a maelstrom of needless incompetence, fears of failure, defensive insecurity, and irresponsibility that certainly winds us toward a national disaster.

Rhetoric at this pitch suggests a strong sense that existing institutions, particularly local school districts and institutions of higher education, have been unable to provide serious learning opportunities for experienced teachers at a level which would improve their competence enough to bring about a step change in the effectiveness of the American educational system.

Certain structural aspects of American schools appear to exacerbate the problem. The so-called "self-contained classroom" is asserted to cause isolation and loneliness among teachers, to minimize personal support and what might be called at-the-elbow consulting help, and to discourage the diffusion and sharing of teaching innovations laterally, except on a haphazard basis. Structural efforts to enable peer influence and joint planning, such as team teaching and the multi-unit school, though they have been actively pushed for about a decade, are still represented in the minority of American school buildings.

And from the point of view of those who hold that educational change can best be approached through a process of systematic research, development and diffusion, it must be said that the "delivery" of tested educational products — both those dealing with the substance of the learning experience and the teaching/learning process itself — is not effective. Far fewer of such products are used by far fewer teachers than their developers had hoped would be the case.

In summary, the college and university inability (or unwillingness) to minister to the operating needs of teachers on a day-to-day basis, the structural features of schools which block lateral diffusion, and difficulties in the delivery of educational products to the user (along with supported opportunities for skill development in their use) come together with the diagnosis that little personal renewal seems to be occurring for the average teacher in America — at least on a scale which would permit more than incremental improvement in the functioning of educational systems.

It should be stressed that (to my knowledge) there has never been a serious empirical study of the nature and extent of in-service education activities conducted for practising teachers. The survey being currently conducted by Samuel Yarger of the Syracuse School of Education on a 10 per cent sample of school district superintendents and approximately 600 deans of colleges involved in teacher education programmes should shed light on the current situation. In the meantime, it seems fair to say that the generalizations made above about in-service education efforts would not be contradicted by most practising teachers and school administrators, those who are nearest to the problems involved.

Teacher centres: the British concept

This essay is about the forces affecting the diffusion of a particular social invention, the teacher centre. The version of that invention which appears to have been most focal in the eyes of the conference organizers is that developed in Great Britain, beginning in about 1965, and so it will receive primary attention here.

Editor's Note: *There follows an account, omitted for lack of space, of a paper, "Teachers' Centres: the British Model", read by Audrey Griggs, field officer of the Schools Council. Then Miles takes up the theme of the functions of teachers' centres.*

It can be seen then (contrary to some assertions made at the conference) that the British teachers' centres came out of a strong curriculum-development emphasis and were not simply aimed at "retooling" or up-grading teaching skills or knowledge.

What functions, in general, might a social invention like the teacher centre serve? During the work conference itself, there was a good deal of discussion of this, and two work group sessions were held on the topic "What are teacher centres for?" From this discussion and the other documents available to me, here is a list of possible functions which teacher centres appear to be capable of meeting, at least in the British setting. In principle, there seems to be no reason to believe that such functions could not also be performed in the context of other educational systems, such as our own.

1. *Access to new materials and curricula.* This seems the central function in many British centres, although the emphasis is not on "delivery", to use the American rhetoric, but more on internalization, adaptation, *ownership* of such materials.

2. *Skill learning.* Teachers can use the centres not only to develop process skills, such as those involved in making the shift to "informal" or "open" education, but skills involved in the use of new materials and curricula.

3. *Renewal, rejuvenation.* Centres may serve the function of generating a

new start, a reconception of one's role as a teacher, with an attendant sense of excitement and development.

4. *Materials development.* Teachers may use the centre to develop apparatus or specific materials which they can take back to their own classrooms.

5. *Lateral diffusion of practice.* Centres, through their peer teaching and exchange function, may encourage the swapping of teaching innovations. They may also enable teachers to experience a wider range of role models, and thus to expand their repertoire of teaching strategies and actions.

6. *Elementary-secondary articulation.* Both at the level of subject matter, and of the development and refinement of new teaching strategies, the centres may enable interaction between teachers from segmented or separated parts of the system (e.g. informal education proponents have more opportunity to influence those in secondary schools; traditional subject matter concerns in the secondary schools can inform elementary education).

7. *Reduction of alienation through social support.* Teacher centres may serve to reduce the loneliness of teachers and their distance from each other. In the teacher centre setting, to quote Griggs:

> Teachers' centres are . . . a concept of co-operation . . . In almost all cases, they are seen as places where people involved in the grass-roots work of education, irrespective of title or background, can meet together as professional equals. In such a status-free setting, catharsis is possible.

"One can cry or brag safely", it was suggested in the conference, safe experimentation is possible, and interpersonal linkages and support can develop strongly. It is also possible that such peer support and influence can serve as a countervailing force to the negative influence of peer conformity pressure (at least as experienced in the United States) in which innovative teachers are treated as deviants from general institutional norms.

8. *Trouble-shooting.* Teacher centres may also serve as a setting where short-run helping and problem-solving efforts can occur when teachers encounter unforeseen or uncoped-with difficulties in their day-to-day work. In principle, such efforts can be far more responsive to immediate problematic situations than can a generalized course or workshop. (Griggs' report of the small group discussion at the conference on this general topic said, "Teachers don't want someone who is not at the problem face" (as a helper).)

9. *Personal and professional ego development.* Teacher centres may provide a setting in which teachers can get more fully in touch with themselves as persons, and with their own professional competence. Strengthening

may occur both in one's personal capabilities in dealing with the ebb and flow of classroom events, and in one's professional abilities and knowledge.

10. *Strategic empowerment.* Teacher centres may also provide teachers with a clearer sense of "fate control", the sense that they are able to influence the immediate educational environment and thereby encourage and enable more initiative-taking in change efforts. Because of increased sense of mastery and personal potency, teachers may be more likely to take the actual freedom available to them to bring about changes in their school building beyond the doors of their own classrooms.

Though this is an extensive and even ambitious list, it should be said that it derives almost completely from empirical reports of the ways in which teachers' centres have, in fact, been used in the British setting, and from experience in American centres attempting to use the basic concepts underlying the British model.([2]) Thus, the functions are not arbitrary or fanciful projections, but are estimates by users of actual teacher centres. Few American educators would assert that existing in-service projects, or college and university graduate courses, serve functions like those listed in any very direct and sustained way; few American educators would deny that such functions are crucial in the process of professional renewal. In one sense, the issue becomes one of assessing the degree to which new institutions can be designed in the American setting which would successfully permit such functions to be carried out.

Recent developments in American teacher education, with reference to teacher centres

The Syracuse conference's reaction to and discussion of what might be called the quintessential teacher centre concept (roughly that described above) needs to be understood in the context of some recent history in American teacher education, in which the United States Office of Education and institutions involved in teacher education played a central part. Disentangling the sequence of events from the documents available to me was not always easy, and I should say immediately that I have made no attempt to be comprehensive about the current status of teacher education in America, nor evaluative about the productivity or efficacy of the various experimental programmes which have been developed in the last few years.

During the period 1966 through 1968, a National Defense Education Act

National Committee on Teacher Education (a project subcontracted to the American Association of Colleges for Teacher Education) carried out an extended series of seminars and deliberations aimed at assessing the long-range needs of teacher education in America, an enterprise widely believed, even by its operators, to be in difficulty and in need of reconceptualization. The publication emerging from the committee's work, *Teachers for the Real World*([3]), was in effect a prospectus for the sort of experimental work which deserved Federal funding and support. Certain concepts were developed in the report which bear on the later development of an American version of the "Teacher Centre". One of these was the concept of "training complex":

> ... an entity sufficiently independent of existing institutions to take responsibility for the training of the classroom teacher and establishment of a system that will interact and be interrelated with those institutions that are concerned with teacher preparation on a continuing long-term basis ... The training complex would not try to displace the existing institutions but rather undertake to do what such institutions currently are not doing.([4])

The training complex was later described as "an institution to facilitate co-operation between schools, other human service agencies, universities, colleges, and communities in the improving of pre-service and in-service training of education and other human services personnel". The training complex was seen as distinguishable from other institutions by its central focus on training, the provision for "active participation for all those concerned with decision-making in regard to the training of educational personnel at the policy level", access to school, university and community resources and greater flexibility in employing and utilizing personnel from a variety of backgrounds.

No precise model for the training complex was suggested; it would "be built upon existing structures such as universities and schools, and yet have an independent life of its own".([4]) The desirability of the training complexes being established on "neutral ground" was advocated but not insisted upon, as an acknowledgement of the fact that existing institutions were somehow not, as presently constituted, able to be fully effective in teacher training.

The report also spoke of "educational service districts" — "bold and comprehensive agencies" which would include perhaps ten schools clustered near a university or college with industrial and community representatives participating. Large cities, for example, might have five to ten such educational service districts. The training complex was presumably to be embedded in such a district.

In August of 1969, the United States Office of Education took initiative to create an *ad hoc* National Advisory Committee on Training Complexes to study the concept in more detail, develop alternative models, and begin work with such models on a pilot basis. In January 1970 the United States Office of Education funded a proposal from Clark University (directed by Sol B. Cohen) aimed at carrying out the enterprise.

In examining the committee's final report (and indeed many other documents dealing with the improvement of teacher education), it is difficult to draw the line between what might be called vigorous use of available expertise and conflict of interest. In the opening meeting of the committee (19 Feb. 1970), for example, it was pointed out by the United States Office representative that three committee members were authors of *Teachers for the Real World*; that three people had had experience in TTT (Training Teacher Trainers), an earlier programme of the United States Office of Education; that one member was also heading a parallel thrust committee on the production of "protocol materials", an additional developmental programme in teacher education; and that funding was already contemplated for training complexes at Clark University, in the Appalachian region, in Dallas, and at Stony Brook in New York (representatives of all these institutions were themselves members of the committee). Thus, the committee's deliberations could hardly be expected to move in directions which would be contrary to the vested interests of those present, and could be calculated to induce a flow of funds in favourable directions. Federal agencies naturally need to draw on the expertness and energy of persons who have been most intimately associated with an institution it is hoped can be reformed, but it is not clear from the committee membership or its products that minority views were thoroughly represented or that heresy was encouraged. It is possible that this process also limited the working assumptions of the group in certain ways. For example, notes of the first meeting indicate that training complexes would have to have "national impact and visibility plus initiative from some institution, and have a defined, specific product if they were to be effective". (British teachers' centres do not make such assumptions.) The notes of the second meeting do suggest that a genuine effort was being mounted to design a new institution.

> The objectives of a university and the objectives of a training complex are basically different.... Training complexes, in order to be effective, must train for change. ... Training both pre-service and in-service personnel is not something which higher education can necessarily take on along with the rest of its tasks.... Unlike universities, a training complex carries the idea of direct accountability to the consumers of its services: the community and the personnel it trains.

The committee's Foreword says,

> A new social technique ought to represent a significant difference conceptually from what is going on now. [Up to now, the training of educational personnel] . . . was an amalgam of existing services — a collection of old ways of doing things. A training complex should represent a new way of doing things — not just bits and pieces and stuffing them together.

The intent is clear. However, of the twenty-two persons invited to participate, only three were affiliated with public elementary and secondary school systems, and of these, two proved unable to participate actively. It seems likely under these circumstances that the interests of colleges and universities historically involved in teacher preparation would be more vigorously served than the interests of teachers and others from local education authorities.

The committee produced a descriptive definition of training complexes stressing "neutral ground" and responsiveness to various stakeholders, variety of staff, simply designed training aimed at improvement of performance according to specified criteria, need-based training, the achievement of goals which neither schools nor universities could accomplish alone, a broad trainee population, commitment to constructive change rather than defence of the *status quo*, continuous evaluation and "building upon the strength of creative educational personnel to make 'good' or potentially good educators into excellent educators". A series of guidelines was proposed for evaluating training complexes, as well. This report appeared in July of 1970.

In November of 1970, Dr. Don Davies, Associate Commissioner in the Bureau of Educational Personnel Development, which had sponsored the Training Complexes Advisory Committee, created an internal office of Education Task Force to study the implications, not only of the training complexes report and its teacher-centre implications, but those involved in four other programme thrusts bearing on teacher education (the "Protocol Materials Programme" aimed at documenting teacher-pupil interaction to aid in teacher education; the Training Materials Programme, the Elementary Education Models Programme; and the Performance-based Certification Programme, aimed at designing teacher education programmes anchored around the achievement of specific output criteria in teachers). The Task Force, in addition to its internal discussions, also discussed the concept of the teacher complex (as one of the central features of the programmes being funded) at professional association meetings and special conferences, covering a total of 13,000 educators. As a result of this process and the internal analysis, two major disagreements with the original concept, as recommended by the *Ad*

Hoc Committee, began to emerge. First, "the requirement of 'neutral ground' as a setting for a training complex/teacher centre was seriously questioned. Almost all educational leaders involved in the process agreed that the training complex/teacher centre concept would not work in the present atmosphere of defeated bond issues, rising education costs, etc., unless related to major educational institutions in existence." Second, "it was also felt that it would be impossible, at least in the beginning, to provide for all training needs of educational personnel. Because of this, as well as the fact that in five years 80 per cent of the teachers are already now in the classroom, Task Force 72 determined that first priority be given to in-service training."([5])

Reading the deliberations of the Task Force leads to the inference that certain working assumptions were central to its work. These include: 1. *Delivery orientation*: "Whatever we do, there must be 'something' delivered which is tangible and usable. Planning activities and new design work must be put aside . . . and not be continued as a discrete, self-justifying activity." 2. *Systems orientation.* "It should be possible to develop a series of general category systems to hold, or 'package', components within teacher education approaches and to fund various institutions to develop alternatives within these categories . . . Although different types of management systems could be used, all the alternatives could be made compatible to a master management system which could be used to guide the implementation, monitoring, and replacement of components at both the pre- and in-service levels." 3. *National scope*: "Operationally the plan calls for . . . an established dissemination, diffusion, and product testing network that works on a national basis." 4. *Institutional linkage*: "An established relationship with a large number of schools and universities across the country which satisfies a major requirement for further development, namely, an on-going change agent reasonably set off from the institutional structure." 5. *Materials emphasis*: "Protocol and training materials are . . . probably essential since in-service training involves work with both concepts and skills." The Task Force commented that "outside track" committees and field sessions produced a stress on the urgent need for in-service materials. "The majority of people I interviewed thought that developing new educational organizations and structures would prove useless unless related to a well-conceived curriculum of concept and skills development."

These working assumptions, with the possible exception of the latter one on materials, appear to flow naturally from the interaction that might be expected between a large federal agency, deeply conscious of the need to produce a systematic, well-thought-through plan for the improvement of teacher education, and the members of the existing teacher education establishment (even though it appears that vanguard, forefront member were selected to work on the Advisory Committee). Note that none of the assumptions, with the possible exception of the materials-based one, appear to have been seen as necessary in the development of the British teachers' centre movement. Teachers' centres, for example, are not seen as part of a national network, but as locally managed and as developing uniquely according to the demands of the immediate situation. No overall "management system" is seen as necessary. Perhaps it is not necessary to underline here that the assumptions underlying the training complex-concept are surfaced here, not for polemical purposes, but simply to make them explicit. The question of whether such assumptions are in fact necessary for the survival, viability and diffusion of something like the teacher centre concept in American education remains open.

Task Force 72 members, as Office of Education personnel, acknowledged that it was "composed of in-house people, who after each meeting would return to their bureaucratic surroundings and biases", and so created three "outside track" groups to work with the Task Force. These included a consortium of directors of programmes labelled "elementary models", a study by the Teacher Educational and Professional Standards Group in the Washington State Department of Education, and a Committee on National Programme Priorities and Teacher Education. This latter group, seen as the most salient, was created in March of 1971 to study the five programme thrusts in teacher education and to analyse and discuss relative priorities for funding among them. The committee, though called "outside track", was deliberately designed to include at least one national leader from each one of the five programme thrusts, and although the intent was to have "strong representatives from both the university and the schools", these six committee members included only one public school representative. The committee for National Programme Priorities work was published in 1972. The report is dense, technical, and hard to follow for a reader not closely conversant with teacher education programmes.[4] It reviews four types of possible organizations for supporting competency-based teacher education, including a statewide consortium of regional centres, a centre based in the university, a centre based in school systems, and a technology-based individual study centre. Prototypes of the first three centres were already in existence at that point.

The report also described an overall 5-year programme development plan costing $114 million and outlined a 5-year programme for developing a network of training complexes on a substantially more extensive basis. The first year included a proposal for 100 training complexes, costing $1.5 million each (assuming thirty staff and 150 trainees). Four hundred training complexes were anticipated in the second year, 900 in the third year, 2000 in the fourth year, and 3000 in the fifth year. "Thus, with the programme in full gear, annual costs for the training complexes would be $4.5 billion, exclusive of the $1.5 billion expended for the three-to-four-year college preparation of the beginning teacher". The report went on to say:

> If the schools are to be saved they will be saved first and foremost by the quality of the educational personnel who must lead the educational process. Unless we are prepared to invest in the professional training of the teacher, school reform will continue to be a mirage. To speak of jumping the number of training complexes from 150 to 3000 in a five-year period might appear wishful and naive, but without a *crash programme*, trainees would become isolated and lost. *Our aim is to change the system, not merely inidividuals.* To do so, a mass impact must be made.

The report suggested that the scope and cost of such an effort was not beyond the capacities of this nation.

> What is required is an organizational effort of unprecedented proportions for educators, parallel although hardly on the same scale to what has been done in industry and in the military . . . If federal funding is to be used to spearhead the programmes, bureaucracy must become directly and operationally involved in its implementation . . . the problem is national and the initiative for its solution should be national.

The recommendations section of the report included analysis of the effects (both positive and negative) of the complex institution on a variety of different groups (e.g. colleges of education, faculty, minority groups, professional associations). Teachers in service were not included among the groups analysed.

Later in this analysis it will be suggested that one of the major blocks to successful diffusion of something like the teacher centre concept is the tendency to giantize – to design very large-scale and largely "non-divisible" programmes rather than developing pragmatically and organically from small-scale success experiences, as in the British model. Some events occurring subsequent to the publication of this report are indicative of the political vulnerability of efforts conceived on such a large scale (if presumably accompanied by lack of political clout). In the fall of 1971, United States Commissioner of Education Sidney P. Marland, Jr., announced a massive educational renewal strategy "designed to help American schools reform themselves". The original concept has as many as a thousand renewal sites serving about 10,000 schools by 1986. Money for these sites would be consolidated by the United States Office of Education from a number of existing programmes including Title III ESEA (Elementary and Secondary Education Act, 1965), some portions of EPDA funds (Educational Professions Development Act), the Cooperative Research Programme, dropout prevention and bi-lingual education programmes. That is, programmes originally designated as "categorical aid" would have funds lumped together for discretionary use for massive renewal programmes at each site. Each renewal site would presumably have a "teacher centre" in it. The initial estimations were rapidly scaled down to a total of between 100 and 200 renewal sites with funding of $50 to $85 million for fiscal 1972, moving to a total in later fiscal years of about $300 million. The final 1972–3 scale was for fifty to seventy district renewal sites, with a minimum of one in each state. The proposal, however, was blocked in the Senate by an amendment in late February prohibiting the use of certain categorical funds for discretionary purposes in this manner. A later amendment to the Higher Education Act, June 1972, extended this action. Thus, the Commissioner's effort to produce funding on a scale commensurate with that envisioned by the United States Office of Education and "external" planning groups was successfully blocked by legislators with an interest in maintaining the intent of the original categorical grants.

There were certain consequences of this large-scale developmental process in which the United States Office of Education interacted vigorously with representatives of major teacher preparation institutions.

One major consequence was that the functions proposed for teacher centres ballooned very substantially. An ERIC (Educational Resources Information Centre) summary of information on teacher centres[7] listed a total of twenty such functions, including curriculum development, general change, dissemination, advancement of performance-based teacher education, research, teacher placement, recruitment of para-professionals, evaluation, certification, granting of credit for in-service work, aid to local school districts with large numbers of low-income families, training of personnel to aid at renewal sites, referral, attack on specific school problems using concentration of federal monies, and being the core of an educational renewal site. In July of 1971, Marsh conducted a study[8] to generate a series of critical issues concerning teacher centres to serve as a basis for further planning, including the rationale, functions, structure, staffing, programme financing, generalized ability and viability of teacher centres. Marsh listed a wide variety of possible functions, including pre-service, in-service, para-professional and other training for persons in public schools and a wide variety of other settings; distinguished between training for skill development, self-improvement, competency, judgement and certification; suggested that the training might deal with teaching skills, subject matter, affective learning, instructional skills or others; and raised the issue of what else educational renewal might include in addition to teacher training (e.g. curriculum development, organization development, research, institutional linkage, materials development); examined the issues involved in the centres' functioning as a "delivery system" for the products of educational research and development. Marsh's analysis was deliberately exhaustive, designed as a sort of armature for later planning and analysis, but like the functions list appearing in the ERIC (Educational Resources Information Centre) collection by Poliakoff, dramatizes how many functions and how much surplus meaning came to be loaded on the teacher centre concept as it went through sustained discussion and interaction in the United States Office of Education and stakeholder groups.

A second consequence of the approach taken appeared to be a strong preoccupation with "parity", a label originally designed to cover the idea that all the stakeholders in teacher education, notably universities, school systems (and early on, members of the "community", industrial organizations, etc.) would somehow have a proportionate amount of influence in decision-making. The usual formulation implied, more or less explicitly, that no one group should be able to control the operations of the training complex or training centre. Thus, in effect, the vested interests of various stakeholder groups could serve as a kind of barrier or block against the arbitrary exercise of control by any one group (such as the university). This version of control means, of course, that teachers, in contrast to the situation in Britain, would be unable to exert primary control over the fate of a teacher centre. As might be expected, Selden and Darland attacked the parity concept:

> On the accepted reformist dogma that the system cannot reform itself, the governing board of the teacher centre or renewal centre was originally planned to include representatives of teacher training institutions as well as representatives of the school establishment . . . later, when community leaders demanded a piece of the action, they were also inserted into the plan, and still later some of the proposals called for student representatives as well, . . . We do not believe "parity" in a governing or operating equality sense can have practical meaning in teacher centre governance . . . There should be an advisory council to guide the teacher-controlled board of directors . . . It would include university, community and administration representatives.

Finally, the reader is reminded that a major outcome of the process we have been describing was the funding (in 1970-1) of seven pilot projects in teacher education; during the academic year 1971-2, funded enterprises included four "major pilots", one a school system consortium (San Francisco Bay area), one centred around a state department of education (Rhode Island), one focused around the university's delivery of teacher-centre-like services (Texas), and one centring on a local education authority (Washington, D.C.). The support for these ran from $250,000 to $400,000 a year. There were six "second-level pilots" (alluded to above) charged with "developing various conceptual components of a training complex which could be exported to other complexes," and fourteen "developmental pilots" concerned "essentially with planning for teacher centres to meet specific local needs". Eleven of the sixteen grew out of the prior 2-year experience of the Elementary Teacher Education Models Project. It seems likely that this pattern of support would, once again, be likely to maximize the interests of existing teacher-preparing institutions.

Editor's Note: *After naming some of the "second-level pilots", Miles gives an account of certain "Other American Developments", omitted here for lack of space. He ends this section:*

To summarize briefly: the past few years have evidently been a time of change, invention and turmoil in teacher education. Collaboration between the United States Office of Education and the teacher education establishment has resulted in rather complex, large-scale — even grandiose — plans, protective of existing vested interests, but of uncertain political viability. Teachers and local school administrators have been minimally involved. A fairly wide range of pilot programmes has been funded. The British teachers' centre concept has not, by and large, informed this planning very directly; the number of British-like centres (many linked through the Advisory on Open Education) is on the order of two dozen. The teacher-centre concept is beginning to achieve visibility in educational media.

Alternatives reported and discussed at the conference

Four alternative types of "teacher centre", operative or operable in the American setting, were discussed at the conference. This section outlines the essential features of each briefly. The discussion points raised by conference participants in general sessions and small groups appear in the section following.

The Teachers' Active Learning Centre.([9]) This Centre, seen as an adaptation of the British concept, began as a pre-service mathematics workshop in 1969-70, continued in the following year as pilot voluntary one-night-a-week ongoing workshops on mathematics open to teachers in the San Francisco Bay area, and now operates on a more comprehensive subject-matter basis with a staff of six, open daily and 3 nights during the week. This centre is described by Buxton *et al.* as "an example developed gradually from observation and experiences in England and adapted to the particulars of the participants, the locale, and the events of the San Francisco Bay area." The authors identify the three major components of the concept of the centre as "(1) a physical environment which is stimulating, flexible but structured; (2) a personal climate which is supportive and collaborative; and (3) dependent upon these two factors, the direct interaction of the participants with the environment on a continuing basis through structured activities — namely, active learning".

Implementing this basic concept required, in the authors' experience, five components. First, *"the centrality of teachers,* the central position of teachers in the work of learning and making of curriculum", is seen as the heart of the process by which a teacher who has identified his or her own needs becomes responsible for his/her own learning and action necessary to change. (It also presumably supplies a model for subsequent child-centred functioning in the teacher's own classroom.)

Secondly, *voluntary participation* is seen as a crucial means of reducing or removing resistance to learning and increasing openness for interacting with the structured learning opportunities in the immediate environment.

Third, *"independence* of the centre from the existing structure of educational institutions", location on "neutral ground", the absence of credits or salary increments, and an actual physical separation from school and college environments is seen as essential — presumably to emphasize teacher centrality and voluntarism as features of the learning climate. The neutral ground setting is seen as enabling more risk-taking and testing of alternative responses: "A teacher is better able to interpret the 'mistakes' and alternative responses of the children in his classroom, to use them for increasing individual learning, and to develop a curriculum with extended content possibilities."

Buxton *et al.* acknowledged that the British setting does supply a supportive institutional context (local education authority, inspectorate, Schools Council, Nuffield Foundation, etc.) but took the position that a free-standing institution was more likely at that time (1972) to achieve the hoped-for outcome.

Fourth, *heterogeneity* of participants is seen as necessary to enable cross fertilization and provide more data on alternative approaches to teaching.

Fifth, *focus on curriculum content* is seen as central to the work of the centre.

> The aim is that the activities in the environment of the centre lead a teacher to become a learner and a maker of curriculum sequences – not only of materials, aids, or processes, although these are certainly important. The approach to curriculum is essentially seen as holistic, doing away with "subject-centred" divisions of curriculum and instead promoting the perception of content as experienced in the environment.

The physical setting is "the second floor of a building at the edge of the central city in a light industrial area, with a variety of learning areas reflecting and encompassing the range of curriculum content". The areas "are used in conjunction with one another as a basis for making interdisciplinary connections". The concept of a curriculum "web" with linkages and connections between disciplines, concepts and learners is seen as central to the centre.

Participation in the centre began with about 400 participants during the pilot year and increases through lateral communication, informal word-of-mouth recruiting by participants.

The Buxton paper does not describe governance procedures, but the use of the label "Teachers' " is taken to signify centrality in, if not "ownership" of, the centre by teachers.

While commenting on the similarity of the centre to the British concept, Buxton *et al.* also emphasize three additional characteristics of the ongoing operation: first, a stress on teachers *doing* and *becoming* as the basic requirement for change; second, the importance of a non-judgemental, resource-providing, "peer" attitude on the part of centre staff; and third, the importance of emphasis on the gradual, developmental nature of change in teacher behaviour and curriculum-making. The essential components and characteristics described above were seen by Buxton *et al.* as the major explanations or accompaniments of effective learning situations in the centre. These components were identified through a good deal of formative evaluation — self-scrutiny, assessment, and corrective action — during the developmental period of the centre.

The basic concept, then, is one of a self-evolving centre, with learning processes essentially adapted from those used in British open or informal education. The institution itself is seen as free-standing, not connected structurally to other existing institutions.

The Philadelphia Teacher Centre.[10] Like the San Francisco centre, this centre appears to be centred around "open classroom" and informal education concepts, and developed organically over a period of several years. It is seen as a "self-education endeavour for all who participate in it — teachers, administrators, parents, para-professionals, and future teachers". Children's learning is seen as the prime target; the authors characterize the centre as

> One attempt at reorganizing the resources of the school system and the community to facilitate simultaneous, voluntary learning for all parties involved in the child's school experience. It is focused on creating stimulating environments, producing knowledgeable teacher-learners, strengthening healthy, honest supportive relationships within and across peer groups.

The history of the centre includes a beginning in "learning centre laboratories in inner city elementary schools attended by teachers and children beginning in 1963". After-school workshops were also offered for teachers. Local funding led to Title I support for a larger Learning Centre Project. In 1967 a prototype centre in a school where the children's laboratory was used as a base for a construction carpentry workshop, teachers from that and other schools participated in daytime and evening work; in the following year, with expanding interests, a five-teacher "mini-school" was placed in the centre as a visitation site. The initiation for the mini-school and the teacher centre came from teachers, with the support of the Philadelphia Curriculum Office. Support came from the Early Childhood Education Study and, increasingly, from the District itself. Released time attendance for teachers, especially those in kindergarten, became more typical. In 1968 the centre moved into the Durham Child Development Centre, a "womb-to-tomb" public school, including components of a programme for junior-high-school-age mothers, an infant-care centre, a Head-Start unit, an ungraded, informal elementary school, and the office of the Learning Centres Project, along with the teacher centre itself (workshop, math lab, library, lounge, dining room, kitchen).

Approximately 10,000 teachers have passed through the centre during its life. The current rate is 5000 or 6000 per year.

The activities emphasized are "making equipment and learning aids of teacher choice for classrooms, sharing ideas among teachers, learning mathematics and science by laboratory methods, and using the mini-school to get models for reorganizing the classroom physically, pedagogically, and content-wise".

Inferentially, certain concepts seem essential to the functioning of the centre, as presented in the papers read at the conference.

1. *Multi-age, multi-role environment.* The mix of persons and functions in the centre and the use of the building as a "community for all ages of man" seem central. Even the hallways "reflect in their 'street life' " the needs of the adjacent homes. Older children aid younger ones; children use the facilities of the Teacher Centre and its shop; teachers and parents mix with the children; classrooms are constantly being visited by other teachers; administrators are involved in planning for the extension of similar environments to other parts of the system.

2. *Physical construction.* Both in the shop and in the Teacher Centre space itself, there seems to be a good deal of emphasis on the construction of materials and spaces:

> "Most of the conversion of the facilities, from their bleak look of an old, typical, inner city elementary school to the new imaginatively redesigned spaces, was done by the staff and parents themselves . . . materials were bought, "found", or donated . . . the rehabilitation . . . represents . . . the living proof of what a school can do on a grass-roots level to change itself when it has an idea.

Donald Rasmussen's accounts of life in the workshop focus very strongly on the construction of classroom furniture, teaching equipment, and other objects, as a sort of symbol of personal empowerment and, perhaps, the durable embodiment of action on the part of teachers, many of whom had never engaged in such activity.

3. *Participant initiation.* As in open classrooms, there is a great deal of emphasis on self-selection and voluntarism in the choice of learning environment, learning goals, projects carried out, etc.

4. *Peer teaching.* A good deal of lateral sharing among teachers and other role occupants is seen as crucial.

5. *Support for change motivation.* Donald Rasmussen says,

> Rarely have we found teachers unwilling to consider making some changes in
> their classrooms or in their methods, and most administrators in Philadelphia are
> generally supportive of many classroom changes teachers would make. Yet it is
> difficult, often-times impossible, to take an initial step in any direction for lack of
> support within the system.

The centre offers support by providing materials and encouragement for
the immediate execution of ideas, by planning with the administrators of
schools, and by follow-up consultation in the teachers' own schools (an increase in this activity is seen as necessary).

The approach throughout is strongly inductive: in describing a learning
encounter with an initially resistant teacher, Donald Rasmussen commented,
"The philosophy can come long afterwards — sometimes weeks afterwards."

The centre appears to be tenaciously built into the Philadelphia system
(e.g. has survived four superintendents). Certain functions have been added
during the development of the centre, including that of field placement for
para-professional pre-service and in-service student teaching, production and
dissemination of curriculum sequences and materials, slides and videotapes;
and the staging of workshops outside the building for informational purposes.
As with the San Francisco Centre, the approach has essentially been organic
and developmental, with a good deal of emphasis on self-selection and voluntarism on the part of participants: "From the beginning, we have been committed to teachers who wish to help themselves." There is strong emphasis on
teacher initiative and individualization:

> We are a kind of open clssroom for adults — a demonstration of one of the
> alternatives teachers consider for themselves . . . Our workshop began with a very
> simple objective — to help teachers get and make the things *they* wanted, the
> help *they* needed to work more effectively with *their* children. We entered *their*
> classroom with *their* consent to effect the changes *they* desired. This objective,
> supporting teachers no matter what they want, remains the same today as
> yesterday.

In contrast to the San Francisco Centre "the workshop is not on 'neutral
ground' "; though it is centrally designed around furthering teacher development, role representatives of many other sorts can enter on their own terms.
Note, however, that there is no formal structural linkage to teacher-preparing
institutions as such.

Governance procedures are not described.

Oakland Schools.([11]) Oakland Schools is a county school district in

Michigan, with headquarters based in Pontiac. The model described by Watson does not represent an adaptation of the British teacher centre model, but describes a rather sophisticated and professionalized consulting and training operation serving twenty-eight constituent public school districts, including 373 schools and 66 non-public schools. With an operating budget of approximately $2 million, it carries out functions such as "stimulating curriculum innovation, improvement and evaluation, facilitating the learning potential of individual youngsters, and carrying out the business and housekeeping aspects of school plant". There is a staff of 130 sited in a $4.7 million building who essentially respond to problems and needs surfaced by participating school districts and buildings, which cannot be handled locally. The services carried out include training, consulting (including "aggressive" consulting in which stimulation of awareness and need for assistance is present), programme design, and the encouragement of cross-fertilization across districts. In the physical setting are included a library, ERIC (Education Resources Information Centre) information, a media display centre, and meeting rooms.

Funds come from local property taxes, and governance is by an appointed school board.

The centre can, if wished, offer courses subassigned to a local university with academic credit.

Projects worked on have included designing an objectives-based set of curricula for vocational high schools; projects in junior high school science; redesigning and retraining personnel for a lower grades reading programme, developing an objectives-based management and curriculum system; in-service courses in social studies. Annually, about 40,000 people use the centre's services.

Though Oakland Schools stresses the principle of voluntarism and choice in the projects undertaken, the choice involved usually appears to be a "corporate" one, in that units, groups, or building staffs are the usual clients of the centre's work, rather than "individuals" as such. Oakland Schools is not on "neutral ground", but a central part of the corporate life of the school systems which it serves (for example, it supplies services including computing, library, printing, and delivery trucks, as well as administering over $7.5 million of special and vocational education funds beyond its regular operating funds). The general approach taken appears to be planful, sophisticated, technically excellent. One does not detect a philosophical commitment to the form or substance of the educational enterprise similar to that present in the

San Francisco and Philadelphia Centres; Oakland Schools' mission appears to be essentially technical facilitation of movement toward objectives to which constituent schools and subsystems are committed.

The Teacher Education Centre. Collins' paper[12] describes a generalized model for university-school collaboration (with State Department of Education participation) in the enterprise of pre-service and in-service education. From the paper itself, it is not clear how much of the model is currently in actual operation. The Scholastic *Teacher Guide to Teacher Centres* (1972) indicates that the centre was then servicing teachers from the Liverpool and Central Square school districts, who have membership in the centre. The focus is reported to be on improvement of instructional skills through workshops and informal discussion groups.

The Syracuse Centre, as indicated earlier, received developmental support from the United States Office of Education. The basic concept of the model also appears to have been in place at the University of Maryland in 1969, in collaboration with the Montgomery County Public Schools.

A "Teacher Education Centre" is defined as the "vehicle or means by which the profession can study, analyse and develop teaching and the effects of teaching for the purpose of achieving improved learning for both that teacher and the student." The essential concept is that of "partnership" among various stakeholders in the educational system; the model stresses

> the importance of bringing together participating organizations into a functioning partnership . . . true co-operation in teacher education is a sine qua non . . . the essence of true co-operation is joint decision-making with the resultant concepts of joint responsibility and joint accountability . . . It draws upon the resources of organizations and institutions which have historically, traditionally, and even legally had some responsibility for teacher education over the years.

Governance is seen as involving a board drawn from "representatives of the teachers, administrators, college personnel, Teacher Association, State Departments of Education, even students that might be in the programme and community members from the school system".

Another core assumption appears in a comment by Collins: "The teacher centre is designed to meet the needs of a teacher in self-improvement while at the same time creating effective learning environments for students . . . That, for me, means that it has to be in the schools; it has to be there where the children are." Note that the San Francisco centre, for example, did not make the same assumption, though committed to very similar purposes.

Such a centre is described as a cluster of geographically contiguous schools

— an environment where teaching and the effects of teaching can be studied. Organizationally, it is seen as a partnership between a school system, institutions of higher education, together with professional associations and the State Department. The centre provides laboratory experiences for student teachers and pre-professionals, along with in-service programmes and activities for existing school system staff.

The functions or purposes served by the Teacher Education Centre include the design, implementation, and evaluation of model teacher education programmes; integration of "theory with practice on campus with the off-campus, and pre-service with the in-service"; individualization of professional development; studying teaching and supervision; and planning and conducting research.

Activities proposed for the centre include in-service workshop seminars and programmes developed responsively to "needs clearly delineated by the centre's staff", designed to promote the study of teaching, including "the teaching act, specific teaching behaviours, instructional strategies, curriculum evaluation and redesign". Other activities include consultation by college personnel on curriculum and teacher education problems; teacher supervision of pre-professionals (student teachers); development of curriculum centres, laboratories, and resource centres; validation and dissemination of promising innovations developed elsewhere; work with teachers in updating content and methodology in specific instructional areas. "Close association between the college faculties and the public school faculties leads to the involvement of public school personnel in professional courses, and the college personnel more vitally become a part of the curriculum in on-going programmes for public schools."

The rationale underlying the Teacher Education Centre includes two basic principles:

> (1) Those who will be affected by the change have to accept it and be involved in it, become agents of change rather than being objects of change; and (2) the necessity for a vehicle or mechanism to facilitate the desired change and enable it to endure the pressures of opposition and rejection — a vehicle facilitating and promoting desired change.

Collins' presentation linked the proposal to the general concept of educational renewal (the model is generally similar to the United States Office of Education concept exemplified in the Dallas Renewal Centre). He suggested:

> Every renewal programme must begin by specifying the competencies and criteria against which classroom performance will be judged [and suggested that]

Teachers themselves would have to play a very significant role in specifying these competencies and finding out these criteria . . . By the same token, they should also have a determining role in designing programs intended to help meet these criteria.

In spite of such claims, however, given the joint governance of the proposed centre and the strong inclusion of teacher-preparing institutions' interests, it is hard to escape the implication that the "Teacher Education Centre" is more designed to serve the interests of institutions than the interests and growth needs of particular teachers, which assume such centrality in (for example) the Teachers' Active Learning Centre and the Philadelphia Teacher Centre. The Teacher Education Centre, as described here, is a classic model of inter-institutional linkage, avoiding the "neutral ground" concept while utilizing the expertise and knowledge (and maintaining the vested interests) of participating institutions.

Research was cited on the effects of the Maryland programme built on the model, showing that student teachers placed in teacher education centres had more favourable attitudes toward supervision, felt their supervisors used clearer evaluative criteria, participated more widely in the total school programme, used a wider variety of instructional approaches, and used more indirect and pupil-centred teaching styles. No data were reported on the consequences of teacher education centre participation for experienced teachers, however.

This concludes the account of the four models for teacher centre presented at the conference — two centres rather like the British concept, one large consulting and service-supplying agency, and one United States Office of Education supported centre linking teacher-preparing institutions and users. What else occurred at the conference?

Discussion themes

During the conference, a wide variety of viewpoints about the nature, implications, desirability, feasibility, and wisdom of teacher centres — either on the British model or a vigorously redesigned American model — took place both in the large group via discussant reactions, in question periods, and in small group sessions.

Editor's Note: *The summary of discussion themes presented by Miles "to acquaint the reader with the flavour of what ensued" has regrettably had to be omitted for lack of space. Miles ended this section in the following way:*

Concluding remarks

Stephen Bailey, in closing the conference, said,

> Hopefully out of the discussions . . . we'll come to a better understanding of each other and of the kinds of cross-forces and pressures and value systems that are in the middle of all this. [The issue is] the spirit underlying teacher centres . . . the notion that you can begin to dignify still further the role of the teacher and give some responsibility [to him or her].

Bailey went on to quote Emerson: "Every great and lasting moment in human history has been the triumph of some enthusiasm", and hoped that,

> with all the necessary analytical and oftentimes contentious controversy, we don't lose our respective enthusiasms . . . It is terribly important that whatever sparks of energy and concern we have are cultivated and maintained and not stepped on.

Contrasting large-scale, federally supported efforts with small, organically evolving centres, Bailey, to illustrate his "philosophical preference" for the latter approach, quoted William James:

> I am done with big institutions and great success. I am rather for those molecular, moral forces that reach from individual to individual and that creep through the crannies of the world like the capillary oozing of water or the action of soft rootlets, but which, if you give them time, will rend the hardest monument of man's pride.

Though Bailey's preferences were clear, it was certainly not clear that everyone in the conference shared them — and it is not fully clear whether "molecular, moral", person-centred approaches to educational reform are likely to be more or less profitable than large-scale, institutionally mounted efforts. We shall naturally return to this question in the latter part of this paper. [*i.e. in Chapter 10, Ed.*]

Summary of relevant events since the conference

The conference took place in a shifting context of federal, state and local support for the teacher centre concept. Some events which occurred through the spring of 1973 are outlined here.

Legislative finding. As indicated earlier, in February 1972, Senator Cranston had introduced an amendment to the Education Act prohibiting the proposed consolidation of funds from such areas as dropout prevention and bilingual programmes to permit substantial educational renewal programmes in a number of sites (including teacher centres). The amendment passed at that time, apparently largely because of senators' resistance to the loss of categorical aid funds, was confirmed with the passage of the Act in June 1972. The creation of the National Institute of Education, the transfer of many research functions from the United States Office of Education to it, and the corresponding reduction in funding for the National Centre for the Improvement of Educational Systems (which was responsible for the renewal strategy) and the generally bleak picture of educational support in the January 1973 Nixon administration budget appeared to make the original vision of widespread funding for educational renewal and continued support for teacher centres (USOE style) much less likely. Interviewed in February 1973, two United States Office of Education officials differed among themselves as to the likelihood of any further support for the renewal sites concept; the probability was estimated at from zero to 40 per cent.

Cuts were made in the budgets of the four major teacher centres (Texas, Rhode Island, San Francisco Bay area and Washington, D.C.); each had been receiving about $400,000 annually, except for Rhode Island (about $250,000); cuts on the order of one-third were made for the three larger-funded centres. Of the four centres, only the Texas Centre appears to have developed a vigorous ongoing programme providing direct service to teachers; the three other sites appear to have been largely preoccupied with developmental and organizational matters and have suffered from shifts in United States Office of Education policy, monitoring personnel and indeed the concept of just what the teacher centres should be like.

One United States Office official, citing such efforts as the Appalachian Training Complex,([13]) the Portal Schools in Philadelphia and Atlanta, and the Learning Exchange Advisory Centre, felt that the six pilot projects and the fourteen "developmental" projects were operating reasonably well, but that the likelihood of forward support for them was relatively minimal.

Secretary Richardson, prior to his departure for the Pentagon, developed a so-called "megaplan" for streamlining and reorienting his Department of Health, Education and Welfare. According to a United States Office of Education official, the central concepts in the education section of the plan emphasize assistance to individuals through grants, loans, and higher education tuition scholarships, revenue sharing, and, to a considerably lesser extent, "skill-building" activities involving the improvement of existing "service delivery systems" and manpower development. Past efforts to provide substantial grants for educational "renewal" had suffered, it was felt, from mixing general institutional support funds for ongoing programmes with funds for institutional change and development. The support in the so-called "megaplan" for the educational renewal effort was, however, minimal.

NEA initiative. In December of 1972 the National Educational Association announced a plan for the development of a "Teacher Centre network".([14]) The NEA would provide planning assistance during the fiscal year 1973-4 for the development of up to four teacher centres, supported by public funds and initiated by local teacher associations. Plans for "co-operation" with other existing teacher centres were also outlined. The four National Education Association Teacher Centres were seen as becoming operational by 1 September 1974. Considerable emphasis was placed in the *Prospectus* on teacher initiation and operation of the centres, absence of "predetermination", and the development of centre programmes out of "real teaching needs and problems as identified by teachers in a particular place". The *Prospectus* also stressed that "the NEA will encourage and promote teacher centres *only* in those locations where teachers have their working conditions defined in a collective bargaining agreement, signed jointly by the local school board and teachers' association". Teachers are seen as "negotiating through their associations with local and/or state school systems for designation of public funds for centres", and it was stressed that funding should not "come from or be provided at the expense of the present level of support for instructional programmes for students".

The *Prospectus* suggests that rewards to teachers will come from the fact that "learning while teaching will become a part of the teacher's regular job, not an addition to it", but it goes on to add that "also a practical incentive system must be built into contracts to provide for such things as college credit, certification, renewal, and salary increments. There should, however, be safeguards to insure that the programme of a teacher centre is not meant to meet rigid certification or salary requirements."

Diffusion extent. How many teacher centres, actual operating organizations, now exist? The National Education Association *Prospectus* suggests that about fifty centres of various types are in operation. As already indicated, the *Scholastic Teacher Guide to Teacher Centres* lists forty-seven as of late 1972; of these, my estimate was that twenty-nine were "British-like" and nine were of the expanded, United States Office of Education-supported type.

An informal estimate in the spring of 1973 from Albert Leonard, aiding Sam Yarger in an intensive questionnaire study of in-service programmes aimed at 1200 school superintendents and 600 teacher education deans, was that no more than two dozen teacher centres roughly designed on the British model existed in the United States.

Thus, while some British-like prototypes and some expanded/adapted American teacher centres are in operation, the diffusion of the concept and its embodiment in actual organizations has been extremely limited to date, probably touching less than 1 per cent of school districts and institutions of higher education alike.

References

1. SILBERMAN, C. E., *Crisis in the classroom,* Random House, 1970.
2. MOORHOUSE, E., The philosophy underlying the British primary school, in ROGERS, V. R. (Ed), *Teaching in the British primary school,* Macmillan, 1970.
3. SMITH, B. O. *et al., Teachers for the real world,* American Association of Colleges for Teacher Education, Washington, D.C., 1968.
4. COHEN, S. B., A five-year goal for training complexes, in ROSNER, B. (Chairman), *The power of competency-based teacher education,* Allyn & Baron, 1972.
5. All quotations are from *Task Force 72,* Final Report, some selected Sections, Draft Version; a mimeographed, unpaged United States Office of Education report, apparently prepared about July 1971.
6. MARLAND, S. P., A U.S. plan for education renewal, *New York Times Annual Education Review,* 10 Jan. 1972.
7. POLIAKOFF, L., *Teacher centres: an outline of current information,* ERIC Clearing House on Teacher Education, Washington, D.C., May 1972.
8. MARSH, D. D., *An explication of issues surrounding teacher centres and educational renewal sites,* Teaching Research, Oregon State System of Higher Education, 1971.
9. BUXTON, A. P., *et al., The Teachers' Active Learning Centre, an American adaptation of British teachers' centres,* mimeographed, copyright, TALC, 1972.
10. Description based on RASMUSSEN, L. and RASMUSSEN, D., *The Philadelphia Teacher Centre, 1972.*
11. From WATSON, R. P., *The county model,* mimeographed, 1972.
12. From COLLINS, J. F. (Ed.), *The Teacher Education Centre: a unifying approach to teacher education,* Syracuse School of Education, Syracuse University, mimeographed.

13.   FUTCHS, M., *A description of the Appalachian State University Training Complex,* Boone, N.C., Working Paper 4, June 1972.
14.   NEA TEACHER CENTRE PROJECT TEAM, *NEA Teacher Centre Network: a prospectus,* Washington, D.C., December 1972.

CHAPTER 10

Reflections and Commentary on the Syracuse Conference on the Teacher Centre

THE teacher centre is, as suggested earlier, a social invention grounded on the assumption that improvement in education can occur if teachers' attitudes, skills, and knowledge are improved. The concept, as developed in Britain, appears reasonably productive in accomplishing the basic objective of teacher "renewal" and has diffused reasonably rapidly there (on the order of 500 centres in 5 years). The inquiry question at hand is: What will happen to the teacher centre concept and its embodiment in the American educational setting? Answers to that question depend on a series of issues in educational change which are discussed below. The intent here is to be deliberately rambling and reflective, not encyclopedic — or even systematic; rather, the effort is to look through a series of different lenses at the teacher centre and its promise (or lack of promise) as a means for accelerating desirable change in American education.

The teacher centre as a diffusible innovation

One basic lens through which to view the teacher centre is that offered by classical diffusion and innovation theory.([1]) This general style of viewing the teacher centre is rooted in the notion that it is essentially a specific, transferable innovation (invention, practice, cultural artifact) which arose in one social system and is adoptable (with varying amounts of adaptation and alteration) in another. Using this lens, or way of viewing the teacher centre, generates certain sub-issues.

British-American differences. One, of course, is whether "transfer" from one system to the other is possible (a process usually labelled as easy and straightforward by advocates and as completely impossible by opposers). The comment of the United States Office of Education official who said flatly that "we have little to learn from the British teachers' centre" and the slightly bent adaptions of the British model described in Chapter 9 (Philadelphia and San Francisco) represent opposite answers to this question.

Presumably, the likelihood of transfer and the relative amount of energy associated with the transfer process are, in part, a function of perceived differences between the two social systems. In the conference discussion group on politics and economics, it was suggested that certain differing cultural assumptions about change were being overlooked. Mary Lela Sherburne, of the Association for Renewal in Education, suggested that British approaches to change were essentially organic and pragmatic in nature, stressing an incremental, adaptive point of view, and that they stressed the centrality of the development of an informal, "living system", with a basic mission of "ministering to people". In contrast, she suggested that American assumptions about change are essentially mechanistic, involving the refinement or development of a part of a larger system, followed by "plugging it back in to see if it works" (examples included the development of national curriculum materials, school decentralization, and American versions of teacher centres).

In reading accounts of the British teachers' centre movement and the various materials on United States Office of Education financed teacher centres, one is struck by substantial differences in scale — perhaps not wholly attributable to the differences in scale of the two countries. Modest, pragmatic, decentralized, effect-responsive enterprises at the local level seem more preferred in Great Britain; the American tendency is more typically to plan large-scale enterprises, set ambitious targets (e.g. 3000 "teacher training complexes" in 5 years; or the projection of 1000 major educational renewal sites, each spending nearly a million dollars), and to be preoccupied with the design of an overall management and control structure for the operation.

Some of the rhetoric at the conference itself seemed to reflect this giantizing or ballooning tendency, emerging in all-or-none, monolithic formulations, like "We should not rush headlong into teacher centres as a solution to all the problems of American education", and "Teacher centres are not a panacea". It seems likely that the effort to overdesign and expand the scale of proposed diffusion, prior to a pragmatic determination of just how well teacher centres work, and what for, may serve as a substantial barrier — both to legislative support (note the failure of renewal legislation) and to immediate adoption, since "divisibility" of the innovation is relatively low under such circumstances.

The differences between British and American culture, and the educational systems imbedded within them, are not minor. Grannis([2]) suggests that British culture is more individualistic and less peer-oriented than American — but that the individualism takes place in a clear context of sharp adult/child differentiation. Yet, such cultural differences do not seem to be over-determining: Grannis points out that "the disposition of informal British teachers to *listen* to children and to respond to what children are actually saying and doing in their classroom activity is wrought by training and counsel in the teeth of British adult/child practices, generally". He goes on to say

> American change agents would do well to pay close attention to how the British educator brings this about. It seems to me that the most successful advocates of open classroom practices in America today are those who have underplayed the importance of child development theory and who have stressed the necessity of supporting teachers' growth in the same practical and sympathetic ways that children's growth is to be supported.

On top of this, Grannis believes that "pedagogy has been less politicized in Britain than in America", and cites the independence of the national inspectorate, the authority of the head, both in relation to the inspectorate and to local parents, and the authority of the local school to determine its own curriculum.

At various points during the Syracuse conference, it was also suggested that British educators were more dignified, more professionalized, more likely to engage in voluntaristic change efforts, and less vulnerable to community or environmental pressures than their American counterparts. Some of this may be the usual New World sense of inferiority at work, but one senses some objective differences as well. For example, it seems clear that the British head is more educationally and less managerially oriented than the American principal, and that the economic and status differences between teachers and administrators are less in Britain than in America.

Perhaps one can conclude that the supposedly pragmatic, developmental British style, along with what Grannis suggests is a strong deference to the independent authority of government (that is, more insulation and protection for the teacher's expertise), can account not only for the relatively rapid diffusion of teacher centres but the presence of informal or open education practices in about 25 per cent of British primary schools.

Rogers([22]) suggests that informal education has prospered in the British educational system primarily because of close staff-head co-operation, the presence of capable teachers (background and quality is assumed to be somewhat higher than in the United States), and very creative use of materials, along with vigorous government support (e.g. the Plowden Report). It is possible that the same general forces could be seen as supporting the teachers' centre movement itself. Rogers suggests that informal, open education is less likely to diffuse well in America because of heavier orientation to disciplines, greater reliance of teachers on standardized support materials, such as manuals ("sneaky telling"), a radically lower aesthetic emphasis on the part of teachers (less interest in art, music, movement), the American split between kindergarten and primary education and (as we have suggested) substantially more pressure from parents and community for teachers to aid children in the academic race. Since in some respects, the British teachers' centres can be seen as "open education for adults", Rogers' analysis of general educational differences retarding the American acceptance of open education for children may be applicable to the explanation of diffusion rates for the teacher centre invention.

More generally, however, the issue is not whether a practice developed in one culture is transferable or usable elsewhere on a go/no-go basis, but how much adaptation and transformation will have to occur before the practice is usable in the receiving system. In a real sense, cultural differences are not (contrary to the usual assertion) a factor making diffusion impossible; they constitute, in fact, the preconditions for it. The British teacher centre, developed in a supposedly less-politicized, professionally protected, and legitimated educational setting, is not non-diffusible to American settings because of these antecedents, but in fact has considerable promise for a setting where teachers feel vulnerable, unsafe, coerced into "professionalism", and the like. The attractiveness of the "neutral ground" concept, and voluntarism in teacher centre attendance are attractive: American teachers can act "as if" they were more expert, professional, and protected from citizen and parent pressures than in fact is the case.

Innovation properties affecting diffusion. What features in an innovation make it more or less likely that diffusion from one system to another will occur? Barnett[3] speaks of compatibility/incompatibility, the question we have been dealing with above, but suggests that this is not nearly enough to explain diffusion. Additional factors, such as efficiency, cost, relative advantage, hedonistic pleasure, ease or difficulty in mastery of the innovation, and penalties that may be incurred by adoption are at work.

To review Barnett's list briefly: teacher centres do not appear to be strikingly incompatible with the structure of American education. Their relative efficiency is unknown. Financial costs, it was suggested at the conference, are not larger than the (admittedly vague) figure already being spent for in-service education by individuals and school systems; they purportedly offer advantage over the existing and widely damned structure of in-service education. The fact that teacher centres are, in many accounts, intrinsically pleasureful (especially where new materials, equipment, and artistic production are central) is not at all minor. Under "hedonistic" pleasure Barnett refers not only to how enjoyable a particular innovation is but whether it is exciting, offers more freedom of action than its predecessor, is more relaxing, and reduces fears. Such "non-utilitarian" features of innovations, he suggests, are rather important in diffusion, in comparison with whether the innovation is seen as "getting the job done". In some respects, the teacher centre, at least as reported during the conference, does have intrinsic satisfactions of this sort.

Rogers([4]) suggests that certain characteristics of innovations are centrally related to their diffusibility: he names relative advantage, compatibility, complexity, divisibility (degree to which the innovation can be subdivided or tried on a small scale or pilot basis), and communicability. My own impression, in passing, is that such properties (of the innovation itself) are likely to have far more weight at the early stages of adoption (awareness, interest, pretrial evaluation) than during the actual trial and adoption stages. It might be commented here that the complexity and divisibility of the classic teacher-centre concept appear to be relatively low and high, respectively: the idea of learning opportunities built around teacher needs on an organic, developmental basis is a relatively simple, even primitive, one in contrast to the existing structures for in-service education and accreditation. There is no inherent reason why such models could not be tried, as they have been in Britain, on a small-scale, local, experimental basis. It is ironic that the energy invested by the United States Office of Education and the American teacher education establishment has, in effect, moved toward complexifying and making *less* divisible what is essentially a rather simple and straightforward idea. For example, the "ballooning" of teacher centre functions from the initial idea of in-service development of teachers by adding such functions as dissemination, advancement of performance-based teacher education, teacher placement, recruitment of para-professionals, certification, and the like makes it considerably more difficult to get a teacher centre into operation — not only because of the extra work load that must be carried but because so many additional constituencies and constraints must be dealt with.

Properties of receiving systems. In general, it is usually safe to predict that properties of an innovation, as such, have a good deal less to do with its diffusion or adoption than do properties of the receiving system — its general innovativeness, its economic constraints and incentives, and the special properties of adopting units, such as size, autonomy and linkage to other parts of the system. Considering, for the moment, schools to be the adopting unit for teacher centres, what are some relevant properties which could affect diffusion? Elsewhere[5] I have emphasized factors such as goal ambiguity with resultant system-environment conflict, low interdependence (Bidwell's "structural looseness"[6]), vulnerability; and non-competitive position *vis-à-vis* the environment (with resultant under-investment in innovation and development, and lagging response to long-run environmental change). Sieber[7] also stresses vulnerability and goal diffuseness, but adds a feature he calls "quasi-professionalism" (implying both low levels of autonomy and a weak knowledge base) which encourages "status insecurity, ritualistic use of procedures, and scanty communication among staff members".

Are such features of schools likely to promote or retard diffusion of teacher centres? The answer is by no means clear. Compare Schmuck and Miles:[8]

> This analysis may be viewed as gloomy; the properties of schools cited appear to make the likelihood of serious improvement small. We do not think so. These properties do account, in part, for the low rates of change characteristic in education, but they also provide clearly defined change goals and "leverage points". . . . For example, it has been our experience that many teachers, because of their individual roles (characterized by a low level of interdependence), often feel isolated, alienated, and lonely. . . . Interventions which increase interdependence and sharing among teachers often liberate a good deal of energy, lift morale, and make the school an exciting place in which to work.

In this sense, teacher centres might well diffuse rapidly, once launched, since they could help to correct, or at least soften, some of the systemic properties of American schools. The Miles and Sieber analyses suggest that teacher centres will be more likely to diffuse to the degree that they increase expertness and a sense of autonomy for teachers, and help to decrease vulnerability to the surrounding environment. Note that this prediction goes counter to the advocacy heard at the conference (that "community involvement" was essential). Given the systemic properties discussed here, successful diffusion of teacher centres in America will probably depend largely on their ability to provide a safe, protected site for the enhancement of teacher skill and inventiveness, and their ability to buffer the teacher from community pressures.

Moving back a step to look at the American educational system beyond the immediate school, one can predict the vested interests of teacher-preparing institutions (and to some extent, state departments of education) will loom very large in deciding such matters as how rapidly the British-style teacher centre will diffuse, and whether whatever new institutions for teacher development which emerge are largely owned and operated by those they are designed to benefit — or are aimed at solving a much larger range of problems, such as the preservation of the educational and financial health of colleges and universities, supporting/extending the existing structures for certification and accreditation of teachers, and the like.

Redesign. One final issue, given the innovation/diffusion perspective we are considering, is that of just how much transformation is necessary in the British teachers' centre concept for it to be viable and healthy in the American system (assuming that reconnaissance suggests that such diffusion is a desirable outcome). Innovations are always transformed to a greater or lesser degree during the diffusion process. The issue is the extent of such transformation, and whether the innovation is pushed so far out of shape that its supposed goals are not achieved. Transformations usually mean that the achievement of a new set of goals not originally envisioned in the donor system is deemed important in the receiving system. It may well occur that movement toward these new goals blocks the achievement of originally intended goals. For example: it seems likely that the British teachers' centre, which deliberately has little or no function in accrediting teachers or aiding salary advancement, is for that reason particularly helpful in reinforcing professional autonomy, expertness, and self-renewal motivation. If the teacher centre concept emerging in American education turns out to have strong components of certification or accreditation, and if participation in teacher centres is tied, like present in-service courses, to movement through salary schedules, it seems quite likely that some of the original goals will not be achieved.

What sort of redesign work needs to be done during the diffusion and adoption process? Judson([9]) suggests that British-style centres (emphasizing self-determination, self-selection, and active personal participation by teachers), to operate effectively in America, will need other support structures such as advisory and consulting services, American-specific resources (such as protocol materials, ERIC (Educational Resources Information Centre) access, computer-assisted instruction), and a capability for educational organization development. He also suggests the development of a voucher plan for teachers, in which in-service education vouchers, controlled by the teacher, could be "spent" in teacher centres, colleges and universities, or elsewhere.

One had the impression at the Syracuse conference that substantially more energy went into either (a) denying that the British model had any applicability or (b) superficially redesigning it in ways which protected the interests of colleges and universities rather than those of teachers — or even of the schools themselves. This was, perhaps, a natural consequence of the heavy weighting of conference membership toward higher education. It does seem apparent, however, that little serious and "dispassionate" redesign work has been undertaken which would allow the strength and benefits of the classical teacher centre to be realized — and to continue to be realized — in the American educational setting. Where such redesign work has been undertaken, as in the case of the Philadelphia Teacher Centre and the Teachers' Active Learning Centre, it has quite naturally been preoccupied with the operations of a particular, specific centre. Perhaps this is as it should be if the aim is to be empirical and developmental.

The teacher centre as a change strategy

The preceding section has discussed the teacher centre as an innovation in its own right — as a more or less transferable or importable invention, with promise for aiding teachers' professional and personal development. It is equally possible to view the teacher centre, not just as an innovation, like team teaching, computer-assisted instruction or "Man, a Course of Study", but as a strategy designed to accelerate rates of change and development in the inhabitants of an educational system.

What are the essential features of the teacher centre seen as a change strategy? Here we shall refer to a half-dozen prior classifications of change strategies to help surface the underlying assumptions which advocates of teacher centres appear to be making about the change process.

Alternate views of change strategies. Chin and Benne,[10] in a comprehensive review of change strategies, suggest that they can be classified into one of three general categories: *rational,* centring around information transfer; *normative-re-educative,* focusing on shifts in the properties of persons; and *power-coercive,* utilizing non-violence, legislation or change in élites. While the classical British teachers' centre does involve utilization of knowledge, its transformatory effects are clearly aimed at altering the attitudes, behaviour and knowledge of role occupants — teachers in particular — and so clearly falls in the normative/re-educative category.

Sieber has a broadly similar classification: rational, co-operative and power-oriented. He also suggests a fourth alternative: a "status occupant" approach, which acknowledges that persons involved in educational change are linked in a network of interdependent statuses. Both in terms of the peer collaboration asserted to be a feature of teacher centres, and the nature of the co-operative helping relationship between teacher-centre clients and staff, one would have to invoke Sieber's "co-operation" rubric.

Leavitt[11] speaks of structural approaches (reorganizations, redesigns); "technical" strategies involving direct intervention in the work flow, with or without shifts in physical technology; and "people-changing" or humanistic approaches, involving attitude change, skill development, and increases in such interpersonal properties as trust. Although the teacher centre is a structural intervention in most cases, whether it occurs on "neutral ground" or involves interinstitutional linkage, one would still have to consider it primarily as a people-changing or humanistic strategy.

Miles[12] classified change strategies as to whether they were initiated by the "target system" (school or college in this case), or by systems in the environment of the target system; and whether they emphasized one or several stages prior to adoption by the target system (design of the innovation, development of local awareness and interest, local pre-trial evaluation, and local trial). Teacher centres are clearly a new structure; some have been initiated by target systems themselves and some by systems in the environment. The teacher centre can be most appropriately classified under Miles' category of "comprehensive strategy", which involves attention to all four states (design of innovations, development of awareness/interest, evaluation and trial). Once again, this analysis assumes that the teacher centre is not only an "innovation" itself but a basic strategy for encouraging the adoption of a wide variety of specific innovations (teaching practices, materials, curricula). (In passing, much depends on whether the adopting unit is seen as a school system, a school building or an individual teacher. As we shall underline later, the teacher-centre concept tends to assume the individual teacher as the adopting unit.)

Havelock *et al.*[13] suggest that change strategies have historically been viewed in one of three major ways; focusing on *rational processes* of decision-making based on information (classically, the research, development and diffusion approach); paying primary attention to the *social interaction* among potential adopters in status systems; or emphasizing the *problem-solving process* that occurs as a potential adopter encounters difficulties in carrying out an educational programme. He suggests a fourth *"linkage"* model in which expert resources and knowledge are brought into conjunction with the needs of users or client systems, usually by the provision of linking roles or groups. Teacher centres, seen from this perspective, are rather centrally a problem-solving strategy; in spite of the emphasis on peer influence, it is not at all clear that most teacher centres have worked systematically on outreach and diffusion across persons or roles within receiving systems. Although there has been a good deal of emphasis in British centres on available curricula and materials, it does not seem accurate to consider them as being primarily a dissemination station at the end of a research, development and diffusion pipeline. Seen at its best, the interaction between centre staff and clients does assume something of the character of Havelock's linkage model, where the user is actively supported in his efforts to surface problems and difficulties, to specify the classes of knowledge he needs, and to work in a collaborative relationship with a linking agent who can interpret and translate material drawn from a broad knowledge base.

Schmuck and Miles speak of *structural* approaches to change (e.g. age-grading, the creation of new roles such as teacher aids, and the design of new subsystems, such as the multi-unit school); of *curricular* strategies (with emphasis on the procedures, materials, and equipment used in the immediate classroom learning setting); and *role-shaping* strategies (e.g. inter-action analysis, micro-teaching, in-service workshops, sensitivity training). They also describe a *"holistic"* strategy, involving the creation of a new or innovative educational system, which avoids the constraints of the existing one and incorporates structural, curricular, and role-shaping substrategies into a grand design for a new learning environment. Teacher centres are probably classifiable as "holistic" in this sense, since they involve the creation of a new system. The primary emphasis, however, is undoubtedly role-shaping, with a curricular secondary emphasis.

This review of the teacher centre, seen from these various change-strategy perspectives, suggests several generalizations.

Motivational supports. First, it seems evident that the root assumption behind the teacher centre, seen as a change strategy, is that it is a person-changing, role-shaping, re-educative strategy which places central emphasis on the alteration of persons. The excitement, enthusiasm, sense of liberation and new-found skills which appear in reports from widely varying centres are congruent with this view.

As I commented at the closing session of the Syracuse conference, the attractiveness — and possibly the future viability of the teacher centre concept — rests on its ability to tap into relatively deep personal motivational streams. Three can be singled out: need power, need achievement, and need affiliation.

First, need power. It will be recalled that the best single predictor of school achievement in the Coleman report[14] — better than any other single measure of school properties or of home and family environments — was "fate control", the sense that the individual is not a pawn but is more like an "origin", to use de Charms' formulation, has a sense of empowerment, ability to act on the environment rather than being run by it. The strong stress on teacher initiation and teacher-centredness in the classical teacher centre undoubtedly serves to increase teachers' own sense of "fate control", and their willingness to be proactive rather than reactive.

A second major source of motivational energy is need achievement, usually defined as "concern over competition with a standard of excellence". Most teacher centres, though minimizing interteacher competition, do stress excellence and the actualization of individual abilities, encourage moderate risk-taking (usually associated with high levels of need achievement), and focus on specific, usable products for classrooms. As in the case of need power, there is a literature[15] showing that need achievement can be increased in students, and that such efforts are associated with increased learning.

The third motivational system which is probably affected by teacher centres is that of need affiliation, the need for warm, supportive, interpersonal relations. Once again, research from classroom learning environments is relevant. Schmuck, for example, showed that students' achievement was greater in classrooms where peer-liking patterns were relatively widespread over the entire class, rather than being focused on a handful of sociometric "stars" in a hierarchical fashion. As with need power and need achievement, it seems likely that teachers, as learners, will move farther and faster when affiliative needs are met. Most teacher centres appear to emphasize peer sharing and support a good deal.

Thus, if the classical teacher centre does indeed minister to basic motivational needs of persons, we would predict they would be not only satisfying but rather productive environments — causing alterations in those who participate in them. The testimony of users tends to support this view (although once again I must emphasize that there are no systematic, empirical data available on the actual person-changing processes or outcomes of teacher centres anywhere).

Person change and system change. The person-centred focus of teacher centres, however, raises a primary issue which deserves attention. Schools are, in fact, meaningful social systems. If a teacher centre places central focus on changes in the *person,* the system surrounding the teacher tends to be largely deprecated, treated as an unfortunate barrier to personal growth, or given up on in despair. At its best, the teacher centre may minister to the organizational pains (e.g. sense of impotence, isolation and alienation) experienced by teachers; at its worst, its efforts may become simply palliative and delusory.

It is only worth noting here that strategies such as organization development, which take the school social system as a change target rather than as an unfortunate set of constraints, are quite feasible – and can alter important system properties (such as interteacher and interdepartmental trust, general innovations, power equalization and general organizational climate). A number of accounts reviewed in this paper stress the importance of active outreach, linkage to existing systems, the provision of advisory assistance, and the like. My own bias is that the consequences of teacher-centre participation for persons will be far more likely to result in sustained change in the actual educational environments those persons create, to the degree that serious attention is also given to organization development programmes in the school system involved. Bigelow,[16] for example, showed that increased peer support and increased "indirect" influence by teachers (both associated with increased student achievement) took place in the classrooms of teachers who had experienced, as a total faculty, an intensive organizational development workshop prior to the opening of school.

Use of education "products". There is one addititional issue which deserves attention in the further development of teacher centres seen as a change strategy: the extent to which educational research and development "products" – curricular materials, specific skill development packages, and the like – are/can be/ought to be actively utilized in the teacher-centre setting. Given active emphasis on teacher initiation and teacher need-meeting, it is not clear that the classical teacher centre can (or cannot, for that matter) serve as some sort of end station in a "delivery system". The British experience suggests that a good deal of "delivery" does take place – *if* it is kept in mind that almost any set of materials, any teaching practice, or even any thoroughly and specifically developed set of curriculum experiences, undergoes a good deal of adaptation and development during the process of becoming "owned" by the teacher. Since teacher centres were not developed out of the classical research, development and diffusion perspective, but from a teacher-nurturant, development perspective, it seems unreasonable to expect them to perform the sort of linking function which occurred in, for example, the United States Office of Education supported Pilot State Dissemination Programme, where a "field agent" served as intermediary between stored educational information (e.g. in the Educational Resources Information Centre) and the needs of users.

The question is: will teacher centres use "the best that we know" (such as it is) about processes of teaching and learning? Seen at the teacher level, the question is a rephrase of the classical worry whether children in non-authoritarian classrooms, whether historically labelled "progressive", or currently labelled "open", "informal", "inquiry-based", will have to invent the wheel all over again — or will in fact make meaningful use of "the cultural heritage". Persons with active experience in informal education and similar models which do not assume knowledge transmission as central to the teaching-learning enterprise, know that such fears are not substantial: children do learn about the world, even when they are not required to do so in a systematically controlled fashion. Nevertheless, the question remains as to the most productive ways to use educational research and development products in teacher centres, and it deserves empirical study.

Installation modes

A third perspective in thinking about teacher centres involves attention to the short-run strategies by which teacher centres can be got "into place", functioning as meaningful subsystems within the larger educational enterprise. The differences in this respect which surfaced during the conference itself were not trivial; they in fact appeared to represent rather basic differences in primitive assumptions about how new institutions are created and actualized.

At the closing session of the conference, I resorted to metaphor as a way of organizing and exemplifying these assumptions, and I shall employ this same approach here.

The Oasis. At the conference, a good deal of the discussion around the "classical" teacher centre appeared to be subsumable within an "oasis" metaphor. The image is one of people voluntaristically clustering around an important but scarce resource (water in the desert) with the shape of the oasis being determined organically and developmentally by the availability of the resource. People are attracted to the oasis because of the water, do some spreading of the word to others, but basically concentrate on the satisfactions of cultivation and association with others which the oasis makes possible. Oasis development is seen as a relatively simple process, resting on basic necessities (water, in the metaphor; perhaps motivational drives, as suggested earlier in this manuscript) rather than on deliberate planning, coercion, etc. In accounts of classical teacher centres, a good deal is made of the inherent joy, pleasure and significance entailed in teacher-centre participation. The range of things growing in the oasis is relatively wide, and the necessity for explicit linkages to other oases, via camel tracks, power lines, etc., is relatively minimal.

The benefits of the oasis model for installation of teacher centres are not minor. This way of thinking produces, in effect, an actualized image of the future, rather than vague rhetoric about "what it might be like"; it enables a direct experience with satisfying, self-initiated inquiry. Because of the modest scale, success experiences for individuals are more likely, and realism in enterprises carried on outside the oasis (that is, in one's own school) is more likely. The oasis approach to installation is also directly focused on user satisfactions and user needs, and can be expected to tap sources of energy usually masked, or blocked, or held unavailable.

However, there are costs involved in using the oasis metaphor. Diffusion planning is relatively minimal (since the oasis life itself is satisfying and productive), and the "real world" (the desert) comes to be seen as an inhospitable place, not seriously subject to man's intervention. It seems possible that inner absorption and self-delusion might be possible outcomes for teachers if the oasis metaphor were dominant. To push the metaphor a bit further than may be profitable, the core question may be whether oasis dwellers only learn methods of cultivating the date palm — or the technology of drilling deep wells to construct their own oases (or larger-scale irrigation systems). The basic attractiveness of the metaphor, however, remains that sources for energy and development are present in persons, and that environments can rather easily be arranged which will run on those energy sources. The epigraphs for the oasis are perhaps "Let it happen", or "Why not?"

The designed building. An alternate metaphor considers the approach to installation of the teacher centre to be rather more like the process which an architect and client go through in planning and deliberately constructing a building. The model here is one of rational, explicit design. Characteristically, a good architect will talk with the client, determine wished-for uses of the building, make forward projections for many years in the future, locate perceived dissatisfaction with previous buildings, and so . on. An architect ordinarily has a very substantial technical bank of options available from which to draw during the designing process, and (if he is a first-rank architect) is also capable of taking substantial creative risks during the design and building process. Expertness becomes far more central than in the oasis metaphor, and, though architects have begun involving building users in social inventions like the intensive charrette, their expertise often leans them in the direction of a technocratic, élitist approach to design. The effort is usually to take the larger context strongly into account; the embeddedness of the to-be-designed system in a surrounding supersystem is of considerable weight — a planning assumption not really present for most oasis builders. ("The camel tracks will happen — we don't need to design them".)

Considering the benefits of this metaphor, one would have to emphasize the centrality and usefulness of rationality. If need assessments are done carefully, it is reasonably likely that the ensuing building (institution) will be able to continue to meet the needs for which it was designed. Survival capability of the institution is higher, and it may be more likely that the wished-for products (in the teacher centre's case, improved teacher competency, changed attitudes, new information, etc.) will be delivered more reliably — assuming that the architect is able to form a collaboration with a good and competent builder, so that the original vision is well actualized.

The costs and risks involved in this model, however, are not minor. As Sarason[17] has pointed out, the creation of new settings of any sort requires enormous and unforeseen amounts of energy. Clarity about the goals of a new institution, along with motivation to achieve them, represents only a tiny fraction of the inputs needed to transform a vision into an operating social institution. Failures in the design of new institutions are more typical than successes; issues of leadership, power distribution, conflict management, allocation of resources, stress and role overload are pervasive and are almost never anticipated during the designing stage. Other risks or costs in the "designed building" metaphor include dangers of over-designing, grandiosity, and wastage of energy on problems which never, in fact, materialize. It should also be pointed out that a serious designing approach does require active dollar and time investment — patron support, so to speak — if it is to be successful.

Interbuilding linkage. A third possible metaphor for the installation of teacher centres invokes the image of a series of perfectly adequate buildings reasonably contiguous to each other, which only need to be linked by paths or covered walkways in order to form an effective, need-meeting system. Telephone, power lines, water and sewage systems, etc., are also to be interconnected. The root assumption in this metaphor is that existing institutions are, in effect, functioning perfectly well, perhaps with some limitation due to difficulties of energy or information transfer among them, and that the creation of linkages is the sole feature required for the creation of an effective, or newly effective institution.

The basic benefits of such a metaphor, of course, are that the resources and expertise of existing institutions are not by-passed or ignored but used more productively and effectively, in a coordinated, planful fashion. The Syracuse conference discussions were full of dire warnings about the folly of ignoring the existing knowledge, expertise, funding power, etc., of existing institutions during the process of designing something called a teacher centre.

The costs or risks of the inter-building linkage metaphor, of course, are that inhabitants of each building naturally tend not only to protect their vested interests, but ordinarily expect that simple extension and expansion of existing procedures is all that is needed to solve the problem at hand. Institutional blinders tend to restrict the development of innovative solutions, and the clash of interests tends to result in mutual vetoing operations (cf. the discussions of "parity", "involvement", "governance", etc., during the conference). Since most institutions are already multifunctional, use of the inter-building linkage model tends to produce a giantized version, a linked system in which each partner institution tends to retain all its old functions and to compete with other partner institutions for scarce resources. The likelihood of close focus on a particular goal (in the teacher centre case, the development of teacher confidence and competence) tends to be obscured, blocked, or watered down amid a maze of competing goals (in this case, accreditation, certification, employment, salary advancement, product delivery, special educational services, and the like).

Exploration of these three alternate metaphors suggests, in addition to the crude cost/benefit analyses made above, two sorts of general comments.

Sequencing. First, it seems possible that the three metaphors — seen as installation modes for teacher centres — might well be sequenced, or used at different points during the various stages of development of the teacher-centre concept in a particular social system. It appears, for example, that the oasis model was far more typical in the early stages of the development of the British teachers' centres, and that movement toward an interbuilding linkage model has occurred as connections between teachers' centres, local education authorities and local colleges and universities developed. One also suspects that serious designing of a new institution called a "teacher centre", with direct relevance to the pressures and demands of the American educational system, can hardly proceed very productively until some prototype oases have been run for a while and examined seriously for evidence of strain, viability, productive capability, and so on. The massive, grandiose and ill-fated over-designing carried out by some of the task forces and committees in the United States Office of Education's renewal/teacher centre effort illustrates the consequences of designing without an adequate experimental base. In fact, the United States Office's funding of pilot teacher centres acknowledges the importance of the oasis metaphor as a basis for later serious design and redesign. It does seem likely that efforts to solve the basic unmet needs of teachers for personal/professional growth and development by "simple" interinstitutional linkage, unless preceded by "oasis" and "new institution design" efforts, are not likely to be productive.

Social architecture. The second general point that seems evident after exploration of these metaphors is that all three installation modes require some attention to the processes of "social architecture".([18]) The organic, developmental rhetoric of the oasis model obscures the fact that careful institutional planning is necessary if a "classic" teacher centre is to deal with teachers' real needs, hopes, and wishes for growth — the oasis model is long on energy but short on design. The "new building" model requires a great deal of explicit planning and design skill. I suspect it is most likely to fall afoul of itself by giving insufficient attention to user needs, and underestimating the complexities of the actual *building* (as contrasted with the *design*) process. Even the interbuilding linkage model requires some careful social-architectural attention to minimize the construction of unnecessary linkages and to develop means of protecting the new institution from the excesses of vested interests. From this perspective, the issue is not whether social architecture takes place — but how explicit it is, how willed it is, what the scale of effort is, the relative balance between *"de novo"* and "redesign" allocation of energy. The need is to design environments which are furthering to humans and their purposes, which enable authentic personal and group relationships while achieving personal and organizational purposes, and which are reasonably flexible and adaptable under stress. This task is not easy, and it is certainly not furthered by the pretence that "everything will happen naturally", the fantasy that "we can plan it out carefully all in advance", or the pious view that "we only need to co-ordinate our resources".

Teacher centres as a social movement

Can teacher centres, in Britain, other countries or the United States, be seen in any sense as a "social movement"? This concept offers a fourth general perspective or lens for viewing our subject-matter.

Here and there, during the Syracuse conference, one encountered the rhetoric that the classical teacher centre was an idea whose time had come, that immediate scepticisms and doubts would shortly give way, and that teacher centres in the United States would diffuse and develop on a scale comparable to that which has already occurred in Great Britain. A sort of latent ground swell or social movement was claimed to be lurking in the wings ready to happen, almost of itself.

Is the teacher centre "movement" anything like a "social movement", in the sense of the Oxford Movement, the Townsend Plan, encounter groups, the civil rights movement, the early stages of the Nazi Party, the worker-priest movement in the Catholic Church? Toch[19] defines a social movement as involving collective behaviour of a relatively long-lasting sort, organized around a programme of purpose, operating on a relatively large scale, and moving from spontaneous beginnings toward promoting or resisting change in society at large. Social movements, from this point of view, are an effort by a large number of people to solve, collectively, some problem they feel they have in common. The social movement may concentrate on altering the environment (e.g. the civil rights movement) or may be essentially self-transforming (e.g. Alcoholics Anonymous). Toch suggests that social movements tend to offer essentially an alerting function – pointing to the existence of difficulties or problems in social systems, rather than providing a clearly transforming or altering function, although the rhetoric of social movements often says otherwise.

If we examine what has been going on in relation to teacher centres, though the rhetoric occasionally invokes the idea of "movement", we must conclude that some distinguishing characteristics of "social movements" are absent. There does not appear to be a large, shared collective need (comparable, for example, to the pains felt by the old people who rallied behind the Townsend Plan or the blacks and whites who fought for integration in the early sixties). The collectivity involved is somewhat diffuse; there does not appear to be a tight orthodoxy or belief system organized around teacher centres (another feature discussed by Toch). So, in some important senses, the "social movement" label does not apply very well.

The relatively rapid diffusion of the teachers' centre concept in Britain (from 0 to 500 centres in 7 or 8 years) suggests something more durable and developmental than the sheer diffusion of an "innovation", and something less than the allegiance and passion of a "social movement". Perhaps we need a new label for the processes involved in the replication and extension of a new institutional form such as the teacher centre. We might wish to speculate here for a minute on the features underlying the British development and spread: in my view, they would have to include a reasonable amount of expertise and sanctioning from a respected body (the Schools Council); the economical use of existing energy and money, rather than the requirement of a substantial "add-on"; the strong and deep degree to which intrinsic local rewards flow to participants; our old favourite, British pragmatism, along with willingness to try what *may* work; and some accelerative support at early critical points (e.g. work conferences sponsored by the Schools Council to share experience across teachers' centre staffs). It is not at all clear, by the way, just how much cross-centre support has taken place since the early stages. In what sense can teacher centres in Great Britain (and those developing in this country, as in the Advisory for Open Education) be seen as a "network"? An informal definition of "network" is: a dispersed structure permitting low-energy access to trusted competence. Appropriate information, energy and other resources can be easily located from physically dispersed nodes to solve local problems. To the degree that network development takes place in relation to teacher centres (and the Syracuse Conference may be seen in some respects as an effort to enhance such development), we would predict more rapid diffusion.

Teacher centres as an alternative institution

A final perspective for examining teacher centres rests on the idea that they are, in many respects, alternative institutions — organizations deliberately designed to meet a particular need (in this case, teacher development) because no existing institution appeared to be coping adequately. During the middle and late 1960s, a good deal of energy began to flow into the creation of alternative institutions (e.g. free schools, communes, group marriages, community development corporations, free churches and others). The original British teachers' centre can be seen in many respects as an alternative institution aimed at restoring, developing and transforming teachers for more effective functioning in an educational system, itself undergoing considerable change in the form of a wide range of new curricula and the basic shifts in teaching/learning style involved in informal education and the open classroom. Any institution billing itself as an "alternative" to existing wisdom, ordinarily has a tough row to hoe. There are severe start-up problems, and the efficacy of the alternative is usually judged in a very short time frame (a year or two). On top of this, most such institutions are trying to innovate without a great deal of social support from the surrounding system, and their viability in accordingly reduced. There is a tendency for alternative institutions to be populated by ideologically pure, idealistic personnel who tend to be disappointed, or critically attacking, when the new institution somehow — as it always must — fails to meet the perfect standards implied in the rhetoric of its founders. Finally, conventional criteria (usually those from the preceding institution which the alternative is designed to supplant) are used to evaluate the undertaking.

Alternative institutions have a number of typical features which turn out to fit the classical teacher centre rather well. First is *small size,* which is seen as enabling more attention to individual needs and more widespread participation, as permitting more-fulfilling human interaction, and as reducing inequalities of influence. Second, alternative institutions characteristically weight the internal *processes* involved with as much or more value than the *products* emitted by the system. Getting there is seen as providing substantially more than half the fun. Accounts of teacher centres often stress the importance of processes, like discovery, sharing, creation, collaboration, help-seeking and giving — regardless of the final knowledge or skill output of the system. The rewards of participation in such processes are seen as intrinsic, rather than only instrumental to the achievement of a specified level of "competence".

Third, most alternative institutions also emphasize *power sharing*, collective decision-making based on the dicta that those affected by a decision should be directly involved in influencing it, and that the possession of physical or technical resources should not necessarily be associated with the exercise of power. There is a good deal of emphasis in teacher centres on self-determination and responsiveness of the centre to the needs and wishes of its clients. (In fact, to term teachers "clients" tends to distort the sense of ownership and initiation which infuses the classical teacher-centre concept.)

The fourth emphasis in many alternative institutions is an emphasis on *wholeness*, the defragmentation of persons, the integration of life activities formerly kept distinct. Much teacher centre practice seems to be built around the idea that a teacher as a person and a teacher as a professional are not to be sharply separated, and that personal experiences of creation, release, liberation and discovery are as essential as "professional" experiences centring around questioning techniques, classroom management, skills, and curriculum development. Finally, it appears that many alternative institutions take a broadly *humanistic value* stance, stressing human needs such as freedom of expression, individuality, autonomy, creativity, relatedness. Such labels naturally are heavily loaded with social desirability. The aim here is only to point out that alternative institutions characteristically do *not* focus on institution-related values, tagged by words such as loyalty, discipline, responsibility, order, commitment. The essence of many alternative institutions appears to be the making of persons and their concerns the centre of the institution, rather than the institution's requiring its participants to serve its purposes.

Alternative institutions do have recurring paradoxes in their operations, as do teacher centres. Kanter and Zurcher[20] describe several.

> The functional declaration of independence from society at large, coupled with the need for selective dependence, in order to support the survival of the alternative form ... the importance of small size, coupled with pressures for proselytizing toward the convenience of numbers ... the importance of process as product, coupled with problems of assessing the impact of process, and rewarding or correcting it ... the importance of participatory democracy, coupled with the difficulty of full collaboration on every decision — the importance of individual diversity, coupled with pressures toward conformity within the alternative form.

They suggest a series of alternative criteria for evaluating alternative institutions, including:

> *Size.* How small, intimate, and connected does a system manage to stay and still do whatever it has to?

Productivity. Do relationships and tasks offer participation, involvement, excitement, and learning?

Adaptiveness. Do relationships and roles change in response to needs of the participants?

Decision-making. How widely is power shared?

Wholeness. How much of a person and his or her life activities does a system or relationship incorporate in an integrated fashion?

Competence. How many roles is a person given the opportunity to play in an integrated fashion?

Paradox management. To what extent are individuals able to understand and tolerate stresses associated with inevitable paradoxes and dilemmas in the institution itself?

Note that criteria labelled "efficiency", "reliability", "productivity" and "stability" are absent from this list.

Seen from this perspective, some of the features of teacher centres which appear "impractical", "romantic" or unconnected to the current pressures of educational systems can be seen not as wilful vagueness or stubborn unwillingness to be hard-nosed about teacher-centre output (as was occasionally suggested at the conference), but as natural and perhaps inevitable properties of any institution posed as an alternative to existing ones. The teacher centre, by any count, must be seen as a modestly alternative institution, without radical differences from the institutions (e.g. in-service training, workshops, academic courses, etc.) it is designed to replace. Nevertheless, the typical alternative-institution features are there. This analysis suggests that efforts to expand the size of teacher centres radically, to emphasize "output" or "performance" rather than process, to make centres less controllable by participants, or to focus them on solely "professional" content may be ways of reducing the fruitfulness of this social invention rather than enhancing it.

Finally, it seems clear that, like many alternative institutions, the teacher centre has not yet found an ecological niche, so to speak, in the macrosystem of American education. The present prototypes are existing precariously on federal grants, partial support from a local district, or personal tuition — and are not yet built into the overall structure of the educational system in the same way that the centres in Great Britain and Japan are. The question of just how such linkages can be made — made in a way that will support the basic intent of the enterprise without enfeebling it in the ebb and flow of vested interests, is a very real one in predicting the future of teacher centres in America.

The future

Will teacher centres "take off", become diffused widely in the American educational system, as their advocates hope? Or will they simply become vulgarized, co-opted, absorbed into the existing educational establishment, like many previous reforms? I do not think it is possible to write anything like plausible scenarios at this point, especially given the reduction in federal funding for education which seems likely over the next few years, and the rather considerable teacher over-supply with which the system is currently faced. Here, however, are a series of plausible events or situations which may well occur during the next 2 or 3 years. These predictions and others should perhaps be run through Delphi technique for a more plausible final view of the future. In any case, here are some possibilities:

1. A few dozen teacher centres, largely on the British model, will continue to operate with some gradual expansion in clientele and overall numbers of centres.
2. United States Office of Education support for the large-scale pilot training complexes and associated teacher centres will be reduced substantially or ended.
3. Teacher ownership of and initiation in centres largely developed under the aegis of colleges and universities will not be protected or supported.
4. Pilot and developmental projects which are able to get commitment and funding from school systems, and/or state departments of education, and which have experienced a reasonable amount of success from operations so far, will probably continue.
5. There will be more experimentation with teacher centres in large cities, largely out of sheer desperation.
6. There will be some co-operation between local education authorities and state departments of education, to experiment with teacher centres on a state-wide basis (perhaps including university co-operation, as in the North Dakota changes in elementary education).
7. Some colleges will develop teacher-centre proposals in collaboration

with local education authorities as a means of attracting funds administered through state departments of education.

8. Continued National Education Association and American Federation of Teachers, interest in the production of teacher-run centres will result in a modest network of such centres, as per the National Education Association's *Prospectus*.

9. Teacher centres will probably continue to have somewhat more impact on elementary than on secondary teachers.

10. The United States Office may generate a wide, but shallow, support programme providing matching funds to local education authorities, possibly mediated through state departments of education, for skill development purposes, congruently with the Richardson "megaplan". Such support may be primarily for planning, and serve a seed-money purpose.

11. A state department of education, in collaboration with some local education authorities, may experiment with a voucher plan in which teacher contracts include a specified amount of money spendable by the teacher for his or her own growth and development, in or out of teacher centres.

12. A large foundation, with United States Office of Education co-operation, will create a "national teaching centre advisory" facility aimed at assisting and supporting the initiation and development of teacher centres.

13. Consultation services and organization development activities will become more widely available in existing centres.

14. The long-term drift is that more sites with the label "Teacher Centre", many of them substantially altered and adapted from the British concept, will be in existence. In-service education will be somewhat more likely to occur in such settings, and somewhat less likely to occur in college or university course settings, or in brief school system workshops conducted by visiting experts.

Which of these fourteen predictions will materialize in the short term is, of course, quite impossible to be sure about. It will be noted, however, that most of the predictions made are "not unreasonable", to use the language of scenario-writers; there is little that is apocalyptic or visionary in the air at the moment. The most likely outcome is that teacher centres, to the degree that they are enjoyable, interesting and not severely draining of funds, will continue to be pressed and advocated by those who care about them, as a means of improving American education.

Concluding comments

Back of the claims of teacher centre advocates (and of the questions of sceptics) there rests an implied causal chain. Teacher centres are seen as inducing certain *desired changes in American teachers* (new knowledge, new capabilities and new attitudes toward teaching and learning). These changes are in turn seen as inducing *improvement* in the American educational system's functioning. It must be said that the links in this chain are relatively tenuous. Even assuming that teacher centres can reliably induce certain classes of change in teachers, the question remains whether the changes are ones inherently likely to improve educational output. Even if that were practically shown to be the case, there still remains the question of the myriad organizational and interorganizational forces which might serve to block the impact of teacher changes on the quality of students' experience, in and out of the classroom.

But, on balance, it seems well worth while to keep pushing the teacher-centre concept. For one thing, it seems almost impossible that teacher centres could be more wasteful of human energy, time and money than the present arrangements for in-service education. For another, teacher-centre experiences have been repeatedly shown to be pleasant, exciting, interesting and personally satisfying. Just as Christopher Jencks([21]) has remarked that although schools do not appreciably contribute to the reduction of economic inequality, there is no real reason not to make them more happy and satisfying places in which to live and learn, there seems no reason why teachers' exploration of the craft and substance of what they are doing with children should not be undertaken in a way that is interesting, exciting, deroutinized and personally supportive.

And finally, there is always the possibility that, by providing a direct, experience-based model for teacher/learner interaction which is more open, collaborative, humane and inquiring than the models many teachers and administrators (and children) now carry around in their heads, teacher centres may in fact help schools and schooling shift in a more human, productive direction. That is what teacher-centre advocates hope, and that hope is certainly not outside the realm of possibility. We shall see.

References

1.e.g. BARNETT, H. G., *Innovation: the basis of cultural change*, McGraw Hill, 1953; and ROGERS, EVERETT M., *Diffusion of innovations*, Free Press, 1962.

2. GRANNIS, JOSEPH C., *Does the school reflect the culture: Who is changing whom?* Teachers' College, Columbia University, 1972, mimeographed.

3. BARNETT, *op. cit.*

4. ROGERS, *op. cit.*

5. MILES, M. B., Some properties of schools as social systems, in WATSON, G. (Ed.), *Change in school systems,* National Training Laboratories, Washington, D.C., 1967.

6. BIDWELL, C. E., The school as a formal organization, in MARCH, J. G., (Ed.), *Handbook of organizations,* Rand McNally, 1965.

7. SIEBER, S. D., Organizarional influences on innovative roles, in EIDELL, T. M. and KITCHELL, J. M., *Knowledge production and utilization in educational administration,* Center for the Advanced Study of Educational Administration, Eugene, Oregon, 1968.

8. SCHMUCK, R. A., and MILES, M. B., *Organization development in schools,* National Press, Palo Alto, 1971.

9. JUDSON, MADISON E., *Teacher Centre development ideas, and Four important components for American teacher centres,* working papers, mimeographed, Reston, Virginia, author, 1971.

10. CHIN, R. and BENNE, K. D., General strategies for effecting changes in human systems, in BENNIS, W. G., BENNE, K. D. and CHIN, R. (Eds.), *The planning of change,* Holt, Reinhart & Winston, 1969.

11. LEAVITT, H. J., Applied organizational change in industry: structural, technological and humanistic approaches, in MARCH, J. G., *op. cit.*

12. MILES, M. B. (Ed.), *Innovation in education,* Teachers' College Press, 1964.

13. HAVELOCK, R., GUSKIN, A. *et al., Planning for innovation through dissemination and utilization of knowledge,* Institute for Social Research, University of Michigan, Ann Arbor, 1969

14. COLEMAN, J. S., *Equality of educational opportunity,* Washington, D.C., United States Government Printing office, 1966.

15. ALSCHULER, A., *Motivating adolescents' achievement,* Prentice-Hall, 1972.

16. BIGELOW, R. C., Changing classroom interaction through organization development, in SCHMUCK and MILES, *op. cit.*

17. SARASON, S. B., *The creation of settings and the future societies,* Jossey-Bass, San Francisco, 1972.

18. PERLMUTTER, H., *Toward a theory and practice of social architecture,* Tavistock, 1965.

19. TOCH, H., *The social psychology of social movements,* Bobbs-Merrill, 1965.

20. KANTER, R. M. and ZURCHER, L. A. (Eds.), special issue of the *Journal of Applied Behavioural Science,* vol. 9, no. 2-3 (1973).

21. JENCKS, C. *et al., Inequality: a reassessment of the effect of family and schooling in America,* Basic Books, 1972, and also published by Allen Lane, 1973.

22. ROGERS, V. R. (Ed.), *Teaching in the British primary school,* Macmillan, 1970.

CHAPTER 11

The Emerging Pattern

Introduction

THE theme of this book is the need for in-service education for teachers and the place of teachers' centres in the emerging pattern. This final chapter makes the point that teachers and those co-operating with them in in-service education would do well to concentrate on the unique problems of teachers as teachers. Any teacher may want a course in some subject discipline or in general background psychology or sociology and fortunately such courses at various levels are now reasonably available.

The importance of such studies is self-evident. It is too easy for a teacher, however, to feel that if he learns up some period of history, masters some new mathematical concepts or devotes himself to science or literature, he is fulfilling his in-service duties. He may be: but only if the knowledge he has acquired helps him to enable pupils to make more sense of the world, and only if his knowledge keeps him in touch with reality.

Like other people, of course, a teacher is free to do as he likes with his own time, building up particular interests or pursuing special causes, but in-service study for teachers as teachers needs to focus upon the classroom and the staffroom. His task is to keep on working out with other teachers and with anyone else concerned, what school is for and what he can do to further these purposes; and to augment his competency to carry these general plans into effect with the actual pupils with whom he happens to have to relate. It is no good his worrying because other people expect the schools to achieve miracles or do what is none of their business. It is his responsibility to be pretty clear about what school is for and about the part he should be playing in it at any time.

According to Tyrrell Burgess in his foreword to Christopher Jencks' tome on inequality,([1]) the schools themselves seldom have any clear objectives of their own and so far as they have any, these objectives are not what society attributes to them. A second point from the same source is that provision of resources and of reforms in organization appear to have little influence on what actually affects children. This chapter is a plea for in-service attention to those matters lying within the power or discretion of heads and teachers, and actually affecting children.

In what follows there are some indications of the climate of opinion in which in-service education is being considered; some account of the changing background of in-service opportunities arising from the establishment of new national educational institutions; some examples of research projects focusing on teachers' problems; some reference to management theory as far as it relates to schools, and some reminders as to who benefits from in-service education.

The climate of opinion

Throughout the Western world there is official recognition that in the near future in-service education for teachers will be in general demand and will need to be catered for adequately. The more advanced the country, in general economic terms, the greater the demand for such further training.

The recent development of teachers' centres in Britain and in a number of other countries is one measure of the response being made by the authorities to this demand. Many of the documents referred to by Matt Miles in his account of the Syracuse conference speak of widely felt concern about these in-service needs, as do the James Report and the government White Paper to which frequent reference has been made by the English authorities in this book. In Australia, the Karmel report[2] says that however high its quality, the pre-service education of teachers was limited in effectiveness — and proceeds to recommend funds for teachers' centres.

Among international reports, that edited by Fauré for UNESCO[3] outlines the case for lifelong education for all, including the third world, and gives examples to show that in the provision of recently established UNESCO-assisted teacher training institutions in countries such as Ethiopia not only initial but also in-service training is included. All this belief in institutional education and in the potential benefits of in-service education of teachers co-exists with wide-ranging criticism of teachers, schools and educational systems. It is as though, in the absence of definitive proof about what education achieves, any weakness in the human condition can be blamed on the professional educators.

Writing about economics-as-if-people-mattered, Schumaker, for example, asks([4]) whether it is far-fetched to suggest that there must be something wrong with its education if Western civilization is in a state of permanent crisis. Later in the same chapter, however, he gives some clue as to how much he hopes from education, saying that it can help us only if it produces "whole men" with their own views on the meaning and purpose of life. He claims that what matters is the tool-box of ideas with which, by which and through which we interpret the world and describes the task of education as first and foremost the transmission of ideas of value, of what to do with our lives. According to Schumaker more education can help us only if it produces more wisdom.

Schumaker is critical but hopeful. Other writers such as the charismatic ex-priest, Ivan Illich, are more devastating. As soon as they see his books or articles, lay readers pick up a ready-made armoury of abuse to hurl at the institutions of education. "School, the sacred cow"([5]) is an easy phrase to remember, as is "De-schooling society", the title of his best known book. Some of his shafts sink deep. He denies the right of those employed in the business of education to control people's freedom and their access to desired ways of living. He wants rid of compulsory schooling and of systems of selection, accreditation and certification. In their place he says he wants education towards personal fulfilment for all. He sees no glimmer of hope of movement towards this end through any modification of the existing educational structures or by means of the in-service education of professional practitioners. Unfortunately, however, he is vague as to the means by which the schooling of an élite with its concomitant rejection of the masses can be superseded by relevant individualized education for all.

We return therefore from this brief excursion into the dream world inhabited by 3700 million fully functioning persons, and consider the task in hand, that of the in-service education of practising teachers. One question that it might be fair to ask at the outset is why teachers, whose whole way of life is teaching and learning, seem to need so much help with further study. As they have already spent more years in school and college than most people, is it not reasonable to expect them to be in a good position to decide for themselves what further study is relevant to their needs, and furthermore, to arrange to get it? Surely their education, initial training and teaching experience have not left them incapable of planning and fulfilling their own programmes?

The reply to this question includes two points. One is that the rate of change is now such that more provision of opportunities for more systematic in-service education is being called for both by the teachers themselves and by those whose job it is to help and assist classroom teachers. The other is that many teachers in fact do undertake their own in-service education and that members of the profession have been doing so for many years: most of those now trying to help in the in-service field have themselves been classroom teachers and have undertaken in-service education to the end that they have been promoted to headships or translated to college, university, research or advisory positions.

Courses and conferences cost time and money. When a teacher attends a course which turns out to be inappropriate to his needs, not only are time and money wasted but some erosion of the spirit takes place. Where an applicant's needs for in-service help are not properly related to the provision, frustration is the result. In the period which may not have ended yet in all areas, teachers were free to apply more or less at random for courses offered by any of a great number of agents. For example, courses promising help with the teaching of reading have been legion — and often over-subscribed: but for a proportion of those in attendance, any one of these courses may have been pitched at the wrong level or in other ways have been quite unsuitable for the particular teacher.

Regardless of whether the teacher was studying in his own time or on paid leave, whether on a short course or for a more exacting theoretical or academic undertaking, it has been rare for much to be done to relate the teacher to the course, let alone to fit the course to the teacher. Some teachers have embarked upon courses of psychology or psycho-linguistics, hoping that such erudition would help them in the classroom — or, conceivably, help them to get out of it — but in few schools or authorities was anything done to give the teacher an opportunity to apply his new knowledge, to share it with his colleagues or to make any return on the investment.

The general assumption was that the teacher knew what was good for him, could find a suitable package on the shelves of the in-service supermarket and that that was the end of the matter. Of course, the employing authorities have been able to decide whether a teacher could be released on salary, whether for a short or a long course of full-time study; whether his place at school could be filled (even in theory) by a supply or substitute teacher; and the extent to which, if at all, subsistence, travelling and other expenses incurred in attendance at a course might be met from public funds. This system worked for many years to the benefit of those with minimum qualifications; but in general, teachers who wanted to push out the frontiers of knowledge about the teaching-learning situation in classrooms got no financial support — and, on the whole, still do not.

The changing background to in-service work

During the last decade there has been a great increase in study related to the task of the classroom teacher. The functioning of examinations, the development of new curricula, the classification of pupils by age and/or ability, the deployment of staff in open school accommodation; all these and many more aspects of the school life of a teacher have been given great attention. Even in these enlightened modern times, however, there has been negligible support for teachers undertaking serious projects, inquiries or observational studies in their own schools. The supporting funds for staffing, travel, equipment and secretarial help have been handled by the Department of Education, the Schools Council, the National Foundation for Educational Research, the Social Science Research Council and various organizations such as the Ford and Gulbenkian Foundations.

Since the 1944 Education Act it has been legal for local authorities to spend money on educational research, but for many years Surrey was perhaps the only authority which made a gesture of supporting school-based educational research. All the authorities were subscribing to the National Foundation and, since 1964, to the Schools Council, and apart from help from their advisory services, authorities did not presume to allocate funds or set up projects of curriculum development or research into school management. Let us turn therefore, now, to consideration of the studies, the projects, the inquiries and findings emanating from official bodies or from research teams whether or not based on institutions of higher education: not exhaustively, but to show some of the kinds of work that have been attempted during the last decade and to indicate their promise for the in-service needs of teachers in the years ahead.

What began the modern period of in-service work was the recommendation of the Beloe Report([6]) that teachers should have control of a certain level of public examination. During the year or two following the diffusion of this idea, some experiments were carried on under the sponsorship of the Secondary School Examinations Council, which published descriptive bulletins aimed at helping teachers to face for the first time the task of setting and correcting papers for the new Certificate of Secondary Education. Once teachers were fairly launched on this task a number of them quickly learned the techniques of assessing and moderating, whilst interest soon developed in the related problems of setting objectives and making objective tests. Throughout the decade since then this nationwide exercise in examining has been supported by regional examination boards elected to advise full-time secretarial and administrative staff housed in new single-purpose offices. The local education authorities maintain this structure by paying the fees of the pupils who enter for examinations. Teachers work directly with their particular regional board.

As regards in-service education, it is clear that a great many secondary teachers have responded to the challenge. They have become knowledgeable about formulating curriculum objectives; have seen the various standards of work obtaining in schools other than their own; and have familiarized themselves with statistical jargon of which most educators contrive to remain innocent throughout life. A number of teachers have extended their experience of problem-solving in the group situation and of committee work in matters of some public concern. On the debit side there is a high incidence of absence from secondary schools of key teachers involved in responsibility for the certificate of secondary education and there is a high cost to the authority in fees for candidates. (According to some calculations as much may be spent on examining as on *providing education* for a pupil who enters for the certificate of secondary education and/or for Ordinary level in the General Certificate of Education. Fortunately for the public purse, no compensatory outlay is made on those who leave school without any experience of these hurdles.) As regards research into the effects of the new teacher-controlled examination: little of it relates to classroom conditions.

The bulk of the (not inconsiderable) research relating to the certificate of secondary education has been on technical matters such as the comparability of the certificate of secondary education in different regions; the comparison with the general certificate of education; the possibilities of item banking; the techniques of analysis applied to examinations. All this detailed research([7]) adds up to useful background knowledge for the teacher but leaves him where he was concerning his classroom problems of how to help children learn. Some of the regional boards have mounted inquiries, but these appear also to be related rather to the examinations as such than to the effects on teachers or pupils of taking part in certificate work.

At about the time that the certificate of secondary education was mooted a working party under the chairmanship of Sir John Lockwood recommended the setting up of the Schools Council. This body met for the first time in 1964 and undertook the twin responsibilities bequeathed to it by the Secondary School Examinations Council and the Curriculum Study Group. The Schools Council was a new form of machinery set up — initially in accommodation belonging to the Department — to help the processes of change in education. Over the intervening years periodic or annual reports have recorded its development, whilst details of its structure, projects and publications are all readily available from the (new) head offices.[8] Additionally, many Schools Council publications are sent free to local authorities and to teachers' centres.

As a rule the work of the Council in any sphere of interest can be readily ascertained. For example, a four-sided sheet on examinations covers the story of 10 years' work, giving Schools Council references. In curriculum, the Schools Council now has upwards of 150 projects on the board or completed, and details of each are issued in *Project News*. The Schools Council influences in-service education not only through such publications but also through the work of its full-time staff, including field officers, through exhibitions and conferences, and through its involvement of teachers in curriculum development.

When an area of curriculum is decided upon it has been the custom of the Schools Council to appoint a director of the project for a limited period of time, and then some project staff. Most directors have been drawn from higher or further education but a proportion of all staff have been appointed or seconded from schools. Each project team plans its work, prepares pilot teaching materials, gains the co-operation of the necessary number of pilot schools, revises the materials in the light of the first trials and gives them a wider try-out in a bigger cross-section of suitable schools. On the completion of these trials further modifications may be made before the materials are published and made available commercially.

By this time the original project team is likely to have dispersed back to posts in school or college. The result is that it can happen that no knowledgeable personnel are free to discuss the use of the new published materials with the heads, teachers or college lecturers who are interested in them. This has been identified as the problem of diffusion and as such is receiving attention. However, some of the criticisms of the project method as adopted generally by the Schools Council go further and deeper.

From the point of view of the in-service development of teachers, the production of Schools Council materials is little in advance of the publication of innovative teaching materials from any other source. It is true that during the pilot and trial stages of preparation, some teachers in schools (as distinct from the small team working for the Schools Council itself) become somewhat involved and have some chance to influence the content or shape of the final product. The position of these teachers, however, resembles buyers being consulted by intelligent market researchers: they are invited to consider a product-in-the-making, not to determine what they thought they really needed.

Unfortunately, unless teachers have been involved in thinking through what curriculum is needed and in helping to plan it, they are likely to resist it or simply not to make the effort required to introduce it when it is packaged. Some of the new materials call for inquiry or discussion methods with which the teacher is inexperienced or which do not fit the pervasive authority/discipline pattern of the school. The teachers in a subject department or the group dealing with a particular cross-section of pupils may not be agreed as to the appropriateness of the proposed package — and the matter of expense may render necessary a commitment on the part of the group as a whole.

All these factors, and many others, may mean that some of the highly innovative curriculum development projects carried through by small overworked teams of intelligent and forward-looking experts will have less impact on school curricula than was anticipated, or than the outlay might seem to warrant. Although by American standards the investment of money and people may seem paltry, the curriculum projects of the Schools Council represent the only major public effort in the United Kingdom to create both a structure for innovation and some new curricula for schools. It therefore behoves all who have at heart the interests of schools and teachers to examine not only the new materials, but more important, the policies and strategies of the Schools Council itself, in so far as they affect the growth and development of practising teachers.

In the early days the Schools Council made some decisions which still seem to influence expenditure policy. Three examples of early decisions whose effects continue to reverberate through the schools are: the separation of the young school-leaver as a form of life requiring special treatment not shared by his peers; the double standard in curricula comprising on the one hand, subject specialisms and on the other hand, integrated studies — with neither of these classifications of curricula based on explicit theoretical concepts; and lastly, the extension and further complication of the system *(sic)* of competitive public examinations at age 16, with the effect that some pupils obtain a form of certificate and some do not, and in neither case does the pupil take home any clear assessment of his various competencies. (some pass, some fail and some do not start; but what can they do, any of them? Do they themselves know? Who is benefitting from the 16-plus examinations?)

These Schools Council decisions are closely related to the two major freedoms to which heads and teachers lay claim: the freedom to choose curricula and the freedom to organize the school as they see fit. However, both these freedoms are inhibited by external examinations which prejudice the position throughout the period of compulsory education.

For many years after the 1944 Education Act created the primary school, its curriculum and organization were influenced by a form of selection procedure commonly referred to as the 11-plus and imposed by the various local education authorities. It largely controlled the transfer of children from the primary to the secondary stage in such a way that the only parents to be offered a choice of school were those whose child stood high according to the instruments used to measure achievement and (it was assumed) potential. Throughout the same period, that is since the 1944 Act, the curriculum and organization of secondary schools have also been affected by examinations, most of them externally determined.

The result of all this on the teaching force is such that there is scarcely a teacher who has not experienced the competitive system man and boy. Most of them emerged through it initially and have taken it largely for granted ever since. They have fairly generally accepted the concomitant propositions that pupils need to be prejudged and streamed so that those deemed most likely to succeed according the accepted examination measures follow a substantially different course from those not expected to be able to meet those requirements.

This is not the place for a full discussion. The only point being established is that when the bulk of the teaching force works in and generally co-operates with a system of selection now giving way with younger pupils, but still entrenched with regard to the 16-year-olds, the profession cannot claim to retain or ever to have had control of curriculum and organization. What they can claim, even boast of, is a greater measure of such freedom than have the teachers in any other country.

The persistence of this examination system and the secondary school pattern of differentiation of courses at an early age makes overseas observers sceptical of our much vaunted claims regarding the teacher's autonomy. According to the report of a recent conference on styles in curriculum([9]) European educators and most Americans laugh us to scorn over our talk of the need to involve teachers in innovation — "our obsession with the teacher's participatory role". In connection with curriculum the report lists British inadequacies of organization, evaluation, dissemination and implementation together with a general lack of theory which means that we risk carrying pragmatism beyond safe limits.

The message to teachers here is that they must demand from their in-service resource persons the kinds of help which will enable them to retain their initiative in school curricula and their control of internal school organization whilst extending their competence in the field of the assessment of pupils of compulsory school age. In this country we are inclined to take our freedom for granted but teachers here should be aware of the list of weaknesses that others see in us, should take them seriously and try to ensure that our freedom is not thrown away in desperate efforts to find remedies. The onus is on the national bodies, the local advisory services and interested academic and professional groups to make available to teachers not only innovative materials but basic curriculum theory in usable form; not just the results of research surveys but detailed classroom observations of the teaching-learning interface.

Since control of curriculum and organization is of such crucial importance, even within the limits indicated above, it is worth trying to find how adequate teachers are to the task.

Regarding curriculum, the first question is one of principle. On what principles do teachers construct their curricula, or what ideas guide them in this task? The quick answer is that there are many ideas but no agreed principles, and that what theory there is, is little known among teachers.

Attempting for the moment to disengage the twin problems of curricula and organization from the stranglehold of external examinations, what (apart from success in examinations) is school for? What do the teachers think they are there for? Are they there to keep the children happy, occupied, interested, even amused? Are they there to inculcate moral rectitude? Have the basic literacy skills a major place in the school? Are teachers there to help the pupils master bodies of useful or prestigious knowledge? Maybe teachers are still trying to build up team spirit, give opportunities for self-expression, meet the need for vocational insights, offer some initiation into democratic practices and help the younger generation to build a new world of peace and international understanding. Any of these aims can be pursued and there is no doubt something to be said for all of them as for any new ideas that younger teachers bring in. The question is then, how do teachers decide what to try to teach any particular child, group or class? On what principles do they work? How do they judge their success or their failure?

It seems that they work by intuition and not according to principles. Trying to get teachers to describe how they plan their courses for pupils, Philip Taylor found that they could not do so.[10] As far as he was able to ascertain, the teachers had not developed any procedure for systematically taking into account the complexities underlying the process of planning. They tended to concentrate on aims and on subject-matter but made few references to methods or to evaluative criteria. Taylor wants teachers to have explicit principles by which to plan effectively and as there is, as yet, no clearly stated set of rules, he proposed a methodology of eight main points as a means of helping the work forward.

Perhaps the most ambitious attempt at devising principles according to which knowledge, skills and attitudes might be classified was Bloom's taxonomy[11] and in the last decade or two various large and small-scale efforts have been made to plan curricula by its light. In England the Northwest Regional Curriculum Development Project under Allan Rudd at the Manchester University School of Education made a thoroughgoing effort to use the taxonomy. Groups of secondary teachers in seven panels of about thirty in each, all planning fourth-and fifth-year courses for early leaving pupils, were supported by the regional centre at Manchester for some years, helping to produce materials which were diffused subsequently mainly within the areas of the local authorities concerned.

Some discussion about the pros and cons of the taxonomy are accessible in a small NFER volume[12] in which Wiseman and Pidgeon also give an account of curriculum by objectives and of how and why evaluation procedures should be included when new curricula are being planned.

Once the teacher abandons the attempt to define curriculum by objectives, he has to seek guidance elsewhere. Most teachers are soon out of their depth in books about philosophy unless it happens to be their special interest. The question is whether the philosophers have any help for the teacher who is still bent on doing the best he can. On what basis do philosophers recommend one type of curricula rather than another: or, even, what do they recommend — whether or not the basis is clear to the uninitiated?

One recent short book offers a practical division into two categories of curriculum activities.([13]) White suggests that category I activities should be compulsory and the rest not compulsory. His lists are not meant to be exhaustive but the basis for the discrimination is interesting. In category I are the activities which cannot be understood without engaging in them. Examples are communication in general, pure mathematics, the exact physical sciences, appreciating works of art and philosophizing. These activities are what White would provide as compulsory curriculum. Examples of other activities, those in category II, are foreign languages, cookery, woodwork, cricket or other organized games, and painting pictures or other creative aesthetic activities. The suggestion is that none of these should be compulsory. It is not proposed that category II activities ought not to be pursued in school, only that compulsory attendance of children and young people need not imply a totally compulsory curriculum. As we all know, there are options on most school timetables but on the whole these are not chosen options but choices between compulsions.

Some research projects focusing on teachers' problems

Discussion of such theories keeps teachers focused on the question of what they are trying to do in school. It is difficult enough to think on new lines: any suggestion of putting innovations into practice brings a crop of problems. Any change affecting the balance of subjects, especially at secondary level, has immediate repercussions on the timetable and cannot be undertaken lightly; and much less radical changes than those postulated in White's book can stretch the internal organization of a school to near breaking-point.

A remarkable account of one secondary school undergoing processes of change has been written by Elizabeth Richardson, who worked as a consultant at Nailsea Secondary School in Somerset over a period of 2 or 3 years, seconded from Bristol University and engaged on a Schools Council project: *Change and innovation in an expanding comprehensive school.* At the time of her research the school had already changed from a grammar to a comprehensive school and was in process of building up its numbers. In her self-chosen role of participant observer and change agent, Richardson worked in partnership with the head and staff but had no dealings with pupils or parents. Each member of staff agreed to being named in the report and to having interpersonal conflicts and intergroup struggles interpreted by the consultant and published in detail.

Although the book is about one school, the experiences are common to schools in general and on this account can sustain the interest of any teacher, head or teacher trainer. The Nailsea project was an example of on-site staff development. The total staff of a large secondary school gained in understanding of the issues that could divide them (and spoil the school) and acquired management competencies to deal with many of their stresses. Proof of this success is contained page by page in the book, *The teacher, the school and the task of management.*[14] Whilst the development of the head and of the teachers in a school is not susceptible to measurement by known research instruments, the evidence of growth is there just the same and large as life. The consultant was also affected by her exacting ordeal. Some evidence of this lies in the fact that instead of writing a summary of this book she has written a new statement of major issues in secondary school management.[15] Examples of its chapter headings indicate the clarity of the theoretical formulation: roles, tasks and boundaries within the staff group; the curricular/pastoral divide in school organization; the individual and the hierarchy.

No doubt heads and teachers will learn what they can from these writings, for to read, think over and discuss such a book is a course of in-service education in itself. Not every reader will accept the author's approach to group tensions. She works on the theoretical structure developed by Bion, Rice and others at the Tavistock Institute of Human Relations. But most teachers have not known that a theoretical structure of any kind was at hand to help elucidate the jungle of obstructions that crops up between good ideas and their being carried into effect; between seemingly straightforward innovations and their actual implementation. The lack of recognition of these complexities accounts in some measure for the non-effectiveness of much high endeavour in the educational field.

Administrators and educators who have left the classroom tend to attribute the gap between their fine plans and any outcome, to the general bloody-mindedness of teachers; whilst the latter are hampered and worn out by daily, relentless and seemingly inexplicable interpersonal and intergroup struggles in the classroom, in the staffroom and in the head's room, to the point that they may (quite rightly) resist change. The question for those concerned with in-service education in general is whether any other schools want experience comparable with Nailsea's. Extension or replication of the project could run into the difficulty of the lack of trained consultants: to which one answer might be that the one consultant with relevant experience might work with a small team of others prepared to undertake school consultancy, not necessarily on exactly the same lines.

To date, however, despite considerable interest on the part of some teachers and advisers and of groups such as the English New Education Fellowship no promise of supporting funds is forthcoming for further projects. It seems likely therefore that Nailsea will be a one-off — at least until the Americans recognize another British "first" and try to put it on the conveyor belt.

Quite a different approach to the problem of what actually goes on in classrooms has been made by a small research team working first at Chelsea but later from a base in the University of East Anglia. Their original study was an analysis of behaviour in the informal, open classroom. Walker and Adelman developed a new technique of uninterrupted audio-visual recordings and in the process they re-appraised their concept of participant observation. Their method created such a new way of looking at classrooms that they began to accumulate some first-hand indications of how informal classrooms function as social settings. The technique offered feedback both to the researchers and to the participating teachers. With such material it is possible to begin to see what happened during some classroom incident or how some bit of curriculum was handled with various children. Since moving to Norwich the team has undertaken co-operative action research with a chosen group of heads, teachers and local advisers.

Some account of this work has appeared in the *New Era*([16]) and full documentation is available.([17]) The action research appears to be a model of how to get a number of initially motivated teachers to undergo learning experiences affecting their competence to teach. The group agreed that among their aims was that of teaching children to reason independently. During the action research these same teachers came to recognize ways in which, unwillingly and unwittingly, they habitually put constraints in the way of such learning to reason.

Once this lesson was swallowed the way was clear for new strategies of guidance for pupils. To recapitulate: the sequence of the in-service experience, arrived at through disciplined discussion between a research team and upwards of fifty practitioners was that they first came to agreement as to an objective: they wanted to increase their pupils' powers of reasoning; then they were enabled to identify ways in which they were themselves imposing constraints on the pupils, inhibiting their chances of reasoning; and also to identify other constraints; and subsequently to get rid of both types of constraint and begin by effective guidance strategies to increase the pupils' powers of reasoning.

The purpose of detailing this particular action research is that it illustrates how simplistic is so much other curriculum development and in-service advice. The outline given above exemplifies the kind of work which can constitute effective in-service education: effective in this case both for primary and secondary teachers and for the research team. The latter had begun with an idea: that of developing a new audio-visual means of recording classroom situations. In the course of this work their interest in the open classroom situation was deepened. Given a chance to work with teachers on a further project, they ascertained what it was that the teachers thought they were trying to do in the open classroom. They helped to clarify all kinds of concepts along polarities of formal/informal, structured/unstructured, guided/open-ended, until the teachers could handle some of their ideas about inquiry teaching, discovery learning and other patterns of teaching/learning.

From all this emerged the project, indicated above, of training pupils' powers of reasoning. In such action research the teachers are neither subjects nor objects but partners. They understand that they are not being manipulated, not being sold a gimmick, but that they are being offered experience which replicates their own back-home situation in the classroom. There, they are the experts: they are the ones in the position of needing to listen to and discuss with pupils what should be done, of having the necessary expertise and the possibility of helping pupils to apply themselves to the learning they want.

In contrast to such laborious but rewarding action research, many in-service projects are planned with a view to implanting the know-how about some teaching method or aspect of curriculum. The teachers who attend the course or conference have not committed themselves, as a rule, to any point of view before arriving, but come in hope of useful knowledge, skills or materials. When the meetings begin it is quite normal for some superficial attempt to be made to identify the needs of the agglomeration of individuals on the course, but such efforts have quickly to give way to the agenda. Although the pattern of courses is changing, it remains fairly usual for a lecturer to give a paper and then to opt out, leaving the members and conference directors to make what they can of it.

Many of the teachers may find the lecture useful: it may give them just the clues they were looking for — this is the luck of the draw. But because the lecture situation mirrors traditional class teaching, a teacher attending such a course gains reinforcement for well-worn methods of instruction and loses an opportunity of experiencing two-way action between teacher and learner. He may have gained knowledge or understanding but without the accompaniment of any additional insight into his own qualities or inadequacies as a teacher. He may have learnt and accepted something about modern education, but such knowledge remains inert unless in the unsupported loneliness of his own classroom he contrives to translate theory into practice.

These comments on typical teachers' courses, old style, reflect the neglect of modern teaching techniques in Higher Education. It has meant that our schools and colleges are staffed with experienced adults, some of whom are talking about modern methods or trying to apply them, but scarcely any of whom has experienced them in his student days. This point was brought out clearly in some research carried on in Bristol.

Before the completion of the researches, an article by Bolam in *Trends,*([18]) the publication of the Department of Education and Science, gave an indication of the nature of some work being carried on with regard to probationer teachers and the induction year. One thing that emerged was the lack of trainers, advisers, call them what you will, with any working knowledge of modern teaching techniques. At Bristol they used the case-study method, the unstructured discussion group, the case conference method, interaction analysis, workshop methods, a curriculum theory approach, team teaching and the pastoral tutor approach. Even with their resources they were not in a position to use simulation methods or microteaching.

This finding regarding the paucity of techniques on call reflects on the tediousness of much of higher education. For some studies, no doubt, reading, discussion and some seminars are adequate. For the inculcation of other kinds of knowledge, however, other methods are imperative. These other kinds of know-how are the very coin of teaching: the habit of working in empathy with some other person, whether teacher or pupil; the experience of communicating with others to pool ideas and of doing so without regard for the hierarchy; some competence in group work in such roles as listening, observing, contributing, evaluating and summarizing; and the confidence to select and use the most appropriate from a whole battery of available techniques.

The reports themselves([19, 20]) offer some useful distinctions between the aspects of induction which might reasonably be considered as a function of the school and those for which the teacher might meet other teachers or advisers at a college or teachers' centre. Since their publication researchers in various areas up and down the country have been discussing and experimenting with proposals for better in-service provision for beginning teachers.

Something of the new ways in which the Department is working with the area training organizations on school management is indicated by Harold Knowlson in an article([21]) dealing especially with the question of the school-based tutor. He clarifies three areas of responsibility: initial training, induction year and continued education, and lists what school-based professional tutors might do in connection with any or all of these areas. Once the need for these has been highlighted the help of resource persons, whether from college, university or the local advisory service, can be directed towards particular skills, techniques or forms of training. Microteaching is such a technique and the use of video-tape in association with an electronic camera is another. As regards the handling of technical equipment, the advice of experts in the media is desirable and reasonably available.

The application of new devices or techniques in the in-service training situation is one, however, calling for constant revision and refinement. It is common experience that many more teachers and teacher trainers know about technical aids than actually use them. According to a useful introduction in *Trends*([22]) microteaching applies to methods of class instruction writ small. Perhaps, however, the idea is capable of application to the individualized and small group teaching which is becoming the norm in England. Microteaching seems to be of great interest to educators in Australia. The Higher Education Research Unit at Monash University has developed a microteaching inventory. After studying the literature they felt that they needed to look again at the complexity of teaching behaviour, and to use a job-analysis approach. Another Australian authority on microteaching is Professor Turney of the University of Sydney.

A final example from Down Under: Salisbury College of Advanced Education in South Australia is building a special relationship with certain schools through the joint exploration of uses of modern techniques. The in-service aspect here derives from the close contact of the schools with the college (whose primary concern is with initial training). The more flexible and imaginative use of microteaching which the authors of the *Trends* article recommended in their conclusion may be achieved by such means as those currently influencing Australia.

Management theory related to schools

Apart from such particular techniques, universities are in a good position to help the whole education service with theory regarding organization, administration and management. The British Education Administration Society was set up on university initiatives and the report([23]) of its first annual conference shows the broad range of its membership and interests. It serves also to throw light on some of the issues relating in-service education to management development. The latter is usefully defined in terms of "processes which foster overall improvement of the competence of staff for the institution in which they serve *and* for their own personal and professional satisfaction". One of the main speakers, Ron Glatter, pins his hopes on new Development Centres in Educational Administration (or Management) whilst the other, Tony Light, argues for a strategy of staff development based on the school but drawing upon the resources of the local authority and the locality. He foresees both on-site and off-site training, complementary to each other, and involving both teachers and the supporting services in new roles.

Through such discussions as those conducted by the British Education Administration Society, and such courses on school management as have been sponsored recently by the Department in association with the area training organizations, words such as administration, organization and management have entered the vocabulary of heads and teachers. In the old days, administration was what went on at the headquarters of the local education authority, and school administration was a phrase largely reserved for the paper work connecting the head of a school with that office. School organization was a fairly straightforward matter of deploying a number — not a large number — of teachers, pupils, subjects and classrooms on a time table. Management theory belonged to the world of business and was rarely thought of in connection with the conduct of major educational institutions, let alone schools. Nowadays, however, all three words are used almost indiscriminately in relation to a school, a college, a teachers' centre, or a whole system of education. The question to be touched upon next in this chapter is how far or in what ways management theories deriving from business are applicable or helpful to schools.

Attempts to compare a school with a business enterprise are not very useful. In industry the general pattern is of input, processing and output. Each of these can normally be calculated and (hopefully) a profit can be made. Although people have their place at all levels they are not a part of the raw materials nor of the output. All this is perfectly obvious but must be said. The teaching/learning situation in a school is different. In school, children are the input; the curriculum used by the teachers in interaction with the children constitutes the process; and the young people 10 years or so later form the output. Although some partial measures can be applied, there is no means of making reliable calculations of the input, the process, the output or the profits. Whatever is borrowed, therefore, from management theory has to be carefully checked for validity in the school situation.

However, at least one of the main lessons from management appears to be entirely transferable to the educational world. It is that healthy development depends upon people being in genuine communication with each other. In school this means at the least, that all those concerned in any proposed organizational or curricular change need to talk the matter through first. It is much better if all those concerned with the on-going programme of curricular and organizational growth were so well in touch with each other that they continually revised their own and each others' thinking.

Such genuine communication needs to be up and down the hierarchy (pupils, teachers, allowance holders, head) as well as across whatever other barriers may obtrude (perhaps sex, age, manner, style of teaching or level of intelligence). Without such communications, such feed back from the less to the more powerful, such contributions from whoever ought to be involved, the message of management theory is that planning is a fallacy and innovation a farce.

No one has enunciated this management theory more clearly than the business consultants, Blake and Mouton,[24] who were prepared to carry through management training by three stages provided they had full access to the whole range of power-wielders in the firm. (In this paragraph, teachers should read "school" for "firm".) First is training in communication — and this may take hours, weeks or years according to the complexity of the business and the degree of ossification affecting it. Then comes the stage of planning the model of what would be happening in the firm and what everybody would be doing in it if everyone were doing what they now realize they should. Finally, they are in a position to begin carrying their plans into action.

However, after the implementation stage is reached it is important to keep on with both the communicating and the planning. In this way, plans are continually revised and action is modified in the light of changing circumstances and experience. The on-going processes provide the staff with regular training so that some develop and take on wider responsibilities whilst newcomers to the firm have the good fortune to step into a living concern. With any luck, such a firm does not need to have further recourse to consultants, nor will it need to buy in much talent ready-made: it will be growing its own people.

Lest it seem that this grass-roots, coal-face type of approach to management is idiosyncratic to one firm connected with Texan oil, some brief reference will be made here to other expositions of management theory. McGregor's classic([25]) has provided us with the shorthand of Theory X and Theory Y. Heads and teachers, not to mention pupils and parents, can readily recognize contrasting types of school in his accounts of opposite climates of management. Theory X leads to an emphasis on control; on telling people what to do; on procedures and techniques for seeing that they are doing it and for administering rewards and punishments. Theory Y, on the other hand, leads to a preoccupation with the nature of relationships, to the creation of an environment which encourages commitment to organizational objectives; it provides opportunities for the greatest exercise of initiative, ingenuity and self-direction. According to McGregor's reckoning, the job environment (read school) is the most important variable affecting the development of the individual. As he defines it, the purpose of the education of managers (read heads and teachers) is to enable them to learn how to create an environment conducive to growth on the part of their subordinates (read pupils and teachers).

One last reference to management theory before looking briefly at its origins. The witty but serious Robert Townsend in his best seller([26]) gives gems of advice based on management theory. For example, acknowledging his indebtedness to McGregor for a sound agricultural approach he says that management should provide the climate and proper nourishment and let the people grow themselves, and that the results are amazing. (One could put a different catch phrase from his book on the wall every day for a term.) All these snippets of guidance from management theory relate rather to people than directly to production. It seems that, in business, the difficulties are less technical than human. Commercial production is through people — and in education production is not only through people but of people. Perhaps business would have fewer problems if the schools and colleges were doing a better job. It appears that the world is falling flat on its face less for lack of mathematics, for example, than for lack of people with any experience of working effectively together.

Psychologists, human relations experts and management consultants such as those at the Tavistock Institute or the National Training Laboratories of the National Education Association of America speak of group work and of human relations training, they even use such a taboo phrase as "sensitivity training". Little wonder that the body of knowledge which has been building up for a quarter of a century has made small impression on the educational world. As a rule such consultants do not visit schools and on the whole the school advisory services have not sought out and experienced the training themselves. The universities of Leicester and Bristol have been focal points for the application of such group theory to teacher training but probably the project at Nailsea referred to earlier in this chapter is the only thoroughgoing consultancy ever conducted in a school.

It must be years since class instruction was the dominant pattern; but schools still seem to be thought of in terms of classes of children confronting teachers rather than of groups of pupils working with a teacher and teams of teachers working together. In the same way, in-service education for teachers is still predominantly considered in terms of courses of study measured in time, instead of in terms of such kinds of inquiry, action research, human relations training or work with a participant adviser or consultant, which might − just might − impinge directly on some of the teacher's intransigent problems.

It is not that the need for in-service education receives no recognition. Not only teachers, but everybody is thought to be due for recycling nowadays. What is difficult to establish is the nature of the in-service process where it is aimed at helping the teacher to interpret fully his responsibilities to his pupils and his colleagues in the school.

It appears that those who were responsible for his initial training had no clear criteria of what they were looking for when they sought a "good teacher". In the report of a conference of the Committee for Research into Teacher Education[27] Fontana quotes a conclusion reached by Wiseman and Start in 1965 to the effect that it was difficult to see with what the professional training course was associated; certainly not with promotion, head teacher's assessment or satisfaction in the profession.

A similar finding was reported from a high-level conference in Washington,

D.C.([28]) The United States Office of Education had made clear at the beginning that it was determined to do whatever was needed to ensure the effectiveness of the teaching force. However, in a concluding chapter Robert Gagne had to admit that up to that time there was no way of answering the question: "What do teacher characteristics have to do with the outcomes of school learning?" because, as he said, there was no satisfactory way of measuring these outcomes, nor, he said, did they know the processes by which a teacher could ensure learning.

At about the same time as that conference was in progress, a team from the National Foundation for Educational Research was studying the teacher's day in primary schools here. The concluding paragraph of the report([29]) indicates that although held within the bounds of objective reporting, the authors, Hilsum and Cane, had wanted to get at crucial questions about teaching. Their overall impression was that the pattern of the teaching day's activities was determined by the teacher as an individual rather than by any other factor. In their view this lent weight to the suggestion that research into educational situations ought to concentrate more and more on what makes the teacher think and act as he does. They thought that much lip service had been paid to the importance of the teacher as the focal point of the teaching-learning situation, yet time and money were only just beginning to be allocated to research into the teacher and his role. However, the parallel investigation, now in progress, into the teacher's day in the secondary school is on closely comparable lines, differing mainly in the greater number of categories being used for analysing how the time of the teacher's day is spent.

What may emerge from the secondary report is some picture of the complexity of secondary school organization. However, local authorities and schools themselves cannot wait for whatever guidance on these matters emerges from such surveys. Already, for example, the Inner London Education Authority has distributed a report ([30]) of a working party on the internal government of schools based on returns made by schools. In conclusion it offers six suggestions for the consideration of teachers regarding such matters as staff involvement, responsibility for decision making and in-service education: all useful for in-service discussion.

Since, however, many of the ideas for major changes in education have been developed within schools, one looks to the schools themselves for accounts of what their problems are and how they are meeting them. A number of books as well as many teachers' courses have been based on case-studies or descriptions by heads and teachers of their response to their particular problems. Three examples of such publications are given in the bibliography,([31]) one relating to primary and secondary schools in Leicestershire, and two to recent developments in the organization and management of secondary schools. Such edited compilations give heads and teachers a chance to formulate and record what is happening at a certain time and perhaps to see it in some broader perspective set by the editor. Whether for publication or not, the writing of such accounts is a worthwhile discipline serving to clarify ideas. Such accounts serve also to illustrate facts that not all teachers recognize; that the thrust towards openness at the primary and comprehensiveness at the secondary stage derive largely from teacher initiative; and that these developments have not failed only because heads and teachers, with or without relevant in-service education, have succeeded in making major adjustments to their outlook and teaching techniques.

An excellent example of a book showing how heads and teachers not only live with their changing problems but also conceptualize what is happening to them and their schools, has been written by the head of Countesthorpe College.([32]) His account of the essence of the new schooling should benefit teachers and influence public opinion. For one thing, he establishes what the end of selection means to schools. Teachers have now to be prepared to do the best they can for all comers: not just for some segregated section of gifted children, disadvantaged children or those thought to have a practical bent. (Perhaps they will soon also learn to accommodate some who need wheelchairs or have other kinds of handicap, physical or mental, hitherto confining them to special education.)

In this situation, complicated by changing expectations on the part of young people in general, the author, John Watts, indicates several distinct kinds of demand on the teacher who in turn has to make new demands upon the system. The teacher has to get to know his pupils personally; he has to be prepared to lose some of his autonomy regarding curriculum in exchange for increased co-operation with a team of colleagues; and he has to become an expert in locating sources of knowledge and putting his pupils in touch with them, including those outside the school itself.

This new pattern of teaching is very demanding. Administrators, advisory services or research personnel concerned to help teachers even to survive in it, must see that although the matter is urgent it is not a case for fire-brigade operations. Teachers need help and support in schools themselves and in teachers' centres rather than in a separate in-service educational institution. Regardless of whether the teacher is a beginner in his first year; a middle-range teacher with behind him years of success according to earlier standards; or the head of a school perhaps suddenly jettisoned by local reorganization into a position where new problems face him at every turn — all these need their help at hand. A reduced teaching timetable with some chance to talk to an adviser or to belong to a small working group may be more to the point for many teachers than off-site courses. Through such opportunities within the school a teacher turns his classroom experience to use; without them, he is more likely to give up, in spirit or in truth.

The emerging pattern of in-service education is school-based. At its foundation is the purposeful discussion of classroom experiences. Whether conducted with pupils and parents, with colleagues and head, or with teachers' centre wardens, Schools Council personnel, local authority advisers or consultants from college, university or research unit, the process serves the same function: to diagnose what the pupils' needs are and to clarify what the school stands for.

As the staff of any school become a little sophisticated in ways of working together they may reach some approximation to consensus regarding education priorities. In a school where a full contribution is expected from everyone, teachers find themselves helping to develop the policies for whose implementation they will bear some responsibility. None of this is easy but in schools up and down the country the new pattern is being carved out by teachers who evidently find it worth while.

A teacher who comes to grips with his task in school in this way — in the collegial mode — begins to formulate what in-service education could do for him and for his school. Once this stage is reached, serious in-service efforts are likely to be harnessed to the school's overriding purposes.

The task of the providers of in-service education, whether in schools, in teachers' centres or elsewhere, is being defined more and more as that of helping the teachers in any school or group with the identification of their problems, with studies designed to enable them to cope more adequately, and with criteria for knowing when they have failed in this aim. When these efforts are conducted mainly in the school itself, financial provision needs to be sufficiently flexible to give the school such consultant, secretarial and material help as is called for in the cause of staff development. Where school-based in-service efforts are coordinated off-campus, there is the same need for support related to demand.

One final feature of the emerging pattern can be seen in new connections between in-service education and promotion. Promotion within the school is being accorded to members of staff who, in the process of working with others, have demonstrably enhanced their qualities as teachers. Promotion to other schools in recognition of these qualities is problematic as many appointed committees are thought to be more heavily influenced by the range than by the depth of a candidate's experience. However, a new move (at the University of Sussex) towards the accreditation of teachers carrying through school-based research and curriculum development could help to focus attention on certain facts of cardinal importance: that classroom experience is the basis for in-service education; that those who attain to the skills and arts of successful teaching ought to be able to reach the heights of their profession without losing their contacts with pupils; and that a school is likely to be an exciting place in which to work and grow up when as many as possible of the pupils and the staff are progressing towards personal autonomy.

References

1. JENCKS, C. *et al., Inequality, a reassessment of the effect of family and schooling in America,* Allen Lane, 1973.
2. *Schools in Australia,* report of the Interim Committee for the Australian Schools Commission (the Karmel report), Canberra, 1973.
3. *Learning to be,* report of the International Commission on the Development of Education (the Fauré report), UNESCO, Paris, 1972.
4. SCHUMAKER, E. F., *Small is beautiful,* Blond & Briggs, 1973.
5. ILLICH, I. D., *Celebration of awareness,* Calder & Boyars, 1971.
6. *Secondary School Examinations other than General Certificate of Education* (the Beloe report), Her Majesty's Stationery Office, 1960.
7. WOOD, R. and SKURNIK, L. S., *Item banking, a method for producing school based examinations and nationally comparable grades,* National Foundation for Educational Research, 1969, *and* NUTTALL, D. L. and WILLMOTT, A. S., *British examinations: techniques of analysis,* National Foundation for Educational Research, 1972.
8. SCHOOLS COUNCIL, 160, Great Portland Street, London, W1N 6LL.
9. MACLURE, S. (Ed.), *Styles of curriculum development,* a report of a conference organized jointly by the Centre for Educational Research and Innovation (Organization for Economic Cooperation and Development) and the University of Illinois, OECD, Paris, 1973.
10. TAYLOR, P. H., *How teachers plan their courses,* National Foundation for Educational Research, 1970.
11. BLOOM, B. S. (Ed.), *Taxonomy of educational objectives,* Handbook I, *Cognitive domain,* Longmans, 1956, *and* KRATHWOHL, D. R. (Ed.), Handbook II, *Affective domain,* Longmans, 1964.
12. WISEMAN, S. and PIDGEON, D., *Curriculum evaluation,* National Foundation for Educational Research, 1970.

13. WHITE, J. P., *Towards a compulsory curriculum*, Routledge & Kegan Paul, 1973.
14. RICHARDSON, E., *The teacher, the school and the task of management*, Heinemann, 1973.
15. RICHARDSON, E., *Authority and organization in the secondary school*, Schools Council research paper, Macmillan Education, 1975.
16. ELLIOTT, J. and ADELMAN, C., Supporting teachers' research in the classroom, in *New Era*, vol. 54, no. 9 (Dec. 1973).
17. WALKER, R. and ADELMAN, C., *Towards a sociography of classrooms*, Social Science Research Council, HR 996 and HR 1442, 1972, *and*
    ELLIOTT, J. and ADELMAN, C., *Innovation in teaching and action-research*, an interim report on the Ford Teaching Project, duplicated, University of East Anglia, 1973, *and*
    ADELMAN, C., *Observing in classrooms*, Methuen, 1975.
18. BOLAM, R., Guidance for probationer teachers, in Department of Education and Science, *Trends in education*, no. 21, Her Majesty's Stationery Office, 1971.
19. TAYLOR, J. K. and DALE, I. R., *A national survey of teachers in their first year of service*, Research Unit, University of Bristol School of Education, 1971.
20. BOLAM, R., *Induction programmes for probationary teachers*, Research Unit, University of Bristol School of Education, 1973.
21. KNOWLSON, H., The school based tutor, in Department of Education and Science, *Trends in education*, no. 31, Her Majesty's Stationery Office, 1973.
22. ST. JOHN-BROOKS, C. and SPELMAN, B., Microteaching, in Department of Education and Science, *Trends in education*, no. 31, Her Majesty's Stationery Office, 1973.
23. PRATT, S. (Ed.), *Staff development in education*, the proceedings of the first annual conference of the British Educational Administration Society, Councils and Education Press, 1973.
24. BLAKE, R. K. and MOUTON, J. S., *Corporate excellence through grid organization development, a systems approach*, Gulf Publishing Company, Houston, 1968.
25. McGREGOR, D., *The human side of enterprise*, McGraw Hill, 1960.
26. TOWNSEND, R., *Up the organization*, Coronet Books, Michael Joseph, 1971.
27. CHANAN, G. (Ed.), *Research forum on teacher education*, based on a conference of the Committee for Research into Teacher Education, National Foundation for Educational Research, 1972.
28. *Do teachers make a difference?* a report on research on pupil achievement, Bureau of Educational Personnel Development, United States Office of Education, Washington, D.C., OE-58042, 1970.
29. HILSUM, S. and CANE, B. S., *The teacher's day*, National Foundation for Educational Research, 1971.
30. INNER LONDON EDUCATION AUTHORITY, *Report of the working party on the internal government of schools*, The County Hall, London, SE1.
31. HARDY, M. (Ed.), *At classroom level*, P.S.W. (Educational) Publications, Forum, 1971, *and*
    HUGHES, M. G., *Secondary school administration, a management approach*, Pergamon, 1970, *and*
    HALSALL, E., *Becoming comprehensive, case histories*, Pergamon, 1970.
32. WATTS, J., *Teaching*, David & Charles, 1974.

Index

247